Architecture and Viole

Edited by Bechir Kenzari

MW00777472

ARCHITECTURE AND VIOLENCE

EDITED BY
BECHIR KENZARI

PUBLISHED BY
ACTAR

I wish to first thank the authors who have contributed essays to this collection. I am grateful to Anna Tetas at Actar for her editorial guidance and patience, and to Dorota Biczel for her valuable precision and expertise in copyediting the final drafts. Finally, I wish to express my gratitude to the Graham Foundation for Advanced Studies in the Fine Arts for its grant.

Libero Andreotti is Professor of Architecture at Georgia Tech and the Ecole d'Architecture de Paris La Villette. His writings on the history of modern art and architecture appeared in *October*, *JAE*, *Architecture and Idea*, *Grey Room*, and *Lotus International*. With Xavier Costa he curated the exhibition *Situationists: Art, Politics, Urbanism* at the Museum of Moden Art in Barcelona (1996), for which he also edited the volume *Theory of the Derive and other Situationist Writings on the City* (Barcelona: ACTAR 1996). He is also co-author of *Sironi: La Grande Decorazione* (Milan: Electa, 2004), a monograph of the exhibition held at the Pinacoteca Nazionale of Bologna (2004) and at the Triennale in Milan (2004). His most recent book *Le Grand Jeu à Venir: écrits situationnnistes sur la ville* was published by Editions La Villette, Paris, 2007.

Annette Fierro is Associate Professor of Architecture at the University of Pennsylvania, where she teaches design studios and seminars on issues concerning technology within the modern movement and international contemporary architecture and culture. Her current research addresses the use of glass in the French *Grands Projets*. She authored *The Glass State: The Technology of the Spectacle/Paris 1981–1998* (MIT Press, 2003) and published work on Japanese contemporary building. Her recent articles include "Popular Construction: Handbooks for Homefronts." Her design work as project architect appeared in various architectural journals, including *Assemblage*, *Architectural Record*, *Progressive Architecture*, and *Lotus*.

Elie Haddad earned his PhD in Architecture from the University of Pennsylvania, with a dissertation on Henry van de Velde. He has published a number of articles based on his PhD work in the *Journal of Design History* and in *Fabrications*, among others. Since 1994, he has been teaching architectural history, theory, and design studios at the Lebanese American University. He participated in a number of international conferences and organized conferences at the Lebanese American University: on the Mediterranean City (2000) and on Contemporary Discourses in Architecture (2004.)

Dorita Hannah is Professor of Design at Massey University's College of Creative Arts in Wellington, New Zealand. A specialized architectural consultant in buildings for the visual and performing arts, she is interested in scenographic, interior, exhibition and installation design, as well as international performance design projects. Her publications include chapters in *Eating Architecture* (MIT Press, 2004), *Exquisite Apart* (NZIA, 2005), and *The Senses in Performance* (Routledge, 2005). Her current research focuses on "event-space" and the twentieth-century avant-garde, and ongoing collaborations with performing artists. In 2007, she was a jury member of the Prague Quadrennial. In 2006, she convened an *International Symposium on Performance Design* in Rome that brought together interdisciplinary architects, artists, performers, and theorists, resulting in the publication of an anthology.

Andrew Herscher is Assistant Professor at the University of Michigan, teaching in the Taubman College of Architecture and Urban Planning, the Department of Slavic Languages and Literatures, and the Department of Art History. His work explores the architectural and urban forms of political violence, public memory, and collective identity, concentrating on modern and contemporary Central and Eastern Europe. A particular focus of his work has been Kosovo, where he worked for the International Criminal Tribunal for the Former Yugoslavia as an investigator and expert witness on the war-time destruction of cultural heritage. He co-founded and co-directed the NGO, Kosovo Cultural Heritage Project, and directed the Department of Culture of the United Nations Mission in Kosovo. His book, *Violence Taking Place: The Architecture of the Kosovo Conflict*, was published by Stanford University Press in 2010.

Bechir Kenzari is Associate Professor of Architecture at the United Arab Emirates University. He holds a doctorate in Architecture from Georgia Tech and has lectured in the areas of philosophy, design, computing, and digital fabrication. He taught at Georgia Tech, the University of Auckland (New Zealand), and the UAE University. He received the ACSA award for the best *Journal of Architectural Education (JAE)* article of the year 2003 and guest-edited the *Built Environment* issue, *Architecture and the Influence of Other Disciplines*. His writings appeared in several international journals such as *JAE*, *Architectural Theory Review*, *The Built Environment*, and the *International Journal of Architectural Computing*. His interest in the issue of violence and architecture manifested itself in the essays on Antonio Tapiès, nomadic dwelling, and violence in French *banlieues*. He published several short stories in the Auckland-based *Pander* and has produced a series of oil paintings. He is currently writing a novel.

Donald Kunze is Professor of Architecture and Integrative Arts at the Pennsylvania State University. He was educated as an architect (North Carolina State University, 1970) and, later, as a geographer (Penn State University, 1983). His is the author of *Thought and Place: The Architecture of Eternal Places in the Philosophy of Giambattista Vico* (New York, 1987) and of articles and essays on subjects such as architectural criticism, landscape perception, literary theory, and film study. He has directed interdisciplinary conferences on philosophy in the spatial arts (1986), the role of kynicism in architecture (1991), synesthesia in the arts (2003), and numerous small symposia on films related to architecture and landscape. He has taught architecture and critical theory at the Pennsylvania State University since 1984.

Nadir Lahiji is an architect, educator, and theorist. He holds a PhD from the University of Pennsylvania in architecture theory. He is a co-editor of an anthology of critical and theoretical essays entitled *Plumbing: Sounding Modern Architecture*, published by the Princeton Architectural Press in 1997, which explores ideology of hygiene in the formation of modernity in the early twentieth century. He is a contributor to the recent book *Surrealism and Architecture*, published by Routledge in 2004. He has published essays in numerous journals, including *Architecture Theory Review, Journal of Architectural Education, AA Files,* and *Any.* He has taught at Georgia Tech, University of Pennsylvania, University of Cincinnati, the Pratt Institute, and the Lebanese American University. He is currently editing a book *Political Unconscious of Architecture: Essays in Honour of Fredric Jameson,* to be published by Ashgate.

William B. Millard is a New York-based freelance writer and editor who has contributed articles on architecture, literature, medicine, music, and culture to a wide range of publications, including *Icon, Oculus, eOculus, Building Design*'s BD magazine, OMA's *Content, Postmodern Culture,* the *Annals of Emergency Medicine, Patient Care,* and scholarly anthologies on Thomas Pynchon, Don DeLillo, and Internet culture. He served as an editor of Columbia University's print/web research magazine *21stC,* holds a doctorate in English and American literature from Rutgers University, and is an alumnus of Amherst College. He lives in New York City's East Village.

Sarah Treadwell is Associate Professor of Architecture and Planning at the University of Auckland, New Zealand. She teaches architectural design studio and lectures on issues of architectural representation. Her research areas include analyses of images of architecture in the South Pacific and New Zealand, and the architecture of volcanic landscapes and unstable ground. She also writes on contemporary fine art practices that reference architecture. Her recent publications include: "Earthquake Weather" in *Drifting: Architecture and Migrancy,* S. Cairns, ed. (London, 2004) and "Architectural Manuals and Pacific Speculations" in *Spatula: How Drawing Changed the World,* G. Shrigley, ed. (London, 2004.)

Since the collapse of the former bipolar system of international rivalry, there has been a tendency among architectural theorists to pay attention to the issue of violence in its diverse spatial manifestations. Following the disintegration of the former Yugoslavia, the dramatic September 11 New York events, the July 7 London bombings, the March 11 Madrid train explosions, and the continuous deterioration of the situation in the Middle East, this propensity has imposed itself with renewed urgency, forcing architecture to acknowledge its relation to violence in a more pronounced way.

Reflecting on the architectural implications of these violent transformations, some theorists have published challenging and focused investigations of this difficult and somewhat slippery subject. A mention should be made here of the 1993 special issue of *Assemblage*, in which some forty authors of heterogeneous backgrounds explored succinctly multiple threads that bind violent events with the violence of space. The brevity of those essays was compensated by the presentation of multiple perspectives. Other treatments of the subject, resolutely more specific to certain conflicts and particular manifestations of violence, have subsequently been published, providing new conceptual tools to interrogate the question of violence from an architectural perspective. They include such tiles as Nan Ellin's *Architecture of Fear* (1997), Rafi Segal and Eyal Weizman's *A Civilian Occupation* (2003), Robert Bevan's *Destruction of Memory* (2007), Eyal Weizman's *Hollow Land* (2007), and Andrew Herscher's latest *Violence Taking Place* (2010). Hence, it could be stated that we are now surrounded by a growing body of literature on violence that aims to examine the critical relation between architecture and the spaces of political, military, religious, ethnic, judicial, philosophical, technical, artistic, and economic power.

Yet, on the whole, the phenomenon of violence is still understudied as an architectural subject, and this is for two principal reasons. One has to do with the boundaries between disciplines, the other with their standard missions. The binary relation architecture/violence is often seen as a category that ought to be analyzed within the bounds of political science, law or psychoanalysis, but not of architecture proper. The other view contends that since the determination and possibilities of architecture are inherently constructive, any attention paid to violence is simply non-architectural. Although the building can be assaulted, the assault itself is not a part of the a priori architectural demarche. Far more than performing an exercise in anti-forms, the architect should strive to propagate a philosophy that looks at destruction as an antonym of performance. For to adopt violence as an architectural strategy would simply mean to declare the end of the architectural project at the outset. According to this view, therefore, the will to build should remain the cardinal principle of any architectural effort.[1]

These are disturbing reservations, with obvious speculative intentions. First, let us stress that the roots of violence often lie precisely in the discourses that openly claim to reduce or exclude violence. As the expression of physical/verbal force against people/objects, violence covers a broad spectrum that can pervade the most serene of places and the most constructive of disciplines. For example, a room—the most pertinent unit of an architectural corpus—can imply a violation of the site, an embodiment of the uncanny, or even a suggestion of the macabre. In Mallarmé's "Igitur," the poet's self sinks deeply into itself, to the point of losing consciousness of the sensuous reality. As a result of this descent into nothingness, the self ceases to be and the room turns into an echo of a sepulchral reality.[2] Precisely because its feasibility depends on the very violence it conceals, the room/house reveals itself as a problematic space at the outset. Haunted or not, the very place that pretends to afford extreme security can open itself up to the secret invasion of terror.[3] To take another example, in Baudelaire's "Double Room," the protagonist is slowly overcome by the infinity of images that in the end appear to negate his original flight into the world of internal self-sufficiency. Inside the room, the dark space of seclusion, the unfolding of images floods consciousness to the point that the interior ceases to function as the space of withdrawal and peace. The long hours of solitude spent in the room, in the contemplation of infinite moments, end with the self's disappointed return to the unbearable "Memories, Regrets, Spasms, Agonies, Nightmares, Nerves, and Rage."[4]

Moreover, there are obvious reasons to argue that buildings and cities, especially in times of war, are obliterated not because they have misfortune to be in the way of a battle, but because they are themselves the target that has to be eliminated. Cato's famous saying *Carthago delenda est* (Carthage must be destroyed) encapsulates this drive. The animosity toward architecture conceals the truth that the discipline itself forms and informs violent functions despite its constructive properties. At the same time, the role played by architects in the crystallization of certain political schemes, often repressed under the pretext of fulfilling their design missions, underscores the doctrine according to which the responsibility of architecture is to design and build realities, regardless of the client's motives. The latter, while trying to preserve the discipline's superficial integrity, in fact contributes to its demise. It is no secret, for example, that fascism used architects to glorify itself at all levels. Suffice to mention the names of Sironi, Speer, and Terragni to recall this truth. Architects, whether they admit it or not, can become powerful leaven for violence.

Without a doubt, the relation of violence to architecture depends on the role taken on by architects in the shaping of the built environment, however, there is little recognition of the negative effects this very role could have on the architects themselves. Positioned at the crossroads of multiple social and political, expectations, architects inevitably run the risk of becoming scapegoats whenever something goes wrong. Such scenarios can take several forms and reveal a nexus of different motivations that cannot be understood without evoking the intricate patterns of historical, political, and professional factors entailed by the practice of architecture itself. Thus, they demand that the concept of violence is rethought not only from an architectural, but also from anthropological, psychoanalytical, and deontological standpoints. Contemporary violence against architects is often subtle and discrete, but it still evokes a complex reality that prescribes patterns of political and professional judgment regulated by the underlying mechanism of rivalry, itself rooted in a distant past.

Hence, we face a paradox: Can architecture take on violence as a problematic object of study and still distinguish itself as a separate discipline, the primary mission of which is propagation of the ideals of construction and harmony? Despite the constructive aspect of the process, keeping the projective energy of architecture oriented towards completeness and coherence, there is an equally destructive side that needs to be acknowledged and analyzed. Rather than elaborate solely the passive view of architecture as a target of violent operations, it is crucial to remember that the discipline constantly feeds the environment with physical objects and images that trigger violent actions.

Even a casual glance at the repertoire of the built environment reveals that structures (from palaces to illegal settlements, from propaganda exhibitions to jails, from barracks to detention centres, from suburban complexes to slaughterhouses, and from separation walls to concentration camps) either sanction violence or give it a spatial ground to thrive. As Bataille once noted, "monuments inspire social prudence and often even real fear. The taking of the Bastille is symbolic of this state of things: it is hard to explain this crowd movement other than by the animosity of the people against the monuments that are their real masters."[5] The space to be destroyed is the space of the dominant party, the very physical manifestation of the sovereign power. Within this context, the element of *jouissance*, often associated with the desire to obliterate physical objects, seems a natural consequence and an inherent feature of violence. As Jean-Luc Nancy rightly remarked, "the violent person wants to see the mark he makes on the thing or being he assaults, and violence consists precisely in imprinting such a mark. It is in the enjoyment (*jouissance*) of this mark that the 'excess' defining violence comes into play."[6]

In accordance with this logic of *jouissance*, the destruction of the World Trade Center's towers was obsessively replayed by TV stations for several months after the bombing itself. This persistent, if not ubiquitous, quality of violence to assert itself has nevertheless been seen as new by virtue of the effect played by the media in its emergence. And so, very shortly after the first episodes of the 2005 Paris riots, a national competition arose between French *cités*, towns, and regions to appear on French and, eventually, international televisions, as privileged sites of violence. The brutal clashes (which ultimately led to the declaration of the state of emergency), the burning of cars and buildings were the main events the (competing) urban pariahs wanted the world to see on TV. As Nancy observed, violence wants to be demonstrative and "monstrative." It shows itself and its effects.[7] This resistance of violence to invisibility necessarily turns it into a spectacle. Etienne Balibar, commenting on the same 2005 suburban riots, noted:

> it is very hard to say "who is using whom" in this process at the limits of the real and the virtual. But, what should be taken from this "virtual violence" is that it transforms real, endemic social violence, to which it responds, into spectacle, thereby at once making it visible in its intensity and invisible in its everydayness.[8]

The concept of visibility leads to another one: surveillance. Recent emergence of comprehensive electronic surveillance networks has instituted an incessant classification of urban subjects and sites, both in time and space. While CCTV cameras have perhaps proven highly useful in deterring attacks, they have also eroded the notion of individual privacy in an unprecedented way. To these networks, one should add other modes of surveillance, ranging from private phone conversations and Internet communications to routinely intercepted credit card and ATM transactions (and so on). This list includes also satellite surveillance and its diverse applications. With remote sensing and commercial accessibility of satellite images, destruction of buildings, villages, and cities can become evidence acceptable in legal proceedings, as well as a useful tool in depicting, promoting awareness of, and protesting various human rights infringements.

Against the incessant emphasis on constructive and harmless roles, the "animosity" towards buildings points to the truth that architecture is itself inherently violent. The discipline's supplementary complicity in objectifying violence ought to be, therefore, directly and overtly faced. Violence should be considered not exclusively within the operations performed by other activities on architecture, nor the opposite, but perhaps at the very borders that separate the discipline from the world around it. It is not sufficient to frame the question in terms of a simple alternative, suggesting that violence originates either from external sources or from within the architecture itself. Architectural "violence" is not simply that what "happens" to architecture (enacted on it from the outside), but rather it is directly related to the meeting of the two realms—the built environment and its other: the architectural and the inviolable world around it, be it ideological, political, religious, socio-economic or ethnic.

Since the idea of violence appears in so many spatial guises, it is meaningful to present corresponding, multiple levels of investigation. Therefore the present book introduces and debates a breadth of associative meanings and methods, but no attempt has been made to treat the question of violence and architecture in any exhaustive way. Nor is there an intention to construct or apply any definite theory of violence based exclusively on philosophy, anthropology, law, psychology, sociology, or psychoanalysis. Instead, several approaches relevant to the reading of each particular case have been selected, provoked by the desire to stress that violence is multifaceted in its spatial manifestations.

Finally, in arranging the articles for this volume, I have refrained from assigning general subject headings. The pieces have been arranged alphabetically according to the authors' last names. No matter how diverse the contributions may be, they all demonstrate practically that the question of violence must be approached drawing on sources from a variety of perspectives and disciplines, and—even more—from their intersections. The authors were invited to suggest their essays under this premise.

Bechir Kenzari
January 14, 2011

Endnotes

1— On this point, see Bechir Kenzari, "Archi-textures," *Architectural Theory Review*, 9. 2 (2004): 16–33.

2— Stéphane Mallarmé, "Igitur ou La Folie d'Elbehnon," in: *Igitur, Divagations, Un coup de dés* (Paris: Gallimard, 2003), 25–61.

3— See Anthony Vidler, *The Architectural Uncanny* (Cambridge, MA: MIT Press, 1992).

4— Charles Baudelaire, "Double Room," in *Paris Spleen* (New York: A New Directions Book, 1970), 5–7.

5— Cited by Denis Hollier, *Against Architecture: The Writings of Georges Bataille* (Cambridge, MA: MIT Press, 1992), ix–x.

6— Jean-Luc Nancy, "Image and Violence," in *The Ground of the Image* (New York: Fordham University Press, 2005), 20.

7— Nancy, "Image and Violence," 21.

8— Etienne Balibar, "Uprisings in the Banlieues," *Constellations*, 14. 1 (March 2007): 47–71.

THE ARCHITECTURE OF VIOLENCE: MARIO SIRONI AND ITALIAN FASCISM

LIBERO ANDREOTTI

Figure 1. Mario Sironi, *Poster for the Exhibition of the Fascist Revolution*, 1932.

THE ARCHITECTURE OF VIOLENCE

"An art of effects, nothing but effects, *espressivo* at any price": the propaganda art of the Italian painter Mario Sironi would seem to exemplify everything that Nietzsche deplored in his famous characterization of Wagner's musical dramas—their grandiloquence, their obsessively repeated leitmotifs, and their use of every available means to maximize the emotional impact of the work on the public. But if Sironi's lifelong passion for Wagner, first pointed out by Mario De Micheli in 1973, certainly deserves the closest critical scrutiny, it is to Walter Benjamin's reflections on shock and the "destruction of experience" that one must turn to understand the essential relevance of this unendearing but arguably most important Italian artist between the wars.[1]

For Benjamin, an "atrophy of experience" was a defining feature of modern life. He traced its beginnings to capitalist commodification and the rise of a mass culture based on technological reproduction whose effects were particularly evident in the daily press. As he noted,

> If the purpose of the newspaper was to allow the viewer to incorporate news as part of his own experience, it would be an unqualified failure, but its goal is just the opposite and it achieves it: to separate as much as possible the news item from anything that might connect directly to the readers' lived experience.[2]

Figure 2. Exhibition of the Fascist Revolution, Rome 1932, nighttime view of the facade.

The tendency toward brevity and comprehensibility was one element that contributed to this effect; another was the newspaper's sensational layout. Both served to screen out the living reality of an event for the distracted and impatient modern-day reader.

Sironi's propaganda art exemplifies these new conditions of reception. The succinctness of his graphic style of commentary, as seen in the many hundreds of front-page political illustrations he made for Mussolini's newspaper *Il popolo d'Italia*, epitomizes a mode of communication that "replaces older narration with information and information with sensation."[3] Much the same could be said about Sironi's monumental installations of the late 1920s and early 1930s, which along with his *consuntivi* (summings up) in the daily press made him the best-known and most recognizable Italian artist between the wars. For Benjamin, quoting André Gide after a visit to one of Sironi's shows, these propaganda settings reflected an "architectural journalism" that was the true essence of fascist monumentality.[4]

Like other writers of the period, including Theodor Adorno, Benjamin recognized that the language of journalism was only one aspect of a more profound modern-day "barbarism" that could not be dissociated from either the long history of capitalist expansion or, in more recent times, from the trauma of the Great War, when, as he put it in a famous passage in "The Narrator," "you could see the soldiers returning home from the

Figure 3. Sironi, *cover illustration for*
La Rivista Illustrata de ll Popolo d'Italia
(Nov. 1932).

THE ARCHITECTURE OF VIOLENCE

front turned silent, not richer but poorer in communicable experience," to which he added, significantly, "and the stream of photo-albums that came out after the war was anything but experience communicated directly from mouth to ear."5

Benjamin's reflections on the war closely parallel Adorno's in *Minima Moralia*. Both recognized that the Great War had dramatically accelerated trends that throughout the nineteenth century had affected only a fringe of "traumatophile types" like Baudelaire, in whose lyrics Benjamin had recognized the first signs of a more general "breakdown of experience."6 With the war, the irreducibility of trauma to normal categories of experience seemed to have penetrated more deeply and widely into the relationship between the subject and the outside world, altering "overnight, and in ways previously thought impossible—as Benjamin noted—our very image of the external world."7 Such profound perceptual shifts affected as much the work of artists and writers of the interwar period as they did the quality and the texture of everyday life. A typical symptom was the feeling that social reality had somehow become "less real," that the boundaries between art and everyday life, subject and object, had become blurred—a recurring theme of late-modernist literature. Sironi's famous *Paesaggi urbani* of the late teens and early twenties, representing the industrial suburbs of Milan as eerily empty landscapes ruled by impersonal forces, convey a similar mood. In the social field, a reverse side of these

Figure 4. Sironi, Paesaggio Urbano, 1921.

perceptual shifts was the proliferation of what Tyrus Miller has called "mimetic practices": role playing, slogans, contagious imitation, ways of speaking and dressing that reflected the general "de-authentification" of social life during these years. Such mass cultural phenomena—the first signs of a "society of the spectacle" where "everything that was directly lived has moved away into a representation," as Guy Debord would write 40 years later—invested every industrialized country in the West.[8] In Italy they were nowhere more evident than in fascism's obsessive preoccupation with symbols, gestures, and ritualized forms of behavior on which its aesthetic, even more than political appeal, was based.[9] Sironi's work was an essential element in this drive to construct a new type of spectatorial subjectivity. His installations offer a unique insight into the way, in Benjamin's words, new forms of perception could be pressed into the service of "ritual values."

In what follows, I examine the most sensational of Sironi's propaganda exhibitions, the *Mostra della rivoluzione fascista* (Exhibition of the Fascist Revolution; EFR), mounted in Rome in 1932, focusing especially on the relationship between the work and the viewer.[10] Like Benjamin

Figure 5. Rome, 28 October 1932. Parade marching down Via Nazionale, with the EFR in the background.

Figure 6. Libera and De Renzi, EFR façade, nighttime view.

THE ARCHITECTURE OF VIOLENCE

describing the poetry of Baudelaire, I take the experience of shock as the key to deciphering the "secret architecture" of Sironi's work, of which we can say that, like Baudelaire's, it involved a high degree of conscious planning.[11] Of special interest, as we shall see, is how Sironi strove to create the feeling of boundary loss, one of the most distinctive features of the "fascist experience."[12] No less central is how he used a whole new range of materials and techniques to construct an ideological narrative whose power and vividness was directly proportional to its ability to evacuate the living reality of an event. To consider Sironi's work in this way is not to dismiss its cultural, stylistic, or psychological dimensions, which have been the subject of a great deal of writing in recent years; rather, it is to highlight the structural forces at work in some of the first media events of the twentieth century, forces that Sironi reveals in a particularly clear way.[13] Contrary to many accounts of the artist that tend to cast him in the role of avatar of a timeless tradition of Italian classicism, however, I argue that Sironi's installations were based on a clear set of journalistic principles; that their driving mechanism was the principle of shock; and that their goal, not unlike that of the emerging culture industry, was to promote the massive reconfigurations of human perception that accompanied the rise of the society of the spectacle.[14]

The longest-running propaganda show ever mounted by the Italian fascist government, now recognized as "the most important cultural and political event of the *ventennio*," the Exhibition of the Fascist Revolution opened in Rome on 29 October 1932 to mark the tenth anniversary of fascism's assumption of power.[15] In Mussolini's words, it was to be "an offering of faith that the old comrades hand down to the new ones so that, enlightened by our martyrs and heroes, they may continue the heavy task" of building a fascist Italy.[16] The first in what would become a series of similar events leading up to the World Exhibition planned for 1939 at the EUR in Rome, the show could hardly have come at a better time for the regime, whose popularity in Italy and abroad was then approaching its peak. The relative stability of Italy's economy compared to other Western countries, along with the widespread belief that fascism represented a "third way" between capitalism and Communism, was echoed in the self-confident tone of the organizers and in the show's uniquely innovative and experimental character. Indeed, the significance of the exhibition in the history of Italian art and architecture can scarcely be underestimated. As the first major experiment in the field of propaganda exhibitions, it helped to focus attention on a wide range of issues related to the development of a "fascist style," stimulating new directions of work in many fields, from architecture to photography and the graphic arts, as well as introducing many fledgling artists and architects to the wider public. Some of these, including the sculptor Mario Marini, became leading figures in Italian and European art after the war.

The building selected to house the exhibition was the Palazzo delle Esposizioni, designed by Pio Piacentini in 1881. Photographs offering views of the palazzo on the day before the opening, commemorating the tenth anniversary of the March on Rome, show files of Blackshirts marching down Via Nazionale on their way to Piazza Venezia, where Mussolini would inaugurate Via dell'Impero, the temporary façade of the exhibition visible behind them. During its entire two-year run, the show effectively became the principal site of fascist worship around the world, attracting

Figure 7. Pio Piancentini, Palazzo delle Esposizioni, Rome 1881.

Figure 8. Sironi and Muzio, Italian Press Pavilion, Barcelona, 1929.

Figure 9. Sironi and Muzio, Italian Pavilion, Press Section, Barcelona, 1929.

THE ARCHITECTURE OF VIOLENCE

an estimated four million visitors, including, among others, Paul Valéry, Auguste Perret, Maurice Denis, Le Corbusier, and André Gide, their recorded reactions ranging from extreme disgust, for Gide, to equally extreme enthusiasm, for Le Corbusier.[17]

As the principal inspiring force behind this event, Sironi already had a long career as propagandist behind him. Even before the March on Rome, his job as political illustrator for Il popolo d'Italia had put him in almost daily contact with Mussolini, designing hundreds of illustrations for the newspaper and dozens of posters and covers for books and magazines. His first propaganda installations dated from four years earlier, when he designed a series of press pavilions advertising the publications of Il popolo d'Italia, first at the Fiera Campionaria di Milano (1928) and then at the Pressa exhibition in Cologne (1928) and the International Exposition in Barcelona (1929). Through these early and still somewhat tentative works, realized in collaboration with the Milanese architect Giovanni Muzio, Sironi had become familiar with the latest techniques of exhibition design, as seen, for example, in the spectacular work of El Lissitzky in Cologne and Barcelona. Photomontage, typographic inscriptions, photographic enlargements, and large relief decorations were among the techniques he and Muzio used to amplify the visual effects of the newspaper's front page. No less important, however, was Sironi's discovery of architecture's potential to underscore the vividness of the presentation through a rhythmic spatial sequence, as seen, most effectively, in the

Figure 10. El Lissitzky, USSR Pavilion, Cologne, 1928.

Sezione Arti Grafiche at the Villa Reale in Monza (1930). The power of a monumental architecture to appeal to the viewer's subconscious was also a recurring concern of Sironi's paintings, and by the early 1930s, amid the debate surrounding rationalism as the new "architecture of the state," it had became a favorite topic of his writings. Here, consistent with the *mot d'ordre* of a constructive synthesis from the experimental phase of the avant-gardes, Sironi called for a new alliance between painters, sculptors,

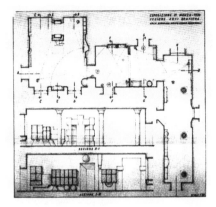

Figure 11. *Sironi and Muzio, Sezione Arti Grafiche, Monza 1930, plan of remodeled interior spaces leading up to the Salone d'Onore (upper left).*

Figure 12. *Sironi and Muzzio, Sezione Arti Grafiche, Monza, 1930. View of Muzio's Salone d'Onore.*

Figure 13. *Sironi, I costruttori, 1928.*

and architects to define a fascist style at once monumental, religious, and warlike, based on "concentration rather than dispersal," and employing unambiguous symbols to achieve a unity in the arts analogous to the one Mussolini had accomplished in the political realm.[18]

The EFR was Sironi's long-awaited opportunity to construct a fascist *Gesamtkunstwerk* on a scale unprecedented in his career as propagandist par excellence of the Fascist Revolution. Organized by the future ambassador to Berlin, Dino Alfieri, assisted by Luigi Freddi, who would go on to play a significant role in the state's cinema industry, the show was designed by a team of approximately twenty artists and architects, many of them young and with relatively little experience. Sironi's part in this event included acting as de facto artistic director, attending frequent meetings with the organizers to determine the overall plan and the principal sequence of spaces, and designing the largest and most important series of rooms (P through S).[19]

The overall plan of the exhibition, cleverly adapted from the old neo-classical order of the Palazzo delle Esposizioni, makes clear the organizers' intentions. The scheme was arrived at only after two earlier proposals were considered and rejected, one by the conservative architect

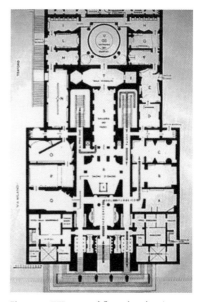

Figure 14. EFR, ground floor plan showing the direction of movement from the entrance.

Enrico Del Debbio, the other by the stage designer Antonio Valente. Both had apparently failed to meet Il Duce's demand for "something bold and audacious, without gloomy reminders of past decorative styles."[20] More important, both schemes would have maintained the centrality of the palazzo's neoclassical plan, with the side rooms opening toward the main sequence of monumental spaces. In marked contrast with these proposals, which would have allowed the viewer a relative freedom of movement, the final plan of the exhibition established a single path leading from the entrance, through a succession of fifteen side rooms, each narrating a moment in the history of fascism, and concluding with a grand procession of major halls down the building's main axis of symmetry toward the final room, the Shrine of the Martyrs. This sequential layout was meant to evoke something like a cinematic experience, a possible precedent being El Lissitzky's USSR Pavilion in Cologne (1928), which Sironi would have seen while working on the Italian pavilion nearby. Unlike El Lissitzky's montage-like assemblages, however, the narrative here unfolded in a strictly linear manner, downplaying the possibility of peripheral vision so as to maximize the impact of the show on the viewer.

Even more telling was the implicit ritual order on which the entire sequence was based, an order that recalled the liturgy of a Catholic mass, with an introitus, a credo, a symbolic reenactment of the passion, and a final rite of communion in the Shrine of the Martyrs. A militarized version of this four-part sequence constituted, in fact, the essential and never openly acknowledged subtext of the ceremony of inauguration, where Il Duce presided over the hymns sung on the front steps of the palazzo, the swearing of the oath in the entrance atrium, the slow procession through each of the fifteen historical rooms, and a concluding rite of communion in the Shrine. Such a ritual structure—itself a textbook case of fascism's use of technology "for the production of ritual values"— was clearly intended to exploit the force of religious traditions in Italy. Through semantic displacements and substitutions like that between the passion of Christ and that of the fascist martyrs, it capitalized on deeply embedded narratives in order to recast fascism itself as a new, secular "religion of the State."[21]

A marked ritual emphasis is clearly apparent in the design of the temporary façade by the young rationalist architect and sometime futurist Adalberto Libera in collaboration with the older and more experienced Mario De Renzi. Photographs depict the façade at nighttime because the exhibition was meant to be visited by night as well as by day. Libera's scheme, evidently based on Sironi's and Muzio's press pavilion in Barcelona of 1929, was poster-like in its concision. A red square block, symbolizing the blood of the martyrs, was flanked by two lower wings in gray, with four giant fasci standing several meters from the wall and connected by a horizontal slab supporting the letters MOSTRA DELLA RIVOLUZIONE FASCISTA. Centered symmetrically on the arched opening, the façade presented itself as a modern reinterpretation of a triumphal arch, with the fasci substituting for the giant order of columns. In Rome it was a direct reference to the nearby classical ruins, a main point of attraction for visitors to the capital. In this way the façade expressed a major theme of the decennial celebrations: the link between fascism and Italy's Roman heritage.

The most striking feature of the design, however, was the way it merged the themes of war and technology. One perceptive viewer, the poet Ada Negri, called it a "war machine . . . sharp and cutting," an aspect forcefully conveyed by the fasci, which were made in bolted copper plates, and by the razor-sharp axes.[22] The entrance consisted of a barrel-vaulted corridor with narrow metal bands filtering artificial light, a poetic meta-

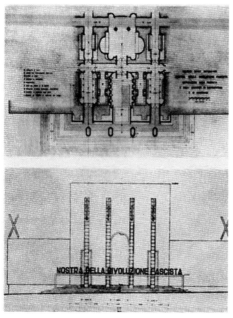

Figure 15. Adalberto Libera and Mario De Renzi, plan of the remodeled entrance and elevation of the temporary facade, EFR.

Figure 16. Libera and De Renzi, EFR entrance.

phor in praise of technology and electricity (the entire show used electrical lighting to the almost complete exclusion of natural sources). Both the façade and the entrance thus reflected the anti-utilitarian conception of technology implicit in Libera's slogan "the machine as a work of art." Both also illustrated Benjamin's remarks on the connection between fascism's cult of war and the tradition of aestheticism. As Benjamin noted in 1935, with prescient awareness of the approaching disaster, "the fascist theory of art has the mark of the purest aestheticism. . . . The 'art of war' . . . incarnates the fascist idea of technology freed from banal use. But the poetic side of technology, which the fascist upholds against the prosaic conception of the Russians, is also its lethal side."[23]

Equally telling was how the design sought to include the bodies of the twelve soldier/apostles standing in front, which the guidebook described as "human decorations." Their posture of attention mimicked the shape of the fasci, the metal of which alluded to the soldiers' helmets, while the blades related to their bayonets. Such mimetic contaminations between an "animated" architecture and mechanized human bodies were a characteristic feature of the show. Indeed, much the same could be said about the façade's relation to the masses of Blackshirts marching by it on the inauguration day; the blocks of people no less part of the total image being conveyed than the building itself. It was through this kind of imagery—which, as Benjamin noted, employed human masses as integral

Figure 17. Soldiers guarding the exhibition.

Figure 18. Giuseppe Terragni, Sala O, view from the entrance.

THE ARCHITECTURE OF VIOLENCE

elements of the composition—that fascist architecture traced a "magic circle" around the work and the viewer, drawing both into an illusory and complete other world in which art appealed as a totality.[24]

Among the rooms leading up to Sironi's monumental sequence of spaces, the most striking by far was Giuseppe Terragni's Sala O, which directly preceded Sironi's rooms and narrated the period of social unrest leading up to the March on Rome. Sironi is known to have taken an active role in its design, determining, among other things, the diagonal arrangement of the space as lead-up to the following rooms. Photographs of the Sala O convey a feeling of lightness and airiness in which the bombardment of optical signals expresses the excitement and confusion of the "pre-insurrectionary" period. Terragni used diaphanous screens to display large graphic compositions that were illuminated by beams of light, producing a vivid interplay of light and shade. A concern for optical effects was especially apparent in what the guidebook described as the "transparency and interpenetration" of the figures in Terragni's narrative. This was most evident in his systematic use of reflective materials and in his superimposing and laterally displacing one image over another, as in the graphic constructions on the diagonal screen, which were supposed to convey "the rapid succession" and the "simultaneity of events" of the insurrection.[25] Their effect was to dissolve the reference planes of the ground, the four walls, and the ceiling. The shiny black linoleum floor, the

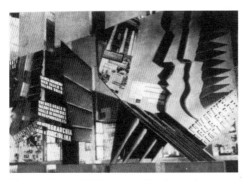

Figure 19. Terragni, Sala O, view of the diagonal screen.

Figure 20. Konstantin Melnikov, USSR Pavilion, Paris, 1925.

silhouetted cross on the ceiling, the copper and aluminum constructions on the diagonal screen that, as one critic remarked, conveyed the effect of a flame, a symbol of religious ardor, all served to abolish the ground plane and walls as firm datums.[26] The resulting sensation of weightlessness, of literally floating in space, was described by the architecture critic Edoardo Persico as a "fantasia terremotata," a seismic fantasy.[27]

The sources for Terragni's design included, interestingly, a number of constructivist precedents. The spatial arrangement, centered on the diagonal screen upholding one arm of a giant X silhouetted against the lit ceiling, was likely based on Konstantin Melnikov's USSR Pavilion of

Figure 21. Le Corbusier, Nestlé Pavilion, Zurich, 1928.

Figure 22. Le Corbusier, L'art décoratif d'ajourd'hui, 1925.

Figure 23. Terragni, Sala O, Photomontage near the exit.

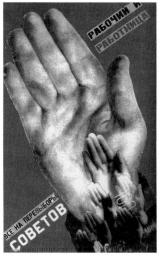

Figure 24. Gustav Klutsis, Poster Workers, Everyone Must Vote in the Election of Soviets! (c. 1920).

THE ARCHITECTURE OF VIOLENCE

1925, which displayed a similar contrast between a diagonal path and a rectangular enclosure and which also included a crossing motif over the open passage. The screen itself, acting as both a billboard and a showcase, was probably derived from Le Corbusier's Nestlé Pavilion in Zurich (1928). The giant photomontage that took up the left wall of the room, showing an immense crowd merging into a field of hands raised in the Roman salute, echoed strongly a poster by the Russian constructivist Gustav Klutsis, while the three spiraling turbines that crossed the composition from the lower left towards the right were likely taken from Le Corbusier's *L'art decorative d'aujourd'hui*, which contained a similar image.

Such borrowings, testifying to Terragni's avid interest in the works of European modernism he would have seen in illustrated journals like *La casa bella*, were far from neutral, however. For example, unlike Le Corbusier, Terragni used the turbine to link technology with modern warfare. A photographic enlargement at the center of the photomontage included a line by the poet Giosuè Carducci: *quando col sangue alla ruota si da il movimento* (when with blood the wheel is set in motion). The reference to the martyrs turned the whole composition into a militaristic glorification of human sacrifice—a fitting illustration of Benjamin's remark that "imperialist war is a rebellion of technology which collects, in the form of 'human material,' the claims to which society has denied its natural material."

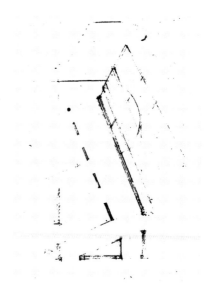

Figure 25. Terragni, study sketch for the Sala O (diagonal screen on the right, escalating sequence of panels on the left, Balbo's column of fire in the upper left).

Instead of draining rivers, society directs a human stream into a bed of trenches."[28]

In much the same way, Terragni's borrowings from Melnikov reflected a different intention that can be seen in a study sketch preserved in his archives, showing an axonometric view of the room. The sketch is an early attempt to define a spatial equivalent for the narrative, with a longitudinal corridor, a semicircular space behind the screen, and a progression of vertical panels on the left wall evoking "the rhythm and the movement" of the narrative in its three main stages, which might be labeled organization, struggle, and sacrifice.[29] Thus the escalating rhythm of panels on the left represented the wave of mass gatherings leading up to the March on Rome, with the lone column in the far left corner standing for Italo Balbo's infamous "column of fire" (*colonna di fuoco*, the scorched-earth campaign against the farming cooperatives of the north that marked the beginning of the insurrection). A comparison between the drawing and the executed scheme shows that Terragni's intention was only imperfectly realized. Nonetheless, a distinctive feature of his architecture, the idea

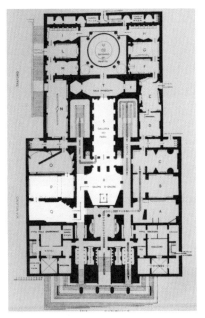

Figure 26. Plan of Sironi's Rooms O through S, the dotted lines in Room P indicate the suspended wall.

Figure 27. Sironi, view of Room P from the entrance vestibule, the suspended wall is visible above.

THE ARCHITECTURE OF VIOLENCE

of a rhythmic and narrative subdivision of space into successive stanzas, made its first appearance in his work here, as a direct response to the practical requirements of the show. The most sophisticated development of this theme would be the Danteum project of 1939, which was based on the textual structure of the Divine Comedy.[30]

For all its richness and intricacy, however, the Sala O's main purpose was merely to prepare the viewer for Sironi's grand finale, offering itself as a lead-up to the monumental sequence that would follow. A glance at the overall plan of Sironi's four rooms (P through S) suggests a very different formal approach than Terragni's. Where the latter sought fragmentation and dispersal, Sironi aimed for unity and concentration, stressing mass over line and tactile over optical qualities. This sculptural emphasis can be seen in what the guidebook called the overall "plastic development" of the four rooms, which moved gradually from flat wall decorations to increasingly bold relief, to architecture, the slow and dramatic pace of the narrative underscoring the transition from a predominantly optical to a tactile register.[31] Two slight modifications to the plan of the palazzo were especially effective here. The first was the small entrance vestibule in Room P, which served effectively to create a single five-part spatial sequence with each space larger than the preceding one. The second modification, made possible by opening a door in the far corner of room P, was the choice of a diagonal path across the first two rooms. Both served

Figure 28. Sironi, *Photomontage of the March on Rome*.

to increase the viewer's presence in the space and to propel him or her forward through an escalating spatial crescendo.

The vestibule was marked off from the rest of the room by a massive wall lifted about three meters from the ground. The wall itself might have recalled a curtain rising on the final act of a drama. Viewers were meant to pass under the wall like spectators onto a stage, the transition from constrained to open space dramatized by the light that flooded the room through a silk screen hung from the ceiling, producing a mist-like haze reminiscent of the steam curtains used in Wagner's operas.

The drive to make the public into an "actor" in the drama clearly dictated the theme and the placement of the large photomontage of the March on Rome, which took up the entire wall facing the viewer as he or she stepped onto the scene. The repeated rows of life-size soldiers shown marching toward the capital, like the pilgrims' march to Rome in Wagner's overture to *Tannhäuser*, were likely drawn from the many photo albums of the Great War published throughout the 1920s—the same ones that epitomized, for Benjamin, the destruction of experience inherent in the press. For the viewing public, however, the most immediate reference would have been to itself, the entire image reflecting the stream of visitors crossing the room diagonally toward the exit. Like Wagner's theater productions, which, as Adorno remarked, aimed to "incorporate the audi-

Figure 29. El Lissitzky, USSR Pavilion, Cologne, 1928, Photomontage of the Soviet Press.

Figure 30. The Roman Salute.

The Architecture of Violence

ence as an integral element of its effect," the representation of the public served to promote to the greatest degree its identification with the scene.[32]

The technique used in the photomontage was likely inspired by El Lissitzky's work in Cologne and Barcelona, which made a spectacular use of this medium. In stark contrast with El Lissitzky, however, Sironi exploited the illusionism of the photograph to draw the viewer forcefully into the space of the picture. The thematic unity, the tiered composition anticipating the great mural cycles that Sironi would produce a few years later, and the evident concern for a seamless narrative continuity (even to the point of erasing by hand the sharp lines dividing one image from the next) all expressed an archaic and magical conception of the photograph that was basically at odds with El Lissitzky's documentary approach. It is no accident that the guidebook—perhaps in memory of the scandal John Heartfield had set off when he introduced two satires of Mussolini in a show of the *Novembergruppe* in Berlin a few years earlier—systematically shunned the term *photomontage* in favor of the medievalizing *photomosaic*, and that Sironi would eventually abandon the medium, perceived as too commercial, in favor of more permanent materials.[33]

Aside from photography, the main decorative device used in the four rooms was the large mural relief, usually combined with a typographic slogan and clearly intended to amplify the percussive force of the artist's own political illustrations. The juxtaposition of image and word evoked

Figures 31–34. Sironi, studies for Room P.

the magical concentration on sight and sound made possible by photography and radio. Likewise, the concealment of the construction process used in the reliefs—a makeshift mixture of disparate materials, from wood to plaster, recalling the hybrids Adorno criticized in Wagner's operas—heightened the fetish-like quality of the figures.

Before we examine the stream of mural constructions that covered the walls of each room in a crescendo from flat surface to architecture, it is useful to consider some of the many surviving studies in a wide range of media, which are a rich source of information on Sironi's intentions. Taken together, they present a surprisingly disparate array of images and ideas that would seem, at first sight, to have little in common with the executed scheme, a fact that has led some critics to overemphasize Sironi's talent for improvisation.[34] On closer inspection, however, it is possible to recognize a consistent set of concerns, relating less to the choice of images themselves than to their visual effect and their placement along

Figure 35. Sironi, Synthesis of the World War, 1918.

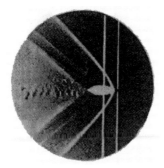

Figure 36. Ernst Mach, photograph of a bullet in flight (1880s).

THE ARCHITECTURE OF VIOLENCE

the viewer's path. Most of these studies display contrasting visual motifs that have a marked gestural quality. Two are especially dramatic: the diagonal and the wedge. Both were common devices in Sironi's work and indeed in much of the graphic art of those years. The diagonal emphasis could be found in any number of earlier drawings, where it served, among other things, to counteract the static geometry of the page. In this case, however, an added connotation would have been obvious to most viewers, who would have recalled the Roman salute, the latest in a series of stylized gestures (including *passo romano*, the Roman walk), which had just recently been imposed as a required custom for young recruits and intended to redefine the appearance of the "fascist man."

Similarly, precedents for the wedge ranged from Luigi Russolo's *La rivolta* (1911) to Sironi's own *Sintesi della guerra mondiale* (1918).[35] In both, the wedge was used as an image of force and speed similar to that of a bullet in flight (as depicted, for example, in Ernst Mach's famous photograph). Its meaning, in this case, was best summed up by Sironi himself when he compared the exhibition to "a giant wedge planted into the heart of the capital to sweep away the last remnants of resistance to modern art."[36] Indeed, whether as a dagger, triangle, flag, or ax, the wedge was the single most common motif used in the show.

Taken together, the gestures of the diagonal and the wedge were complementary—as may be seen in Sironi's cover illustration for the guide to the EFR which brought them together in one image. In reality, however, the gestures were meant to be played out successively, alternating like the tonal and dominant motifs of a musical score to suggest the movement of an arm raised and lowered repeatedly to strike a blow.

If one now turns to the mural decorations as built, one can see how these two essential images/gestures, embedded like subliminal signals in the figures of the narrative, structured the entire spatial sequence from beginning to end. The barrage began in the first room, with the Roman dagger cutting the heavy red chain representing the downfall of liberalism, followed by the eagle and flag with the bold white characters LA MARCIA SU ROMA evoking the ascent of fascism. Conceived, like all the other reliefs, as unframed and integral with the wall so as to place the viewer inside the space of the picture, they activated the basic rhythm that would structure the entire sequence, the downward thrust of the first playing off the sideways sweep of the second. Even before entering the second room, the wedge motif returned in the violent thrust of the letter R of the word ROMA over the entrance door, which appeared to cross the wall from side to side, the force of the image recalling the power and precision

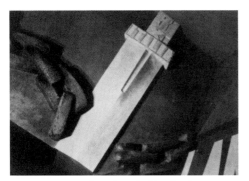

Figure 37. Sironi, Sala P, The end of the Liberal Era, sideway view toward the ceiling of the dividing wall, with dagger and chain.

Figure 38. Sironi, Sala P, The Ascent of Fascism, view towards the exit.

Figure 39. Sironi, Sala Q, view towards the exit.

Figure 40. Sironi (left) near the entrance to Sala Q.

THE ARCHITECTURE OF VIOLENCE

of the printing press. Projecting over the viewer as he or she moved into the room, the word ROMA framed the view of two giant warriors raising the Roman standard of victory. Lifted high above a pedestal, their stone-like texture soliciting the viewer's sense of touch as well as sight, their strong diagonals recalled those of the earlier relief of the eagle and flag. Consistent with this basic rhythm, the exit displayed the massive typeset characters of Mussolini's declaration of victory in another forceful push downward, similar to that of the dagger in the first room.

Distilled to their bare essence and redoubled in strength, the same two gestures could also be found in the Salone d'Onore, representing the apotheosis of Mussolini, whose more-than-life-size statue dominated the space from the top of a high niche. Their effectiveness was due in no small measure to the powerful structural rhetoric through which Sironi dramatized the effects of load, support, and structural penetration—as seen, for example, on the end wall, where the square characters of the word *DUX* seemed to physically support the upper projecting portion of the wall. The first gesture took its place over the two side doors, hence directly above and facing the viewer as he entered the room, where in a direct transposition of *Sintesi della guerra mondiale* a massive triangle appeared as if forced energetically between the top of the pier and the lintel of the doors. The second gesture was even more prominently displayed over the exit in the form of the two crossing diagonals of a gigantic Roman

ure 41. Sironi, Salone d'Onore,
w from the entrance.

Figure 42. Sironi, Salone
d'Onore, side entrance.

Figure 43. Sironi, Salone d'Onore,
view of the exit.

numeral ten, symbol of the fascist decennial, cantilevered dramatically over two massive piers. The overall effect, suggesting an epic battle of conflicting structural forces, was summed up by Margherita Sarfatti when she wrote of Sironi's art that "its only law is struggle," noting also that the exhibition owed its dominant character to "le meilleur des nos peintres italiens d'aujourd'hui, Mario Sironi, qui a donné a l'exposition l'autorité de son haut talent et de son âme fière, puissante et tourmentée: une âme et un talent tumultueux et vraiment Michelangelesque."[37]

Sironi's understanding of how architecture could be used to bind the viewer forcefully to the scene was nowhere more evident, however, than in the last of his rooms, the Galleria dei Fasci. Here, in a grandiose recapitulation of fascism's heroic history, ten colossal pilasters lined the hall, five on either side. Each symbolized one year of the fascist revolution. Looming gigantically over the viewer with their oblique projections, the pilasters were vaguely reminiscent, as Giorgio Ciucci notes, of Melnikov's Rusakov Club in Moscow (1928).[38] A more direct and obvious reference,

Figure 45. Konstantin Melnikov, Rusakov Club, Moscow, 1928.

Figure 44. Sironi, Galleria dei Fasci, with Italy on the March on the back wall.

Figure 46. Sironi, cover for Gerarchia, 1926.

THE ARCHITECTURE OF VIOLENCE

however, would have been the Roman salute. Structurally encoded in the shape of the new "fascist order," the repeated gesture served efficiently to frame the image of "Italy on the March," which took up the end wall. Executed by Quirino Ruggieri, a well-known and respected sculptor, this plaster relief of five meters in height presented itself as a nearly exact replica of one of Sironi's cover illustrations of the journal *Gerarchia* from a few years earlier. Ruggieri's scrupulous adherence to Sironi's sketch left no room for the expression of his own very different plastic sensibility. The result reflected the coercive relations underlying the Wagnerian idea of the *Gesamtkunstwerk*, which as Adorno noted, anticipated the methods of the culture industry.[39]

Like Libera's façade, but in a more powerful because literal way, the Galleria was meant to be a backdrop for files of saluting militiamen, the mimetic exchange between architecture and the human body emphasized by the pilasters' relentless repetition of a single unvaried image/gesture of the diagonal. In point of fact, a curious feature of the Galleria was precisely the absence of a second theme. In the rooms preceding it, the diagonal and the wedge were always clearly presented in pairs: from the downward thrust of the dagger in the first room to the redoubling of the diagonal at the exit of the Salone, the orchestration of shocks and countershocks formed a regular and escalating rhythm of ABABAB. At first sight, the Galleria appeared to contradict this rhythm. Instead of returning to the theme of the wedge, as one might have expected after passing under the giant Roman numeral ten in the Salone, it insisted on the single theme of the diagonal.

Like everything else in Sironi's settings, this effect was not accidental but calculated to obtain two distinct results, one temporal and one spatial. First, the relentless and monotone repetition of a single motif served to create a feeling of a hypnotic suspension, the lack of closure contributing to the darkly romantic *angst* of the space, which would have recalled ancient precedents such as the giant statues that lined the hall of the temple of Abu Simbel. Even more important, however, was the Galleria's function to prepare the viewer for the last scene of the exhibition, the Shrine of the Martyrs, where the theme of the wedge would return for the last time, and with the greatest possible force, in the gruesome image of a cross thrust like a dagger into the ground and surrounded by a pool of blood. Spatially and temporally, therefore, the Galleria acted somewhat like a prolungato in music to draw out the dominant key in the next-to-the-last note in order to heighten the force of the closing finale. This feeling was even more pronounced in the exhibition because the Galleria was separated from the Shrine by a small transverse room. Made by Leo Longanesi with the affected simplicity of *Strapaese* to illustrate Il Duce's biography, this room marked a further gap, or "a moment of silence," as the guidebook put it, before the final room.

Designed by Adalberto Libera and the stage designer Antonio Valente but clearly inspired by Sironi's political imagery, the Shrine of the Martyrs was based on the most famous site of Christian martyrdom, the Colosseum in Rome, which also had an iron cross standing in the center of the arena to commemorate the blood of the martyrs. Libera's militaristic rendering of the theme, with bolted copper plates similar to the fasci on the façade, served effectively to annex this religious symbol to fascism's own iconography. The same objective explains why, just a few months before the opening of the exhibition, Mussolini had the cross in the Colosseum removed, under the pretext of archeological excavations, only to have it reerected—with suitable adjustments—at the heart of the EFR.[40] Libera's design was thus a particularly explicit example of the syncretism of ritual events like the EFR—the migration of symbols and displacements through

Figure 47. *Libera and Valente, Shrine of the Martyrs.*

Figure 48. *The Colosseum.*

THE ARCHITECTURE OF VIOLENCE

which fascism, like any other mass political ideology, constructed its own discourse of self-legitimation.[41] The same could be said about the obscure fascist funerary rite to which the Shrine alluded, a rite in which the assembled mourners would gather in a circle around the body of the dead comrade, the eldest would call out the names of the martyrs and all those present would answer in unison "*Presente!*" ("Here!"). The word *presente*, recalling the litanies of a Catholic mass, was repeated ad infinitum on the six metal rings surrounding the cross in the Shrine.[42]

Like the façade, the architecture of the Shrine exploited the magical effects of new materials and technologies such as metal and electrical lighting, its illusionistic effects made possible by Valente's long experience in the art of stage design. Here, however, an added touch was provided by the sound recordings of the songs of the martyrs, which could be heard echoing from afar. Like Il Duce's voice on the radio, the martyrs could be heard but not seen. The sensory split between sound and sight, image and word that was part of the effect of estrangement produced by photography and radio was evident here no less than in the juxtaposition of images and slogans recurring throughout the show.

In conclusion, it is important to emphasize the social function of the EFR as a "representative rite" intended to reaffirm and articulate a consensus around fascism as a new secular religion.[43] This overriding imperative largely determined the EFR's symbolism, its ritual organization, and its representation of the public as a protagonist in a mythical narrative. The same imperative to celebrate consensus also explains the importance of Wagner's methods, which as Jonathan Crary notes, were "all about the transformative effect that could be obtained through the collective experience of a ritual communal event."[44] The EFR also shows, however, that "the rational production of collective dream-like states"—as Crary aptly describes Wagner's project—involved issues of organization, narrative structure, and perceptual control that were neither simple nor obvious.[45] The question of how to effectively lead the audience toward a blind, oceanic immersion in the scene, to experience what Freud called "the sense of an indissoluble bond, of being at one with the world as a whole," was only one of many issues inherent in Wagner's project.[46] The EFR shows how Sironi approached it with purpose, not hesitating to borrow ideas from his ideological rivals if necessary, and lifting a great many themes from the Catholic Church.

At the heart of Sironi's strategy was the idea of a rhythmic repetition of blows, encoded in the figures of the narrative and carefully calibrated in their tone, formal register, and intensity. Central to this orchestral strategy, which as Nietzsche said of Wagner, "used music as a means to hypnotize," was Sironi's unique understanding of the effects of shock in both the print media and more recent fields such as photography and radio. No less central, however, was the capacity of architecture to instill more deeply (because less consciously) the structures of feeling, the gestures and slogans through which the new fascist subjectivity was to be displayed. To a degree possible only for someone with the figurative sensibility of a painter, Sironi used architecture for its capacity to immerse the viewer in the scene and to focus his or her attention hypnotically on the repeated, signal-like motifs of the narrative. Ultimately, Sironi's work shows how, through the cyclical repetition of gestures, architecture's mode of *tactile* reception could be used in the *tactics* of mass mobilization to break down the subject's resistance and entrain a whole series of automatic responses in the viewer. That Benjamin saw architecture's mode of reception as the "canonical model" for the way new media could be used to exercise "covert control" over the audience was no accident.[47]

Finally, the EFR shows how Sironi was able to use the forms of distracted perception to construct powerful new narratives that both responded to and intensified the subject's psychic fragmentation. Nowhere is this more evident than in the images of war that were one of the most obtrusive and disturbing features of the show, their endless repetition not unrelated to Sironi's own experience of the battlefield and to the war neuroses that were common during those years. Indeed, the duality that Freud had observed in the symptoms of shell shock—the closing up of the ego on the one hand and the blind immersion in the scene of trauma on the other—was also a crucial component of the aesthetic experience generated by the EFR, where a passionate identification in the drama unfolding in the sequence of rooms took the form of an endless series of hammered blows, as violence was repeatedly and relentlessly staged in both the percussive design of the rooms and in the version of events represented in the narrative, culminating in the apotheosis of violence—literally the bloodbath—of the last room.[48] The whole function of the oceanic feeling, including its capacity to compensate in some way for the alienations of modern life, was thus dependent on a categorical separation of the public as spectator, at once immediately present on the scene, yet vastly removed from it. It was in this way that Sironi's work both destroyed and rebuilt its relationship with the viewer: first by externally eliminating any possible distance, through theatrical and other more invasive devices; then by recreating that same distance internally, as spectacular distance, through the objectification of the viewer as a mere

THE ARCHITECTURE OF VIOLENCE

element of the décor. As Benjamin noted, in the paralysis of the viewer at the mass rallies of fascism "art gains in its suggestive effect what it loses in its power to enlighten."49

Nowhere is the profoundly destructive aestheticizing double logic of the spectacle more evident than in the incessant replaying of the ur-image of the EFR, *Sintesi della guerra mondiale*, which was produced in September 1918 while Sironi was still mobilized on the northern front. Recurring insistently, in all its archaic muteness like the compulsive repetition of a traumatic dream, it stands as a figure for the shattering of experience to which Benjamin alluded when he wrote,

> "Fiat arts, pereat mundus," says Fascism, expecting from war . . .
> the artistic gratification of a sense of perception altered by technology.
> This is evidently the consummation of l'art pour l'art. Humankind,
> which in Homer's time was an object of contemplation for the
> Olympian gods, has now become one for itself. Its self-alienation has
> reached the point where it can experience its own annihilation as a
> supreme aesthetic pleasure. Such is the aestheticizing of politics,
> as practiced by fascism. Communism replies by politicizing art.50

Endnotes

1— This essay is a development of my article, "La Mostra della Rivoluzione Fascista" in *Mario Sironi: La grande decorazione*, exh. cat., ed. Andrea Sironi (Milan: Electa 2004), 241–264. Its earlier versions have appeared in *Grey Room* 38 (Winter 2010) and in Gevork Hartoonian, ed., *Benjamin and Architecture* (London: Routledge 2010). On Nietzsche and Wagner, see Karin Bauer, *Adorno's Nietzschean Narratives* (New York: State University of New York Press, 1999), 145. Mario De Micheli's "Un wagneriano in camicia nera" appeared in *Bolaffi arte*, no. 26 (1973).

2— Walter Benjamin, "On Some Motifs in Baudelaire," in *Walter Benjamin, Selected Writings*, ed. Michael Jennings (Cambridge, MA: Harvard University Press 2003), 315–316.

3— Benjamin, "On Some Motifs in Baudelaire," 315–316.

4— Walter Benjamin, "Pariser Briefer (1)," in *Walter Benjamin, Gesammelte Schriften*, vol. 3, ed. Hella Tiedeman Bartels (Frankfurt: Suhrkamp, 1972), 482–495. Translated into Italian in *Benjamin, critiche e recensioni: Tra avanguardie e letteratura di consumo* (Turin: Einaudi 1979). Benjamin borrows the phrase "architectural journalism," coined by André Gide to describe the Exhibition of the Fascist Revolution, from André Gide, *Nouvelles pages de journal* (1935), republished recently as, *Journal (1926–1950)* (Paris: Gallimard, 1997), 448. On Sironi's work as political illustrator, see Andrea Sironi and Fabio Benzi, *Sironi illustratore* (Milan: De Luca, 1994).

5— Walter Benjamin "Experience and Poverty," in *Walter Benjamin: Selected Writings, Volume 2: 1927–1934*, ed. Michael Jennings et al. (Cambridge, MA: Harvard University Press, 1999), 731.

6— Benjamin "Experience and Poverty," 731–732.

7— Walter Benjamin, "The Storyteller: Observations on the Works of Nikolai Leskov" in *Walter Benjamin: Selected writings, Volume 3: 1935–1938*, ed. Michel Jennings et al. (Cambridge, MA: Harvard University Press, 2002), 143. See also Tyrus Miller, *Late Modernism: Politics, Fiction, and the Arts between the World Wars*, (Berkeley and Los Angeles: University of California Press, 1999), 41–45.

8— Guy Debord, *The Society of the Spectacle* (Detroit: Black and Red, 2002), 2.

9— See Simonetta Falasca-Zamponi, *Fascist Spectacle: The Aesthetics of Power in Mussolini's Italy* (Berkeley and Los Angeles: California University Press, 1997), 119–139.

10— On the EFR, see Dino Alfieri and Luigi Freddi, eds., *Mostra della rivoluzione fascista*, exh. cat. (Bergamo, Italy: Istituto Italiano d'Arti Grafiche, 1933). Recent literature on the EFR is quite extensive. See, for instance, Jeffrey Schnapp, "Epic Demonstrations: Fascist Modernity and the 1932 Exhibition of the Fascist Revolution," in *Fascism, Aesthetics, and Culture*, ed. Richard J. Golsan (Hanover, NH: University Press of New England, 1992), 1–37; and the special issue of the *Journal of Architectural Education* 45: 2 (Feb. 1992), with essays by Diane Ghirardo, Jeffrey Schnapp, Brian McLaren, and myself.

11— Benjamin, "On Some Motifs in Baudelaire," 318.

12— See for example, Alice Yaeger Kaplan, *Reproductions of Banality: Fascism, Literature, and French Intellectual Life* (Minneapolis: University of Minnesota Press 1986), 6 ff.

13— For an example of a cultural reading of Sironi's work, see Jean Clair's challenging "Nato sotto Saturno—Su due allegorie di Sironi," in *Sironi 1885–1961*, ed. Claudia Gianferrari (Milan: Mazzotta, 1985), 28–44. A useful discussion of contemporary media events is Daniel Dayan and Elihu Katz, "Articulating Consensus: the Ritual and Rhetoric of Media Events," in *Durkheimian Sociology: Cultural Studies*, ed. Jeffrey C. Alexander (Cambridge, UK: Cambridge University Press, 1988), 161–186.

14— See Jonathan Crary, *Suspensions of Perception: Attention, Spectacle, and Modern Culture* (Cambridge: MIT Press, 2001). On Benjamin's attitudes toward the mass media, see Hans Ulrich Gumbrecht and Michael Marrian, *Mapping Benjamin: The Work of Art in the Digital Age* (Stanford, CA: Stanford University Press, 2003); and Andrew Benjamin, ed., *Walter Benjamin and Art* (London: Continuum, 2005).

15— Jeffrey Schnapp, "Ogni mostra realizzata è una rivoluzione ovvero le esposizioni sironiane e l'immaginario fascista," in *Mario Sironi 1885 61, exh cat, ed Fabio Benzi* (Milan: Electa, 1993), 47 (my translation).

16— Alfieri and Freddi, 1.

17– See Gide, 448, and Le Corbusier to Paul Otlet, 29 June 1934, in Archives Le Corbusier, Paris. Le Corbusier described the exhibition as a "miracle de visualisation et d'enseignement" (a miracle of visiualisation and teaching). On the public reception of the EFR, see also Emilio Gentile, *Il culto del littorio* (Turin: Einaudi, 1990), 136.

18– See Ettore Camesasca, ed., *Mario Sironi, scritti editi e inediti* (Milan: Feltrinelli, 1980). On the Cologne and Barcelona pavilions, see Sironi and Benzi, *Sironi illustratore;* and Emily Braun, *Mario Sironi and Italian Modernism* (London: Cambridge University Press, 2000).

19– On Sironi's role in the EFR, see my interview with Mimi Costa, in "Architecture and Politics in Fascist Italy" (PhD diss., MIT, 1989), app. B. For a detailed account of the planning history of the exhibition, see my "Mostra della rivoluzione fascista," in *Sironi: La grande decorazione.*

20– Alfieri and Freddi, 8.

21– For a more detailed description of the opening ceremonies, see my "Aesthetics of War: the Exhibition of the Fascist Revolution," *Journal of Architectural Education* 45: 2 (Feb. 1992): 76–77.

22– Ada Negri, "Madre di Martiri," *Corriere della sera* (Milan), 11 April 1933, 3.

23– Benjamin, "Pariser Brief (1), 261 (my translation). On Libera's anti-utilitarian stance, see his "Arte e Razionalismo" (1928), in Vieri Quilici, *Adalberto Libera: L'architettura come ideale* (Rome: Officina, 1981), 229–233.

24– Benjamin, "Pariser Brief (1)," 261 (my translation).

25– Alfieri and Freddi, 176.

26– Gigi Maino, "La Mostra della Rivoluzione Fascista" in *Rassegna Italiana* (Mar. 1933), 207.

27– Edoardo Persico, "La Mostra della Rivoluzione Fascista," *La casa bella* 30 (Nov. 1932).

28– Benjamin, "The Work of Art in the Age of Its Technological Reproducibility," 3rd vers., in *Walter Benjamin, Selected Writings,* vol. 4, ed. Michael W. Jennings (Cambridge: Harvard University Press, 2008), 268.

29– Alfieri and Freddi, 176.

30– See Thomas Schumacher, *The Danteum* (Princeton, NJ: Princeton Architectural Press, 1996). A letter from the historian Emilio Arrigotti in Rome to Terragni in Como, dated 16 August 1932, and preserved in the Terragni archives along with other material relating to the show, suggests a concern for sufficient circulation space in the room. Arrigotti wrote, "sono sempre più convinto che la Sala del '22 rimarrà spaziata—di 'respiro.'" (I am more than ever convinced that the room of 1922 will have enough space and breathing room). This is probably the reason for Terragni's last-minute substitution of the panel sequence with the Adunate photomontage. Arrigotti supervised the work until Terragni's arrival on 3 September 1932.

31– Alfieri and Freddi, 193.

32– Theodor Adorno, *In Search of Wagner* (London: Verso, 1991), 30.

33– Alfieri and Freddi, 195 passim.

34– See Schnapp, "Ogni mostra realizzata," 60, but also my own PhD dissertation.

35– Similarities may also be noted between Sironi's *Sintesi della guerra mondiale* and El Lissitzky's famous poster *Beat the Whites with the Red Wedge* (1919).

36– Mario Sironi, "L'architettura della Rivoluzione," *Il popolo d'Italia,* 18 November 1932, 132.

37– "The best of our Italian painters of today, Mario Sironi, who has given to the exhibition the authority of his high talent and of his proud, powerful, and tormented soul: a soul and a talent that are tumultuous and truly Michelangelesque." Margherita Sarfatti, "L'exposition du fascisme," *Formes* 31 (Jan. 1933): 3–4 (my translation).

38– Giorgio Ciucci, "L'autorappresentazione del fascismo: La mostra del decennale della marcia su Roma," *Rassegna Italiana* 10 (June 1982): 48–55.

39– On Wagner's working methods, see Adorno, *In Search of Wagner.* The few detectable differences between Sironi's drawing and Ruggieri's sculpture—namely, the mechanization of the horse and of Italy's outstretched arm—go against the flowing style of Ruggieri's work.

40– One of the historians working on the show, Antonio Monti, recalled that the final design of the Shrine was "merito precipuo del Duce" (principal merit of the Duce). See Antonio Monti, *Rapsodia eroica, dall'interventismo all'impero* (Milan: n.p., 1937). This view was confirmed in a discussion I had with the wife of Antonio Valente, who recalled that during one of several visits to the exhibition while preparations were underway, Mussolini discussed the design of the Shrine, suggesting the idea of a cross against the initial proposal for an altar to an unknown fascist martyr. (Interview with Maddalena del Favero Valente, Rome, 15 September 1985).

41– On the syncretism of political rituals, see Mona Ozouf, *Festivals of the French Revolution* (Cambridge, MA: Harvard University Press, 1988); and Cristel Lane, *The Rites of Rulers: Ritual in Industrial Society—The Soviet Case* (Cambridge, UK: Cambridge University Press, 1981), 229–239.

42– For a description of this rite, see Ion S. Munro, *Through Fascism to World Power* (London: Alexander Maclehose and Co., 1933), 323.

43– I take the notion of representative rite from Emile Durkheim, *The Elementary Forms of Religious Life* (New York: Macmillan, 1965), 419. On fascism as a "secular religion," see also Gentile, *Il culto del littorio*.

44– Crary, 148. See also Brian MacGee, *Aspects of Wagner* (Oxford, UK: Oxford University Press, 1988).

45– Crary, 148.

46– Sigmund Freud, *Civilization and Its Discontents* (New York: Norton, 1961), 12.

47– On the connection between tactility and tactics, see Esther Leslie, *Walter Benjamin: Overpowering Conformism* (London: Pluto Press, 2000), 166.

48– On Freud's theory of shock, see Ruth Leys, *Trauma: A Genealogy* (Chicago: University of Chicago Press, 2000), 19–40.

49– Benjamin, "Pariser Briefer (1)," 258.

50– Walter Benjamin, "The Work of Art in the Age of Its Technological Reproducibility," 2nd vers., in *The Work of Art in the Age of Technological Reproducibility, and Other Writings on Media*, ed. Michael Jennings et al. (Cambridge, MA: Harvard University Press, 2008), 42.

INSCRIPTIONS OF VIOLENCE:

LONDON'S LANDSCAPE OF COMMEMORATION

ANNETTE FIERRO

Unreal City,
Under the brown fog of a winter dawn,
A crowd flowed over London Bridge, so many,
I had not thought death had undone so many.
Sighs, short and infrequent, were exhaled,
And each man fixed his eyes before his feet.
Flowed up the hill and down King William Street,
To where Saint Mary Woolnoth kept the hours
With a dead sound on the final stroke of nine.
There I saw one I knew, and stopped him, crying: "Stetson!
'You who were with me in the ships at Mylae!
'That corpse you planted last year in your garden,
'Has it begun to sprout? Will it bloom this year?
T. S. Eliot, *The Waste Land* (1922)

It is perhaps the impossibility of capturing the trauma of large-scale destruction of a city that prompts the incessant, inevitably unrequited desire to do so. Certainly, this is so in London, the greatest of case studies of major Western cities subjected not only to the destructive event, but also to its incessant replay. The most obvious of these, at least in terms of number of books, documentaries, historical fictions, and films, is the

Figure 1. *Why does the V+A choose not to refinish the pockmarks of bombs on its walls?*

INSCRIPTIONS OF VIOLENCE

devastation of the city by the German bombings of World War II. (The BBC on-line alone lists some 500 pages of documentaries, archives, and source material.) These attempts point to remedial psychologies intended to assuage by replay, to heal through a desperate search for rationale through repeated inquiry: a self-inflicted therapy to forget by remembering. Nietzsche dismissed the obsession to recapture history as a liability of civilization's responsibility to the present, a pathetic tendency.[1]

London can claim particularly righteous status in the cadre of major Western cities whose cataclysms have been numerous and devastating. As early as the Great of Fire of 1666, which saw the damage of eighty percent of the city's fabric, through the incomprehensible fifty-seven consecutive days of bombing during the Blitz of 1940–41, to the more sporadic damage due to IRA bombings in the 1980s and early 90s, and most recently, to fundamentalist Islamic terrorist attacks on the city's infrastructure, London can be regarded as the quintessential Western site of devastation. Consequently, London has also earned folkloric stature for effective aversion to and management after such crises. With its significant range of recuperative and documentary measures, London can rightly be called an *archival* entity—a seminal site where past violence has been enfolded in the city's many morphological and iconographic structures.

It is curious to note that in contrast to literary media, in London's architecture and urban design, references to the numerous cataclysms are relatively absent, relatively silent, certainly in the most conventional notion of encountering monuments commemorating former sites of destruction. Found scattered throughout the city are discrete memorials to various events, various military units or particular groups, the most recent of which was dedicated in 2005 to "The Women of World War II" in Whitehall. Yet, within the physical fabric of the city itself—the actual site of destruction, there is scant evidence, and little if any reference, to major points of cataclysm. In maps showing the destruction of the Blitz of the City of London and surrounding Holborn (figure 2), for example, it is precisely the erasure of the destruction within the familiar modern city that intrigues and seduces study. While specific markers are dedicated to commemorating particular involvement, the largest testament to past violence, the city itself, has been repressed from ever acknowledging its wounds. London, ever the capitalist machine, seems more attendant to property lines and profit from reconstruction than to testifying to more personal forms of loss.

As Paul Virilio noted in *A Landscape of Events*, in the very potency of the violence there is a latent question: What happens to that violence?[2]

Does it linger immanently in whatever form it manages to leave its trace or does its painful residue simply disappear into the past? How previous destruction and violence is made legible in London's urban context is the topic that this essay hopes to address, positing first of all that vestigial traces of these violent events are indelibly inflected onto the imagery of the architecture of the city: from surface markings, to long evolutions of referent iconography (particular to London and its architecture), to, as Virilio also observed, newer types of recordings in media of electronic journalism and surveillance apparatus. The latter suggests a pervasive subtopic to be encountered in this article—not simply how imagery/iconography appears and reappears, but how the emergence of imagery is palpably affected by the influence of different scales of time. It is not only about how imagery records events of violence, but also, how it is affected by complicity with structures of time.

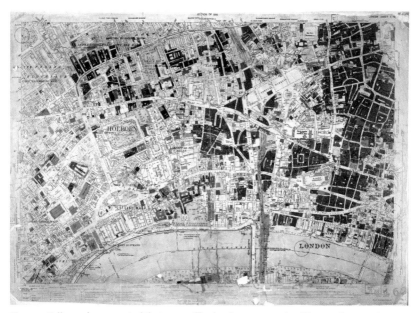

Figure 2. Holborn, circa 1945. And that great coffee shop last summer, site of devastation or not? Courtesy City of London, London Metropolitan Archives.

For the Sake of Argument: The Monument

Buried in every tourist guide is a curiosity that impresses only particular readers. "The Monument," a classical column found in the City of London, completed by Christopher Wren between 1671 and 1677, commemorates the Great Fire of London. The very extent of destruction makes it noteworthy, despite that it was not caused by a violent act—in 1666, 430 acres (80% of the city) were destroyed by simple neglect, a careless fire in a bakery. Very few casualties resulted: only five were documented, though eighteen were rumored. These figures do not include an unfortunate Frenchman who was made a scapegoat for the accident, tortured to the point of confession and then hanged as a papist interloper, a testament to long-standing political resentments between France and England, Canterbury and Rome.

The effects of the Great Fire on the developing metropolis, however, were enormous, stemming directly from the impetus to rebuild. Fueled by the huge influx of immigrant labor needed for construction, London's demographic growth in the aftermath established it as Europe's largest city. London's well-known legal culture was also developed and structured in this period, as laws and governing entities grew to meet litigious contentions by owners and tenants looking for all types of compensation, from settling preexisting leases to accounting for storage charges for property after the fire.[3]

Figure 3. Which Monument? The Monument, Christopher Wren, 1676. Photo: Christopher Junkin, 2006.

Figure 4. No Monument. Foster and Partners, 30 St. Mary Axe, 2004.

The consequence to the London's physical context was subtle but equally profound. As in recent years, there was very little impulse to take advantage of the opportunity created by the fire to re-envision the city at the largest urban scale, as for example, in Haussmann's operation in Paris a few centuries later. Christopher Wren's immediately drafted ambitious plans to modernize London through the imposition of axial boulevards were quickly rejected because of the rights of ownership involved in preexisting property definitions. More subtle effects were, however, dramatic in their pervasive scope. The scale of the typical city street was substantially altered as standard widths were expanded to accommodate fire prevention vehicles. Building heights were allowed to vary depending on the prominence of the street. More drastic was the complete change to the street's material density: new structures were required to be reconstructed out of masonry rather than wood, transforming not only the texture of material to be encountered on the street, but the rhythm of vernacular London facades.

Historians have granted the Great Fire responsibility for configuring modern London, in physical, economic and governmental terms. When one considers the magnitude of the effects instituted by the Great Fire today, The Monument looks paltry indeed. The column, once the tallest free-standing column in the world, now appears insignificant, its stature challenged by the building boom of the last twenty years. Ignored by all but the most diligent tourist, the diminishing status of The Monument is symptomatic of a much larger failure. Severed from original social, historical, and cultural attributes, the veracity of the column as a commemorative object slowly falls away, especially as time passes. Without the volumes of narrative that constituted the original event, The Monument does not succeed in its fundamental principle of communicating meaning, or of recreating the significance of the event, be it in historical or visceral terms. But is this not a dilemma that exists due to the inability of any discrete, "typological" object to continue a didactic mission over centuries? If a glance at The Monument teaches anything, it is the inability of such conventional commemorations to collapse the spatiality and multiplicity of a complex event into a point of singular legibility, observed in detached time.

The institutionalization of meaning in the traditional monument inevitably neutralizes the viscerality of the original event as much as it deadens the event's field of originary complexities.[4] The pure symbol of the column does not internalize the content that formed it: it evacuates it. Yet the opposite impulse, to ignore the violent event altogether, is fraught with an equally problematic set of consequences. These are endemic to London, describing the generic relationship of the city to its violent events far closer than that of the conventional monument. Instructive in this argument, and located in close proximity to The Monument, is the newest iconic imprint on the city's skyline, known to Londoners affectionately as "The Gherkin" but more officially as "30 St. Mary Axe." A private speculative corporate office building opened in May 2004 by the developer Swiss Re, the building markets itself as the new landmark of London comparable in its significance to The Monument.[5]

Designed by Foster and Partners, this building is well known for the environmental engineering, which prompted its shape and the configuration of the interior spaces. Taking advantage of the potential of existing wind currents on the site, the building form was conceived to allow the pressure differential created around the curvilinear shape to draw natural ventilation through spiral lightwells, shafts of air running around the building's exterior.[6] The dimensions of the floor plate are configured to maximize daylight, thereby minimizing the need for artificial lighting. Retrofitted with blinds within the building's double ventilated skin, locally controlled mechanical ventilation, low energy light fittings, and even surplus bicycle storage space in the basement, Swiss Re claims that 30 St. Mary Axe is London's "first environmentally progressive working environment."[7]

Given the trumpeting of advanced technology in this union of geometry, function, space, and environmental performance, it would seem that these attributes would become the basis for the building's notoriety. Despite, however, the razor-sharp scientific rationale of its conception, most Londoners respond primarily to the novelty of the iconic shape and the iconoclasm of its extreme departure from vernacular historical surroundings.[8] Yet buried within the circumstances surrounding the building of St. Mary Axe is a fact unknown to most. The site for the building became available only after the IRA exploded a massive fertilizer bomb there on April 10, 1992, completely destroying the beloved Baltic Exchange Building, killing three people and injuring ninety. Besides the physical devastation to the entire urban block, it was this particular bombing that also prompted the British government to open greater lines of communication with the Irish terrorists, signaling the effectiveness of their strategy.[9] Like most other sites of major IRA bombings, the particular facts of the event go as unacknowledged as the event itself. Whether it was a strategic or cultural gesture on the part of the government to maintain the stereotypical British "life as usual" attitude after such terrorist incidents,

A NNETTE F IERRO

59

the developers and tenants of St. Mary Axe do not, for obvious reasons, go to lengths to advertise this bit of the building's tragic birth rite.

That the building sacrifices its potential for commemorative function is no surprise to those acquainted with the eventual debacle involved in the proposed construction on the World Trade Center bombing site in New York. When commercial interests of such magnitude are involved, the need for a commemorative rite is quick to be diminished if not entirely obliterated.[10] Not only is this a question of economics and politics, but also of governance. Ultimately, which municipal authority decides what site and what degree of devastation merit an obligatory mention of tragedy? Do the forces of a market economy work inherently to repress ancestry of violence, intervening in whatever psychological function is granted by whatever form of commemoration to the recovering city? The particular iconic dimension of 30 St. Mary Axe makes this particular disjunction poignant: the most prominent of the buildings within the public gaze is strangely divorced from the violence through which it was created.

The particular mechanism of eradicating memory by the glitz of high commerce is at extreme odds with intensity of violence itself, yet is hardly unique. The burial of the sacred dimension of the violent event, its *animality*, into normative urban typologies—a park or a museum—drove Bataille's reflections in his "Abattoir" and "Musée."[11] This pregnant silence between objects of note and their recumbent events is omnipresent in contemporary London—a veritable landscape of unrecognized, unvoiced sacrificial sites, nestled within the highest trappings of commerce and fashion in the Western world. It is here, however, within this set of circumstances that the possibility of a new commemorative urban structure might emerge. Rather than being formed by singular, didactic (and impotent) points of a monument proper, this commemorative structure might be conceptualized as a *field*, located pervasively throughout the city, but signaled only through barely legible but highly-loaded, emotive artifacts: a field of Proustian moments.

Déjà Vu: War and Its Machinery

On September 7, 1940, close to a thousand German bombers and fighters appeared over London beginning the infamous "Blitz" that continued for eight months, the most intense period of which was the first fifty-seven consecutive days of bombing that continued throughout day and night. Changing his original strategy to weaken England by destroying military targets outside the city, Hitler's new plan was to completely demoralize the country by the incessant destruction of its major cities. In terms comparable to the Great Fire, the first five months of bombing of the City of London led to the destruction of more than a third of the City's fabric. Four years later, bombs continued to fall at rates of sometimes seventy-five a day, but this time from pilotless missiles—the V1 and V2s—which intensified destruction of selected targets as they heralded modern intelligent warfare. Unlike the immediate rebuilding of 1667, the shock of WWII to England's fading colonialist economy resulted in more than a decade of stagnation when rebuilding was delayed and enormous portions of the city lay in ruins. As after the Great Fire, the incontestability of property definitions prevented any substantial change to the city's morphology. If traces of the war are to be found, they are to be uncovered within a few limited sources: official histories, minor art forms, and most unlikely, the city's architectural iconography—through a particularly tricky lineage of radical proposals of the 1960s which ultimately reemerged in the city's most prominent contemporary architecture, that of its home-grown British Hi-Tech.

London under siege was a city obsessed with its own survival. While the military weaponry of WWII has its own vast history that has inspired decades of study in the recounting of the war through its architecture, it is the apparatus of daily survival, the quotidian gadgetry of the civilian population, which has become most indelibly inscribed.[12] There are many examples that can be examined. Most prominent was the appropriation of London's transportation infrastructure for unintended uses. Even before the bombs began falling, the municipal transportation system was requisitioned for various wartime causes, from evacuating London's children to the country *en masse*, to moving goods and war-time supplies across the city. At the height of the bombings, the depth of the London Underground made it the ideal shelter; the beloved "Tube" was taken over for housing as well as light industry. Offering refuge for as many as 177,000 Londoners at night, many of the new and disused extensions of the subway tunnels were eventually retrofitted with standardized systems of partitions, bed-frames and other domestic fittings, as well as machinery for war-time industrial production. Particularly impressive was the Plessy Tunnel, so named for an entire factory set up inside the tunnel between Leystone and Gants Hill, replete with its own system of entries and a miniature railway for moving materials and parts through the tunnel.[13] The Underground became a series of discontinuous networks, a patchwork of overlaid infrastructures within the larger transportation system, which remained fully functional, providing continuous movement across the city throughout the war. The emergent organizational structures are as important to future architecture as the multifarious nature and wild diversity of functions inside. Housing makeshift domiciles and small industries, furnished with scattered libraries, wandering minstrels, refreshment stands, and vendors, the Underground was a life-line for the city of many descriptions and dimensions.

Can it be serendipitous that only twenty years later, members of Archigram—the now grown-up and iconoclastic children of the Blitz—became obsessed with mobilizing transportation infrastructure as the fundamental organization of their early visionary cities? Peter Cook's "Plug-In City" (1962–65) proposes a tube-like structure, similar in proportion and scale to the Underground, for the movement of everything, at different speeds: goods and services, pedestrians, as well as his kit of retrofitted temporary elements ("plug-ins") which made habitation not only feasible, but dynamic. In his vision, Cook ascribes the "quality of urban life: its symbolism, its dynamic, its gregariousness, its dependence upon situation as much as established form."[14] In this project, as well as Dennis Crompton's "Computer City" of 1964, the new infrastructures are overlaid on the pre-existing Underground, in a new cannibalization of the city's infrastructure, which programs fun and vibrancy in place of shelter from falling missiles. In the systems proposed there was a tangency to the hierarchies of the war-occupied Underground: between permanence and

Figure 5. Deep inside Michael Hopkins's Westminster Underground Station (1999): are we finally experiencing Plug-In City?

INSCRIPTIONS OF VIOLENCE

temporality, between retrofitted and durable systems, between infrastructures proper and parasitic sub-networks. In the 60s version these levels of infrastructure are hyperbolized, but continue to draw on the notion of wildly diversified modes of inhabiting the substructure of a city. Thus, as during the war, infrastructure is granted the primary role of maintaining the vitality of the city.

Archigram's infrastructures were compelled by the same machinic scenography of services and networks found in the furtive Underground, but assumed magnificent proportions. As landscapes and skyscapes of unbounded gadgetry, the speed and vibrancy of temporary occupation and configuration could be felt in the very pieces and parts of Archigram's systems of construction. Imbuing war machinery with the graphic potency of science fiction and the studied veracity of master draftsmanship, Archigram's images were to become the fascination of the subsequent generation of British architects, dominating new architecture in London for decades. As recently as the 1990s, we see London embarking on the building of the "Jubilee" underground line, in which this lineage of iconography—the particular marriage of technological iconography and appropriated infrastructure—materializes significantly. By commissioning many of the most prominent Hi-Tech architects, who freely deployed imagery of advanced technology in deep underground networks, in this latest chapter of reemergent language, a curiously extra-vigorous architec-

Figure 6. Nurses and their well-sheathed infant charges. Courtesy Imperial War Museum, London/ IWM D.654.

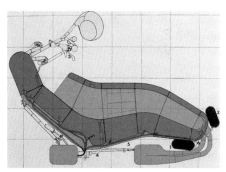

Figure 7. Michael Webb's environmental playsuit: The Cushicle, 1966–67. Courtesy Archigram Archives.

tonicism emerges, which cannot be explained simply by either technology or function, but which sustains its virility through pure expressive excess.

Examples continue. Different types of life-sustaining gadgets meant to buttress the vulnerabilities of the body appear in every historical account of daily life during the Blitz. Most memorable of these were the thirty-eight million gas masks furnished to the entire population of Britain, described repeatedly in popular reminiscences. While most of these were the familiar hoods worn over the head, some, especially those for children, were designed to envelop the body: full suits were designed for toddlers and gas "tents" were provided for babies. Many of the more amusing images in these accounts concentrate on these suits

Figure 8. Elevator capsule, just another pod, at Lloyd's of London, Richard Rogers, 1979. Photo: Jenny E. Sabin, 2004.

Figure 9. Cook's pods, reappearing behind a Nicholas Grimshaw Sainbury's supermarket in Camden Town, 1990.

INSCRIPTIONS OF VIOLENCE

and hoods being used by groups in otherwise familiar settings: families on the beach, all with headsuits; groups of children on playgrounds, balancing gas masks on see-saws.[15] The concept and incongruity of the body-encapsulating protective sheath reappears incontestably in Michael Webb's Cushicles (1966–67) and Suitaloons (1968). These devices, while meant for a sole inhabitant, are also garments intended for an entire population; the individual body is protected but joined within a larger collective. The Suitaloon is itself conceived primarily not simply to encapsulate the individual but to provide a technological interface—through a coupling device—with others wearing similar Suitaloons. There is a consistent aspect of social collectivity in these proposals that goes far beyond a fascination with space suits as gadgetry. While the members of Archigram delve into war apparatus as well as futuristic technologies for the source of their concepts and images, the devices are to be used by the whole population very much on earth, whether in cities or wandering together through rural landscape, but never as sole explorers on distant planets or undersea. Read this way, Archigram's proposals might be more nostalgic than futuristic: longing not for the war itself, but for the legendary collectivity of the population casting off all social conventions and coming together under tremendous duress, aptly captured through funny, machine-like suits, worn by everyone.

Webb notes, "Clothing for living in—if it wasn't for my suitaloon I would have to buy a house."[16] Indeed, as environmentally-independent body/living units, the clothing is very similar in concept to the capsules found in many of Archigram proposals, especially in Chalk and Herron's housing or Cook's "plug-in" modules, which allow for varying amounts of independence from their parent infrastructures. It is this trajectory of forms that ultimately informs the latter Hi-Tech's fascination, appearing in scattered fragments throughout their oeuvres: from the elevator and bathroom plug-ins of Richard Rogers, to all the different pieces and projects of Nicolas Grimshaw, which either connote encapsulation or actually provide it.

There are even more examples of the war apparatus that refuse to disappear. During and soon after the Blitz, London was populated by a plethora of temporary devices contrived to perform basic functions for a population cut off from ordinary living.[17] Lean-tos—small, temporary coverings attached to existing buildings—were, for example, outfitted with plumbing to furnish ad-hoc outdoor lavatory facilities. The washing of the city's dirty clothes was provided by a fleet of mobile laundries in the small trucks of the "National Emergency Washing Service." In the texture of the wartime fabric of the city there were also "balloon barrages," silver dirigibles on cables that floated above standard house height to foil enemy aircrafts flying low. Balloon-filled skies were quickly made iconic by the war memorabilia as well as national postage stamps. Twenty years later, they appear in uncannily similar images in Archigram's work. In the drawings *Instant City, A Typical Night Scene* (Cook, 1968), *Instant City in a Field* (Cook, 1969), and *Instant City at Bournemouth* (Cook, 1969), the skies are full of similarly scaled balloons, hanging outdoor movie screens and advertisements, while small incidental trucks and vehicles furnish temporary infrastructural services on the ground. Here, the vital infrastructure to equally needy provincial outposts is not laundry, but popular culture. While Archigram may have been very aware of Buckminster Fuller's similar attraction to deployable structures and dirigibles, the group was less interested in these as utilitarian objects, as they were by their potential role in constituting a coherent architectural theatrical vision, a horizon of temporary props and vehicles working to provoke a spontaneous and dynamic urban life.

All of these vestigial references of the war were confluent in the young counter-cultural group's titillation with contemporary space, naval and communication technologies, woven together under the spell of American technological optimism of the 60s.[18] Nevertheless, despite the abundance of these other sources, the lineage of images that continually re-emerge in different forms emanates most viscerally from the apparatus of the war. Vidler contends that in Archigram's visions, the new paradigm of postwar functionalism was united with the psychological terrorism of war, and overlaid with the aesthetic and scientific connotation of cybernetics and all things biologically disposed.[19] It is the fundamental psychological dimension of such imagery that grants the work a commemorative function. The phenomena of the irrepressible emergence and re-emergence of the imagery over the decades, in the work of many different architects and engineers, and across a diverse urban geographic field, make this a very different historical event than one emanating from a conventional art historical tracing of referential connections. In Archigram's fantastic recreation of the war apparatus and later in the Hi-Tech is our *Proustian field*, an encrustation of the city's surface with fragmentary memories, an indelibly inscribed recording of life under siege.

The period between the war and the emergence of Archigram is an interesting architectural chapter in itself. Archigram insinuated themselves into the scene at the end of a period of heroic challenge to the strict objectivity perceived as part and parcel of canonical modernism. It was this challenge, in London spearheaded by the Smithsons and their cohorts, which was fundamental to the emergence of post-modernism in the next decade. Embedded within this trajectory was the quintessential figure of James Stirling, hero and mentor to the young Archigram members. Particularly significant was the tremendous public debate raised by his Engineering Building at Leicester University of 1959–63, designed with James Gowan. Stirling's many but nuanced departures from a strict structural/functionalist vocabulary instigated a generational call-to-arms of traditional modernist teachers and critics against the rising tide of the youth culture, bent on decrying the offenses of the past modernist generations. Historian Nicholas Pevsner, representing the former, satirically labeled the impulse as a development of the "radically original," a signifier of a cult of personality present in the youth, or, he says, an *Expressionistic* throwback to Gothic nostalgia.[20] To Pevsner, the departures from strict functionality in many elements of the Leicester building were nothing, but a search for "emotional effects."[21] And indeed, if post-modernism's seminal roots were present in the debate, Pevsner's scoff at expressive tendencies ultimately found its most profound realization in Giorgio Grassi and Aldo Rossi's search for primal melancholy in the tradition Italian vernacular. In England, in contrast, the desperate search for meaning embarked upon in this period resulted in the evolution of a highly wrought, highly articulate, highly excessive techno-industrial language, a characteristic which appears in only one other country across the world— the country equally subjected to devastation at an unprecedented scale— the Japanese post-modern bubble world of Shin Takamatsu, Hiroshi Hara, Itsuko Hasegawa, and Riken Yamamoto.

The psychological dimension of Archigram's imagery has one more element peculiar to its evolution in London. Richard Rogers's autobiography has noted that his first acquaintance with the potency of architecture was through a late-adolescent visit to the Festival of Britain in 1951.[22] The Festival, a landmark event, was to have a powerful influence on British architecture, especially on all young British architects, including the members of Archigram. Instigated by the British Government, from its inception the Festival was intended to alleviate the psychological depression of the long, post-war recovery effort: "a tonic to the nation." Consciously instilling the Festival as "the place of fun and fantasy, escape and edification," its planners undertook nothing less ambitious than coaxing the tired British public into recasting their own national identity. At a time of pressing financial need, the governing Labour Party, with considerable controversy, committed eleven million pounds to the cultural celebration dedicated to constituting a new sense of being "British" in the post-WWII world: "the autobiography of a nation."[23]

In the initial planning of the Festival, the government consciously constituted the leadership committee from the ranks of architects, designers and engineers, rather than politicians or financiers. The result for British design culture was a windfall, to be felt for the next fifty years. Chosen as the primary theme of the Festival, the union of cutting-edge modernist design, art, and British technology was an exuberant concoction posed as the remedy for Britain's lagging self-esteem. Celebration of the new British technologies would hypothetically assuage perceptions of having been marginalized to second-world order status. In the exhibit's displays, British advancements in television, radar, and jet engine technologies were featured prominently. From public architecture—of which the Festival architecture itself was the showpiece—to building techniques and new everyday utilitarian technologies, the Festival attempted to inject new life into staid British sensibilities. This was more than the intent to boost British manufacturing: Labour's agenda, to improve human nature through clean lines of modern design, was decidedly utopian.

Figure 10. Ralph Tubbs, Dome of Discovery, Festival of Britain, 1951. Courtesy Museum of London/ IN16681.

The lasting symbolism of the celebration is attested to by Richard Rogers's almost literal recreation, in 2000, of the Festival's most prominent piece of architecture, Ralph Tubbs's Dome of Discovery. With Powell and Moya's Skylon, the Dome formed the visual emblem of the Festival of 1951. Tubbs's original design featured a fully aluminum construction, in support of the British initiative to revitalize its traditional industries by producing cladding systems of the imported material.[24] Continuing shortage in metals, however, caused the aluminum intended as the primary material for the dome to be ultimately wedded to a concrete primary frame structure. Nevertheless, the Dome, the largest of its kind in the world at the time, was perceived as a vanguard for advanced technology. Rogers's latter-day version, the Millennium Dome, was built in north Greenwich across the Thames from Canary Wharf, as a part of a vaguely conceived plan to initiate development in eastern London. Taking the profile and trussed construction of the columns holding up the Dome of Discovery, Rogers recreated them as suspension members above the roof, suspending a tensile fabric from below. Both tensile principle and profile of the suspension elements made further reference to the Skylon. With this clever

Figure 11 All over again: Rogers's dome, "The New Millennium Experience, 1996–98.

marriage, Rogers's heightened the emblematic function of the Dome and its allusion to an earlier moment of heroic recovery.

Prominently isolated at an extreme bend in the river, the "New Millennium Experience" was intended to use the millennium celebration to project the future of a new sector of the city. How exactly this was to be done, was left to the impetus that the celebration would hypothetically provide. As a result, the lack of real urban planning left the Dome completely vacant for years after the celebration. Indeed, it was not until the 2012 Olympics was awarded to London that enough interest was generated to believe that the enormous development plan, the "Thames Gateway," the project encompassing the entire Lower Lea Valley, might actually come to pass. Until then, however, Rogers's Dome, its surrounding fairgrounds, and huge transportation hub completed by Norman Foster lay completely fallow, underscoring the notion that this most recent dome, like that of the Festival of 1951, was meant to perform primarily as an emblem rather than a functioning facility, and employed the language of advanced technology to do so.

The theme of uniting technology, art and modern life is familiar to every student of modern architecture, and the similar coupling of spectacle with technology, and nationalism with consumerism, is familiar from the tradition of early twentieth-century world expositions. What distinguishes the Festival of Britain is the central idea that it was to be primarily a form of national therapy; that "fun" could be doled out to the masses in order to make them, simply, happy. That "fun" signified by design and technology was exactly the ludic inspiration adopted by Archigram. Provoked and inspired by the celebration, Archigram adopted "fun" as both mantra and ideology against previous social and architectural orders. Because the group fed on the elation generated by the 1951 Festival, it is important to note that even though this elation was a product of the spectacular nature of the exposition, it was also keenly dependent on the emotional history of the recent war and its destruction of Britain's cities, economy, and world prominence. Archigram's expressive vehicles for this conjecture of "fun" were founded on the overlay of fun-house spectacle upon war machinery, and in the contrived mechanical scenography of the Festival architecture, this iconography was tinged with the memories and effects of the war. Similar in spirit to the Dadaists revolt against the ravages of WWI with absurdist contraptions mimicking war machinery, the incongruous images and proposals of Archigram were equally conflicted, though their protest was directed primarily against post-war sobriety and was mixed with more than a healthy dose of technological positivism.

It is no surprise that Archigram's machine obsessions as well as graphic style abutted many popular forms of science fiction. Since the 1920s, science fiction in Britain had functioned not simply as an alternative literary media but, just like Archigram, as a challenge to established cultural institutions of all forms. In the early days, it had been relatively easy for the elite, properly literate circle of Bloomsbury to dismiss the work of H. G. Wells as simplistic and shallow, but by the 1960s science fiction joined the ranks of the avant-garde art. The British New Wave, composed of J.G. Ballard, John Sladek, Kurt Vonnegut, and other considerable figures, threatened the hierarchy of high literature by assaulting conventional thematic genres. In both mainstream and counter-culture journals and magazines, science fiction's explicit reworking of violent futurism with confrontational sexual and racial themes resulted in a literary form which no longer distinguished between high and low art. Literary critic Roger Luckhurst notes," Ballard's work was so much stronger [than his stylistic followers] because—again, very perversely—he actually remained committed to science fiction as the only literature capable of recording the transformation of human subjectivity by the technological revolution of the 1960s."[25] Ballard's work hinged on the potency of the "technological sublime" to subvert normative consciousness, as theorized by media critic Marshall McLuhan. Luckhurst notes that together with an obsessive interest in biological violation and a stream of consciousness incorporation of the effects of violence, Ballard detailed "the exact specification of coming violence to their [the authors'] own psyches."

As an active part of the avant-garde scene in London in the 1960s, Ballard and the other New Wave writers launched their psychologically disposed brand of science fiction very much in the public eye. Inhabiting the same artistic sphere in London, the two prominent groups—the literary New Wave and the architectural Archigram—were certainly aware of each other. Operating at the same moment, the two groups shared similar impulses—from hyperbolizing the machinic to terrifying dimensions, to embracing consumerist media techniques to inflect "high" art with "low"—with the ultimate common goal of destabilizing previously enshrined artistic institutions. The exaggeration of technology in Archigram's work has been often discredited as a product of precocious post-adolescents ignorant of the larger critiques of its propagation. However, consideration of the atmosphere of London says otherwise, as this was the exact moment when science fiction ascended to higher literary status and ignited both popular as well as more rarified imaginations. That violence is latent in Archigram's imagery is certain—but so is the group's conscious understanding of the effect that it had in problematizing the topic of technology. This is clearly attested to in the explicit photographic imagery of wartime bombing included the Greene and Webb's 1963 *The Story of the Thing,* or the end captions in Herron's appropriated science-fiction cartoon strip in *Archigram* 4 (1964), which announced: "Destroy Man. Kill All Humans." Could the machines in Ron Herron's infamous *Walking City* be read as anything than immense apocalyptic war equipment cruising through air and water toward vulnerable cities? Is it inconceivable that buried within Archigram's exhilarated sensibility is a self-aware confirmation of technology's dangerously seductive properties? Can their entire oeuvre be read, as New Wave science fiction was, as technology's ample store of libidinal desire, a draw, which as Virilio says of the conjunction of man and machine is, essentially, that "of loving one's own death?"[26]

What reads at first glance as fetishism of technology in Archigram, through the High Tech must be understood as a highly wrought concurrence of psychic effects. The technological tropes function both as mnemonic devices to the trauma of the war and as iconoclastic absurdities, which, through agencies of humor, therapeutically compel the populace to look to the future. It is these impulses latent within the ubiquitous constructions of the Hi-Tech and their many followers that finally constitute our Proustian field as an immanent substructure of iconography existing in contemporary London. Yet, this field is a nebulous one, an unconscious collection of fragmented sentiments where the erotic and visceral dimension of violence surfaces discontinuously, as in a dream. While operating within the oneiric was the surrealists' life-long quest for the fulfillment of consciousness, within the scope of the commemorative, it comes at a price. While the particular details of our Proustian dream field may be recapitulated successfully, the numerous rounds of semiotic recoding have resulted in a lack of legibility equal to that of the traditional monument. While the details of our field may indeed perform as emotive triggers, no cognitive function is possible, as these fragments are not comprehendible without an accompanying text. And so, they remain buried, floating across London's field of contemporary architecture in constantly reemerging moments, whose meanings, nonetheless, have been ravaged by the passage of unforgiving, on-going time.

Time and its Replay: Coincident vs. Emergent Circumstance

If we have been successful in constructing the notion of an immanent, wildly fragmentary field continually calling forth buried memories of violence, it is the problematic component of time, which neutralizes inherent meaning. Certainly, the reemergence of iconographic language must be considered as time/era-dependent. The meaning of any recreation hinges on the particular historical moment in which it appears. Imagine the difference in a referent of a commemoration emerging immediately after a catastrophe rather than fifty years later, mixing within the semiotic code of diverse origins. In London these are implicated especially in the postpostmodern latter day, in contexts usurped by real estate, marketing and the techniques of corporate branding that financed most of the Hi-Tech buildings.

Rather than calling forth meanings latent in iconographic codes and historical juxtapositions, however, we now turn to examine how violence may lie as a latent component of a building, to emerge only through a particular construct of time. Two examples—Foster's Millennium Bridge and Rogers's Reuters Technical Center—will serve to outline such cases of *potential* violence. The third example, Alsop Architects' Peckham Library, serves to expound on Paul Virilio's thesis of the change wrought upon the very content of violence as it is captured and replayed ubiquitously by contemporary electronic media. The three examples probe into the final type of recordings of violence within the city that exist in tenuous and virtual, but yet, very public realms.

Foster and Partner's Millennium Bridge was built across the Thames as a major gesture to the newly vibrant South Bank, connecting Herzog and de Meuron's highly touted Tate Modern with much older, established setting around St. Paul's Cathedral. The commission of the bridge, the first to be built over the river in over a century, was awarded out of a RIBA-sponsored competition calling for visionary solutions, convoked without the funding necessary for its actual construction. Upon winning the competition, Foster's office, in collaboration with engineers Ove Arup, undertook not only the design of the project, but also the development of financial and political support necessary for its completion. Both architects and engineers worked toward producing a bridge that would minimize vertical structure while maximizing the visual and structural concept of an abstract horizontal line spanning across the river. In the structural design, Ove Arup proposed a lateral suspension structure composed of eight steel cables forming a horizontal support network spanning between concrete pylons, with a pedestrian walkway held up by steel cross-members. Foster's office was equally concerned with the contradictory concept of the bridge as a piece of urban furniture, with a high degree of attention paid to material finishes and lighting. Significant to this notion were the transition points to the ground at either end—Foster's notion of the "architectural moments" of the structure.

A worldwide notorious episode occurred, when upon the completion of the bridge in June of 2000, the first collective walk was to be taken to celebrate its official opening. The event monumentally turned sour. In a phenomenon familiar mostly to military engineers, a crowd moving across a bridge has an inexplicable tendency to unify its footfall. The considerable kinetic load produced by a large crowd marching in military step initially produces a minor swaying of the bridge. Prompted by that initial movement, the footsteps synchronize even closer, consequently accelerating the sway of the bridge—a phenomenon that can be explained in mathematics only by non-linear dynamics. Unfortunately for Foster and Ove Arup, when the frequency of the crowds' steps coincided with the natural resonance of the bridge's structure, the sway became extreme and the 690 tons of aluminum and steel began to twist horizontally as well as undulate up and down. Even though the bridge only moved a few centimeters and was never in danger of failing, according to those participating in the event, the eeriness of the experience caused visitors to be frightened enough to hold onto each other or to the railings. As the amplitude of the

Figure 12. Arup, Foster and Partners, Sir Anthony Caro, Millennium Bridge, 2000.
Behavior and structure, human and machine, synchronized in time.

bridge's vibrations grew higher and higher, each person felt in their every footstep responsibility for the movement of the entire bridge.[27]

The phenomenon was deemed traumatic enough to lead to the closing of the bridge for the next year in order for the engineers and architects to add £5 million of structural modifications, consisting of spring-loaded mass dampers and x-shaped lateral stiffeners. The event, extremely embarrassing for Foster and Arup, was originally televised live, but consequently was replayed over and over again, and continues to be on various Internet sites. The element of time conquered material in several ways. The structural capacity of the bridge was overcome by time's mathematics: as the sinusoid wave generated by the synchronization of great number of individual sources coincided with the resonant frequency of a huge material structure, the conjunction brought the bridge to a complex, unstable state that made it vulnerable to even very small stimuli. As tragic bridge failures at Tacoma and Angers attest, this moment of infinite expansion of force through time has only been stopped in the past by the final overwhelming of the physical by the temporal: the collapse. But in the present day, there are also very different modes of time and event to consider. In the recording of the incident and its infinite replay in electronic journalism, the event is never complete. It can be replayed at will, downloaded, expanded and/or contracted infinitely. A doubly infinite expansion of time and state is instigated: a sinusoid theater, eternalized.

In a series of accruing gestures, the coincidence of those inhabiting the structure meshed completely with the structure itself. The two became inseparable. In the union between humans and machines that occurred in those split seconds of synchronized time, a truly androidal moment emerged, as the structure assumed terrifyingly human dimensions. While literal violence never actually occurred, the nature of exchange as corporeal, as vacillating between intimately personal and enormously monumental, proved all too real psychologically. Virilio's remark becomes appended: while the representation of the android in war apparatus might signal the love of one's own death, the moment of its actualization, when flesh and machine become one, is the moment of death itself.[28]

The second example to which we turn is a little-known building by Richard Rogers, the Reuters Technical Service Centre. Built in the late 1980s to house the data delivery headquarters for the financial news conglomerate Reuters, the primary mandate was that the building remains, for security reasons, completely anonymous. Rogers's building, a mute box articulated mostly by mechanistic stairwells and upper-level mechanical floors, is noteworthy in the architect's oeuvre for its restraint, especially that it was designed just a few years after his exuberant and contro-versial Lloyd's of London in the center of the City.

True to its anonymous mandate, the building is unremarkable in its configuration and planning. The first five floors of the nine-story colum-nar structure are occupied entirely by equipment, and having little need for natural light, are almost entirely windowless. With vertical building circulation moved outside of the envelope proper, the articulation of these spaces is limited to the one-meter floor depth that accommodates miles of linear cable transferring data to and from ubiquitous databanks and pro-cessors. In addition, the floors are punctuated by six vertical electrical ris-ers which contain safety networks should any part of the electronic system collapse. If there is any spatiality to be described on these floors, it is the endless grid of tight corridors and fluorescent lighting between the banks of full-height processors, through which an occasional technician might be seen navigating. In contrast, the upper floors of the building house administration and the control center inspired by NASA's, fashioned to convey the intensity of Reuters operation to visiting high-profile investors.

Built in the late eighties, the primary attraction offered by the site, located just outside of the Docklands near the east entry to the Blackwell Tunnel (seen in figure 13), was its affordability and the anonymity offered by the vast and vacant acreage around the defunct shipyards. This all changed dramatically upon the completion of the financial center Canary

Figure 13. Richard Rogers, Reuters Data Centre, 1987–92. A massive block of real-time vulnerabilities.

INSCRIPTIONS OF VIOLENCE

Wharf, which brought hundreds of new corporate headquarters to the area and prompted considerable growth of housing and support services. In fact, the area has become so attractive to businesses that the traditional publishing and administrative headquarters of Reuters itself are currently being relocated nearby, after several centuries of residing in a Lutyens building at 85 Fleet Street in the City.

Originally housing 400–500 employees within the building, Reuters is systematically phasing them out, reducing staffing from general administration to a skeletal technical support crew. Britain's financial boom after the deregulation of its stock markets in the mid-eighties caused the demand for Reuters services to increase dramatically, almost instantly rendering the technical center under-capacity. With increasing amounts of space devoted to processing equipment and rapidly depleting human presence, the building will soon be rendered entirely an intelligent machine, an impenetrable humanless labyrinth humming with the transfer of enormous volumes of information. Science fiction emerges again in this manifestation of a dense architectural body composed entirely of intelligent systems. If Foster's bridge crisis leads to the creation of science fiction's terrifying android, in Rogers's building an equally familiar dystopic entity emerges: the super-sized, quasi-architectural brain run amok, with nary a human in sight. Known in such far-flung but cultish moments as Kubrick's spaceship brain Hal in 2001: A Space Odyssey and in the Wachowskis' recent Matrix, this concept appears even in architectural visions, notably Superstudio's third mystical city in Twelve Cautionary Tales for Christmas—the New York of Brains, an electronically sensitive cerebral mass with little need for human bodies accompanying their instrumentalized brains.

The statistics involved in the informational transfer at the Technical Center are the subject of every computer geek's fantasy. Reuters claim to uniqueness is in its ability to relay fluctuations in stock prices, translated into user-friendly format, to subscribers internationally in 14 milliseconds, coming close to its goal of attaining "real-time" speed. The capacity of the facility is also considerable. At the daily opening of New York Stock Exchange, engineers at Reuters wait apprehensively for the impact of 100,000 updates/second on their systems. With this type of volume of financial data critical to worldwide markets, it is not difficult to understand Reuters anxiety over potential crises. Initially, this anxiety was centered primarily on the threat of IRA street bombings. In 2004, a catastrophic failure did happen, but due to mere human shortcoming, not bombs. When two risers of electrical power went down, engineers overrode automatic safety measures designed to shift power delivery to back-up systems, contributing a calamitous human factor that incapacitated the system for hours. The exorbitant cost of human meddling could be measured by the seconds the system was down.[29]

This event contributed to Reuters decision to build secondary data centers in Clerkenwell (London), Geneva, Frankfurt, Chicago, Sydney, and Hong Kong. The most urgent factor, however, in the decision to expand safety network came upon the horrifying post-9/11 realization that despite all precautions in choosing a suitably secure and anonymous site, the building had ended up on the flight path for planes departing from the nearby newly-constructed London City Airport. As the threat of terrorism expanded from locally-based IRA ground vehicles to globally deployed planes, the threat to the building was not to human life or property, but to the millions of bits of information suspended in a real-time issuance around the world: the threat of violence transposed from flesh to time. The potential devastation, an intervention into infinite events of milliseconds, is made only more daunting by the realization that it would occur with the sublime singularity of one jet moving at high speed intersecting a building at one particular moment: the signature image of violence of the twenty-first century.

In the case of both Foster's bridge and the Rogers's technical center, a particular moment emerges as a potential site of massive destruction. At that single moment of realization, the potential for devastating violence becomes exponentially enlarged, opening a vast transformation in the notion of the structure as a finite entity operating in discrete time. This moment happens at the intersection of material and virtual time, but also at the critical juncture of human and machine. In the case of the Foster's bridge, this occurs in the exact moment of corporeal and scalar exchange. In the Rogers's building, however, the moment exists in a more attenuated volley: just as the human being is being made obsolete in the realm of the intelligent global machine, that same machine is destroyed by the singularly acting human, devoid in principle of any official affiliation with a group or nation.

The last example to be undertaken, Will Alsop's Peckham Library, is poignantly local. Built in the late 1990s by Alsop Architects, Ltd., the project was the emblematic highpoint of an £275m initiative to regenerate the increasingly crime-ridden African and Caribbean neighborhood of Peckham in the southern borough of Southwark. This enterprise consisted of both enhancing the potential for effective civic moments in Peckham as well as funding an extensive network of CCTV surveillance. Thus, the program for Alsop's library was not simply for an information facility but it encompassed actively rebuilding the community's sense of self-esteem and security—reflected in the mandate to provide civic outdoor space, as well as community meeting and vocational training spaces.

Alsop's concept of civism consisted primarily of identifiability: "a civic space is defined as a place where you go and meet someone outside, name the place, and know where to go." Alsop's response was an inverted L-shape building held up by angled columns and crowned with large metal letters pronouncing it indeed as a "LIBRARY." It is willfully cartoonish, but strategically so. Configured to provide visibility to a small public plaza, the building's exuberant architecture announces itself as unabashedly populist. By virtue of its colorful exterior, and interior spaces both playful and genuinely functional to their many callings, Alsop's library was immediately claimed by the neighborhood. As a reading facility the library generated a wildly unexpected number of visitors, populated to capacity by adults and children at all hours. Instantly becoming known throughout greater London for its unconventional and award-winning architecture, the building became immediately used within the neighborhood as its town center.

Figure 14. Alsop Architects' friendly Peckham Library, 1999.
Photo: Jenny E. Sabin, 2004.

Events which followed, however, were not equally encouraging. On November 27, 2000, a ten-year-old schoolboy named Damilola Taylor left the library after spending his after-school hours there. Only a few minutes after having been filmed by the plaza's CCTV cameras as he left the library, Taylor was attacked and stabbed to death on a stairwell outside his home at the North Peckham Estate, a housing project notorious for its crime statistics. A model student, Taylor's case was deemed photogenic by the press and taken up with fervor, instantly broadcast throughout Great Britain, becoming a cause célèbre for the plight of the neighborhood and immigrants throughout the city. As the backdrop in the footage capturing Taylor's last moments, the fame of the Alsop library was recast overnight. The CCTV footage of Damilola Taylor running from the building was played incessantly over the public news networks for months. Images of the exuberant building were immediately associated with the tragic event of the boy's last minutes and became a symbol for the neighbors' continuing sense of decline in the face of economic powerlessness. Significantly, six months later, hundreds were organized by neighborhood churches and marched in tribute and protest, ending their vigil in front of the library, once again captured on film and once again, re-symbolized.

The story continues to unfold, but only sporadically holds the public's attention. Five years ago, after several mistrials and failed attempts to capture Taylor's assailants, police finally seemed to be close to convicting the gang-members the neighborhood was originally too frightened to

Figure 15. Far-better remembered: Peckham Library's plaza on 27 November 2000, the day of Damilola Taylor's murder. Courtesy PhotoNews Service.

INSCRIPTIONS OF VIOLENCE

implicate. Meanwhile, Taylor's home and murder site, the North Peckham Estate, has been symbolically razed and is now the site for 25,000 new homes. Yet, it is still plagued by only slightly lower statistics of violent crime. The neighborhood of Peckham has become marginally gentrified, but only in its southern-most reaches. Greater Southwark has witnessed more pervasive gentrification and its benefits, dropping from second to ninth in the city for gun-related incidents. Despite the inflammation caused by the notoriety of the case, it seems that the tragic case of Damilola Taylor can be relegated to the annals of sensational journalism. Even the Peckham Library, however unlikely to recover its sunny innocence, continues in large part unaffected, not suffering any appreciable effect to its attraction of local visitors.

A comparison between the incident at the Peckham Library to the Foster's bridge and Rogers's Technical Centre is first based on actual versus potential violence, but this is not its most important distinction. The first two cases represent excruciating singular moments when exact circumstances of the building program, site and occupation construct a possibility for major, devastating violence. In contrast, despite the fact that Taylor's murder was a singular event, it was also one of many similarly violent occurrences in London, which remain largely ignored, unless captured by the caprice of the local media for whatever tantalizing human dimension they might seem to portray effectively. Perhaps if there had not been the famously poignant CCTV footage, Taylor's case may have never caught the public eye.

Damilola Taylor's case was plucked from a vast continuum of events constantly being recorded in London by an immense network of surveillance media. Compared to the cases of the Foster's bridge and Rogers's Technical Center, the Taylor/Peckham case represents a singular moment defined in time but extracted from a sea of equally likely situations. Of all world cities, London has distinguished itself by the pervasive use of the closed-circuit microwave-transmitted camera system. As of 2004, there were 4 million CCTV cameras in Great Britain, some equipped with facial recognition capabilities. In 1996 three-quarters of the crime prevention budgets in London were spent on CCTV surveillance. These cameras record events continuously at every stop and vehicle of mass transportation, at every public and many private buildings, at every ATM machine, at every street and intersection within the City's infamous district, the "Wall of Steel," propelled by the very same IRA bombing of the Baltic Exchange in 1992. The amount of footage continuously capturing events in the city produces unprecedented, comprehensive record of life in the city. This far surpasses the filming of significant events: it is a silent recording of *all* events, despite their relevance to crime or violence. Because the sheer volume of recording makes real-time monitoring by the police impossible, the surveillance systems have little if any capacity to anticipate or interrupt crimes in progress. As manifested by the camera's use in the apprehension of the perpetrators of the 2005 London infrastructure bombings, the surveillance footage is of use only after the incident.

CCTV footage offers thus the most infinite, voracious archive ever to be constructed, continuously capturing events of all levels of significance, offering a vast amount of incidental information made instrumental only after the event. If the Proustian field constructed in the second part of this essay was ultimately understood as nebulous in structure and principle, this most recent field of on-going, ubiquitous collection of information is infinitely so. As Virilio contends in *A Landscape of Events*, reflecting on the nature of images from the first Gulf War, when history is compressed into an image played on the television alongside the Nintendo game, the event itself is destroyed.[30] In the case of Damilola Taylor, the sensationalism of the replayed image, followed by the rise and fall of public attention, corresponds exactly to Virilio's observations. In the ubiquity and infinity of the CCTV collection, however, a very new and different type of archive and recording of violence is opened. Its distinguishing features are the ubiquity and lack of hierarchy. This is an archive of infinite generality, where all events are considered potentially violent, yet forever remain silent in vast digital memory, entombed until deemed noteworthy to peruse and reexamine. In this type of archive, violent events are not remembered but reconstituted, and a very different sort of commemoration emerges. Out of the act of repeated replay, often in the full gaze of a spell-bound public trying to come to terms with the nature of the violence committed, occurrences just prior to the event are typically focused upon. The world is recreated before the act was perpetrated; a play of before-and-after time, which ultimately attempts to posit the possibility of an act caught and never committed, of destruction not felt, of lives not lost.

We began this examination with the observation that the singular monument will never be adequate to capture the multiplicity of the complex event, in terms of its fact and figures, its circumstances and effects, and certainly not in seizing the viscerality, the trauma, even the eroticism of violence. And yet, the appearance of the monument throughout history is itself evidence of an irrefutable desire to do so. If this examination of London has served any purpose, it is the contention that it is not in the singular reference to an event that the viscerality of violence re-emerges, but only in the most vague and most oneiric of field constructions. This field is akin to the condition of landscape, at least landscape defined as a connective medium between events, processes, and relationships through which the multiple dimensions of that violence can be reconstituted and comprehended. It is an immanent, pervasive state of the fragile referent structure, present in London through the work of Archigram and the Hi-Tech, and in the pathos of reconstructed time flickering in an infinite field of CCTV replays.[31]

Endnotes

1— Nietzsche contrasts the ahistoricity of animals, unable to record and replay the past moment, to the shaping power of a human being to develop a singular—and often detrimental—character of itself through cognition and recording of the past. See Friedrich Nietzsche, "The Utility and Liability of History," in *Unfashionable Observations*, Vol. 2, trans. Richard T. Gray (Stanford, CA: Stanford University, 1995).

2— Virilio's book, a set of essays written after the first Gulf War, examines the residue of a series of violent events through/on contemporary culture and media, posing a challenge to all forms of remembrance. From his introduction: "So many questions that give meaning and direction to the temporal depth of our history remain unspoken, to the point where the threat of 'negationism' is now everywhere rampant." Paul Virilio, *A Landscape of Events*, trans. Julie Rose (Cambridge, MA: MIT, 2000), x.

3— Thomas Fiddian Reddaway, *The Rebuilding of London after the Great Fire* (London: Jonathan Cape, 1940).

4— There is in my reading inherently a vast difference between a monument constructed to symbolize the totality and/or authority of either church or state—the monsters of Bataille's discourse—with the monument constructed to commemorate a singular event, especially an event of violence and destruction suffered by a whole population at one historical point in time.

5— The Swiss Re's promotional brochure even mentions that the building's stairwells have three times the number of steps of The Monu-

ment. See "Facts," accessed Dec. 8, 2010, http://www.30stmaryaxe.com/fact.html.

6— These facts are all very well-known. For a detailed synopsis, A+U: 2004, 408 (September 2004): 10–18, or *GA Document* 80 (2004): 84–95.

7— "Specification Summary," accessed Dec. 8, 2010, http://www.30stmaryaxe.com/accomm.html.

8— The particular shape of 30 St. Mary Axe leaves open attribution of all kinds of popular nicknames. The London newspaper, *The Guardian*, coined the term, "erotic gherkin." According to *Wikipedia*, the building has also been called the "Towering Innuendo" and the "Crystal Phallus." On the occasion of a rare opening of the building to the general public, the *Evening Standard* titled their article: "See inside the Mayor's Gherkin."

9— Matt Dillon, *Twenty-five Years of Terror: The IRA's war against the British* (London: Bantam Books, 1996), 310–11.

10– Denis Hollier notes that Bataille's attraction to slaughterhouses comes from their evocation of ancient religious rites. (He cites "Abattoir" in Batailles' *Oeuvres Completes*). In Paris, it is Bernard Tschumi's Parc de la Villette that now occupies the city's original slaughterhouse and meat-distribution district. See Dennis Hollier, *Against Architecture: The Writings of Georges Bataille* (Cambridge, MA: MIT Press 1992), xii.

11– The building of Foster's St. Mary Axe set off a furor in preservationist circles. After carefully collecting pieces from the original Baltic Exchange building and announcing the intention to rebuild the building as it once stood, municipal authorities buckled to developer pressure and did not reconstruct the heritage building, opting for far greater profitability of the Foster Building.

12– Thanks to my seminar student Christina Yaron for making this uncanny observation and providing some of the initial research into possible tangible linkages.

13– Sheila Taylor, ed., *The Moving Metropolis: A History of London's Transport since 1800* (London: Laurence King/London Transport Museum, 2002), 236–268.

14– Peter Cook et. al., eds., *Archigram* (NY: Princeton Architectural Press, 1999), 36.

15– The literature of the effects of war on Britain's children is considerable. Especially prevalent in depictions are accounts of the evacuation, but also the incongruity of gadgetry developed to protect the children. The mythology of children during the Blitz continues; concurrent with this writing is a BBC science-fiction series titled *Doctor Who's: The Empty Child*, an account of an "unearthly child" terrorizing London in a gas protection mask. Given that the average age of the six original Archigram members was seven at the beginning of the bombing, all were familiar with the indelible apparatus.

16– Cook, *Archigram*, 80.

17– Sources for these accounts and statistics are varied. See Maureen Waller, *London 1945* (London: John Murray, 2004), Tom Harrisson, *Living Through the Blitz* (London: Collins, 1976), and John Ray, *The Night Blitz, 1940–1941* (London: Arms and Armour, 1996).

18– Deyan Sudjic speaks of Harold Wilson's contention of the "white-hot heat" of the technological revolution sensed in many spheres of life in 1960s Britain. See Deyan Sudjic, *Norman Foster, Richard Rogers, James Stirling: New Directions in British Architecture* (London: Thames and Hudson, 1986).

19– Anthony Vidler, "Toward a Theory of the Architectural Program: Between Cybernetics and Utopia." Lecture presented at the University of Pennsylvania, September 2004.

20– The term "expressionistic" was one used by Pevsner, which is arguable.

21– In the third program of his "Radio Talks," Pevsner, legendary teacher and popular critic, attacked the Stirling building through a critique of the afunctionality of its elements—especially the configuration of the window and ramp elements. See Stephen Games, ed.,

Nikolaus Pevsner: Pevsner on Art and Architecture (London: Methuen, 2002), 293–300.

22– Rogers's biographer, Bryan Appleyard, tells of Rogers's experience of the Festival of Britain as seminal to inspiring the young rudderless Rogers: "His second experience [of modern architecture], however, seems to have kindled some small and incompletely recognized flame." See Brian Appleyard, *Richard Rogers* (London/Boston: Faber and Faber, 1986), 46–48.

23– For a much more thorough description of the Festival, see Becky E. Conekin, *The Autobiography of a Nation: The 1951 Festival of Britain* (Manchester/NY: Manchester University, 2003).

24– Mario Bowley, *Innovations in Building Materials: An Economic Study* (London: Duckworth, 1960).

25– Roger Luckhurst, *Science Fiction* (Cambridge, UK: Polity, 2005), 151. Much of my account of science fiction in this era is indebted to Luckhurst's thorough research of both British and American evolution of the genre.

26– Virilio, *Landscape of Events*, 35.

27– Much of my account here is based in a March 2005 interview with Catherine Ramsden, project architect for the bridge in Foster's office.

28– Virilio, *Landscape of Events*, 35.

29– These facts and accounts, I owe with thanks to Dave Carney and Mike Bowles at the Reuters Technical Center during their kind and extensive tour of the Reuter' building in spring of 2005. No doubt most of these statistics have already been surpassed.

30– Virilio, *Landscape of Events*, 24.

31– My thanks go to my research assistants Zhongjie Lin and Jennifer Cramm for providing necessary background, as well as now four years of general research (2006–10) done by students in my seminar at the University of Pennsylvania, *Archigram and its Legacies: London, A Technotopia*. Thanks also go to deans at PennDesign, Gary Hack and Marilyn J. Taylor, for providing necessary funding for copyright permissions and travel expenses for my students and myself. General research and travel funding was also provided by a grant from Penn's University Research Foundation. All photographs are property of the author unless otherwise noted.

ARCHITECTURE AS EXQUISITE VIOLENCE

ELIE HADDAD

*The architect represents neither a Dionysian nor an Apollonian state:
here it is the great act of will, the will that moves mountains, the frenzy
of the great will which aspires to art. The most powerful human beings
have always inspired architects; the architect has always been under
the spell of power. His buildings are supposed to render pride visible,
and the victory over gravity, the will to power. Architecture is a kind of
eloquence of power in forms —now persuading, even flattering, now only
commanding. The highest feeling of power and sureness finds expression
in a grand style.*

Friedrich Nietzsche[1]

Architecture and Violence: A Prelude

Nietzsche's statement provides a good point of entry to the discussion
of the relation between architecture and violence. For the thinker who
philosophized with a hammer, violence was a positive factor in the human
drive to master the forces of destiny. The philosopher's late writings,
especially his *Twilight of the Idols*, are replete with statements that exude
an original animus, a call to take possession of things, a call to "frenzy."
This is expressed vividly also when he speaks about art:

*If there is to be art, if there is to be any aesthetic doing and seeing, one
physiological condition is indispensable: frenzy. Frenzy must first have
enhanced the excitability of the whole machine; else there is no art. All
kinds of frenzy, however diversely conditioned, have the strength to
accomplish this: above all, the frenzy of sexual excitement, this most
ancient and original form of frenzy. Also the frenzy that follows all great
cravings, all strong affects; the frenzy of feasts, contests, feats of daring,
victory, all extreme movement; the frenzy of cruelty; the frenzy in
destruction; ... and finally the frenzy of will, the frenzy of an overarched
and swollen will. What is essential in such frenzy is the feeling of
increased strength and fullness. Out of this feeling one lends to things,
one forces them to accept from us, one violates them —this process is called
idealizing. ... What is decisive is rather a tremendous drive to bring out
the main features so that the others disappear in the process.
In this state one enriches everything out of one's own fullness:
whatever one sees, whatever one wills, is seen swelled, taut, strong,
overloaded with strength. A man in this state transforms things until
they mirror his power —until they are reflections of his perfection.
This having to transform into perfection is —art.*[2]

In this statement, Nietzsche defines the main attribute of what he considered to be the essence of art: frenzy in all its forms, even those that veer towards the destructive. For Nietzsche, art is fundamentally a violent act; it is a "countermovement" to religion, morality, and philosophy.[3] Art is reminiscent of "animal vigor," an "excess," and an overflowing of images and desires.[4]

Architecture as a "great will that aspires to art" is not immune to this frenzy, although it appears to take a more moderate position between the Dionysian and the Apollonian, between passion and reason. It is interesting to note that in his rendering of art, Nietzsche did not provide any specific examples, although the notion of "animal vigor" certainly evokes images that go back to the origins of art, to the Paleolithic period. At the time of his last writings, the findings of the caves of Altamira, which would create a sensational discovery in the world of art, were just being published. Was Nietzsche aware of these raw paintings that pre-civilized men had scraped, possibly in a state of frenzy, in the caves of Spain and France?[5] Years later the Lascaux caves were discovered in Southern France, which became the material for Georges Bataille's own discussion of art and eroticism.

Discussions of violence in relation to architecture have been largely centered on the urban manifestations of violence, or the role that institutionalization plays in fostering the development of violence leading to its ultimate manifestation in wars and destruction. From Freud to Foucault, many thinkers have explored the underlying connections between civilization and its instruments, like architecture, and some of their consequences, like violence. This is explicit in Foucault's reference to architecture as the locus of authority and repression. Alternatively, Bataille explored the symbolic dimensions of architecture within the frame that investigated the themes of violence, eroticism, and death.[6]

Eroticism, Death and Violence

In *The Tears of Eros*,[7] Georges Bataille inquired into the connections between eroticism and death. His point of departure were the caves of Lascaux and the mysterious engravings discovered on their walls. How could eroticism be related to death? It is hard to conceive such perverse assumption as Bataille himself recognized:

> *It is indeed difficult to perceive, clearly and distinctly, how death, or the consciousness of death, forms a unity with eroticism. In its*

*principle, exacerbated desire cannot be opposed to life, which is rather
its outcome. The erotic moment is even the zenith of life, in which the
greatest force and the greatest intensity are revealed whenever two
beings are attracted to each other, mate, and perpetuate life. It is a
question of life, and of reproducing life; but in its reproduction, life
overflows, and in overflowing it reaches the most extreme frenzy.*[8]

Frenzy, the Nietzschean notion, reappears in Bataille, where it is
explicitly associated with the erotic, the very act that sets the boundaries between the animal and the human. In addition, awareness of death
appears at the beginnings of history and manifests itself in the architecture of burial places, which are concrete expressions of human anxiety.[9]
The erotic and the awareness of death are for Bataille the two constituents
of our "difference." Furthermore, violence seems to underlie both the
erotic and death:

*"Violence" overwhelms us strangely in each case: each time, what
happens is foreign to the received order of things, to which each
time this violence stands in opposition. There is an indecency about
death, no doubt distinct from what is incongruous about the sexual
act. Death is associated with tears; and sometimes sexual desire is
associated with laughter. But laughter is not so much the contrary of
tears as it may seem: the object of laughter and the object of tears are
always related to some kind of violence which interrupts the regular
order of things, the usual course of events.*[10]

This "violence which interrupts the regular order of things" can be
related to specific architectural settings, propitious for the enactments
of specific rituals, where in opposition to the expressive manifestations
of destruction, other latent forms can manifest themselves, which can be
characterized as "perverse," troublesome, or upsetting established norms.

Perverting Architecture

A few years after the end of the civil war (1975–1990) in Lebanon, a war that
resisted any commemoration, a nightclub named B-018 was built at the
site of what used to be a Palestinian refugee camp in the Karantina area
in Beirut, which had witnessed one of the earliest operations of ethnic
cleansing. The architect, Bernard Khoury, polemically situated his project

ARCHITECTURE AS EXQUISITE VIOLENCE

underground, in a gesture that brings to mind Adolf Loos's famous correlation between architecture and death.[11]

Before discussing the project in its architectonic aspects, it is important to contemplate for a moment the contextual parameters of the project. Not only is the nightclub in question located in the zone that was "cleared" during the war, but it is also in close proximity to the city slaughterhouse and the quarantine zone, where in the nineteenth century foreigners used to be screened and kept in isolation for forty days before being allowed into the city. The project thus takes place on the very margins of the city, in an area of exclusion and elimination, of a "double-dépense," to borrow Bataille's term (figure 1). The historic connotations of the place were not lost to the journals, that first published Khoury's project alongside the iconic photograph of a hooded militiaman facing a pleading woman, lost in the midst of a landscape of death and desolation.[12]

From the outside the project appears as a simple marking in the ground—a large metallic lid of several steel plates. This gesture hides the underground "reality" or, one should say, the history of the site. A circular rim of concrete encloses the rectangular lid, surrounded by the path that organizes the cars parked around the marked, yet hidden, space. The flatness of the construction appears in sharp contrast to the densely

Figure 1. B-018, *view from the outside. Courtesy Bernard Khoury.*

built context that surrounds it. It is a minimalist statement, a negation of "building," but it also connotes a "withdrawal" (figures 2, 3, 4).

From this flat platform on the surface the visitor is led down the narrow stairs to the main entrance, opening up to a space of regimented seating areas. All of a sudden, one finds oneself in a sacred interior space. Red curtains line the walls, lit by spotlights, framing the internal "plaza" occupied by folding pieces of furniture that constitute different "shrines," each marked by an iconic musician's portrait and decorated with a flower vase, all arranged in strict order (figures 5 and 6). In plan, the project hints to possible historical references: a basilica plan, with a central axis, a nave, and the culminating bar, a linear transversal element that plays the role of a theater stage, or better, of a sacrificial altar. Behind the bar lies the service area that takes the form of an apse.

With its uniform ceiling height and the absence of any openings, the space appears claustrophobic. However, the mechanical opening of the roof releases this tension in a double-exposure that simultaneously opens the space to the sky above, while reflecting through ceiling mirrors its internal spectacle to the outside.

This early work by Bernard Khoury has received widespread recognition and was published in a number of international magazines, which have celebrated its provocative aspects: underground placement, mechanically-operated roof, macabre interior, etc.[13] One reviewer praised it for its appearance as a bunker while the interior with its red curtains appeared "tragic yet theatrical."[14] In another review the project is described as a "big machine" sunk into the ground.[15] Yet another assessment noted its "ancient temple" appearance, in which the central axis, like a nave, leads to the bar that takes the place of the "altar." Finally, others associated it with a sacrificial tomb, a night temple, and an intergalactic vessel.[16]

When Khoury presents this work, he typically underplays its symbolic content, focusing only on its technicalities and logistics, intentionally stripping the work of any symbolic pretenses at the very outset.[17] The arbitrary name of the project itself, B-018, reinforces this banality that the project assumes.[18] In this intentional reduction of the structure to a mere function and the resistance of its author to interpretation, one can also read a position comparable to Walter Benjamin's rejection of monuments as forms of symbolic mourning.[19]

But besides its obvious references and allusions, how does the space of B-018 relate to the idea of violence? Bataille's notion of transgression offers clues that could be of significance in reading this work. In her analysis of Bataille, Suzanne Guerlac noted:

Figure 2. B-018, view from the outside. Courtesy Bernard Khoury.

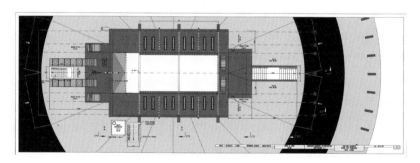

Figure 3. B-018, plan. Courtesy Bernard Khoury.

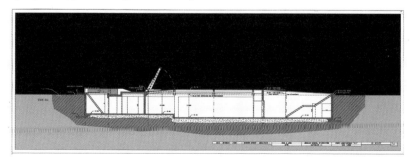

Figure 4. B-018, section. Courtesy Bernard Khoury.

In l'Erotisme, Bataille insists that the two moments of the dual operation of eroticism are so intimately bound up with one another as to be all but indistinguishable. The terms 'interdiction' and 'transgression' become meaningful only subjectively, that is as affective experiences of attraction and repulsion, which distinguish the two realms of the sacred and profane. Bataille presents this as a dance, a ronde, for the experience of seduction moves us toward the sacred object and the feeling of horror that repels us from it are closely interrelated.[20]

Bataille's assertion that eroticism is intimately bound to the idea of death finds a resonance in this particular work. The idea of inserting a polemical project on such specific site cannot be attributed to the architect's will alone, even though in this case the architect was a partner in the decision. Arguably, any project built on this site could have had similar connotations. However, in this case, the architect as a polemical artist raised the issue to the highest pitch by projecting a structure that not only sits on the site of death, but also incorporates the idea of death and celebrates it by confronting it with the erotic.[21]

B-018 seems to be precariously situated on the borderline between the sacred and the profane, and thus assumes the position of a space of transgression. Recalling ancient monuments, the project traces a circumference on the ground, a "ronde," where people gather before they enter. It is also not a coincidence that Khoury chose to play on the theme of death by resurrecting memories of the musicians whose framed portraits decorate the tables, which play a dual role of memorial altars and dancing stages. Hence, the project operates on two levels: it is metonymical, in its direct quotation from the repertoire of death, and metaphorical, in its allusion to the cave, the underground, and the realm of the dead. The opposition is constantly present in the space: velvet curtains contrasting with a rough floor; the mechanical roof, with warm wooden tables.

In the cavern of B-018 there are no erotic engravings as in the caves of Lascaux, but transgression is nevertheless felt in this space that has been reclaimed from the memory of war to become neither a memorial nor a museum, but a space of hedonistic pleasures. The red curtains are suggestive of the "erotic" in its vulgar interpretation: the color of blood, of sexuality, of prostitution. Architecture becomes a catalyst in an expiatory operation, and the space as such aptly fulfills its role as a space of transgression. In the midst of the rituals of dance and music late at night, the opening of the roof takes on an added symbolic significance as deliv-

Figure 6. B-018, interior view.
Courtesy Bernard Khoury.

Figure 5. B-018, interior view. Courtesy Bernard Khoury.

erance, a culmination, re-linking with the *axis mundi* of the sky and the earth. The psychological effect on individuals experiencing this effect may approach the religious, in the original sense given to it by Bataille:

> *Religion is doubtlessly, even in essence, subversive: it turns away*
> *from the observance of the laws. At least, what it demands is excess,*
> *sacrifice, and the feast, which culminates in ecstasy.*[22]

Khoury has projected here a space that recalls some of the themes suggested by Bataille. The nightclub becomes a site of *exquisite* violence, negotiating a fine line between death and eroticism. The confrontation of music and dance with memory and death takes place within the boundaries of this anti-building, sitting on an anti-site, which has been turned into a site of transgression. There is no question that Khoury's work was impregnated with the memories of war, which had been affirmatively reinterpreted into a mechanistic vision of the world, of armored forms that swivel and open up like prosthetic devices.[23]

The prosthetic in art and architecture first appeared with the historical avant-garde after World War I. Hal Foster identified different interpretations of this manifestation: on one hand, the Constructivist, which projected technology as the extension of the body, acting as a means of self-transcendence in a new Communist society, and operated by the artist-engineer; on the other hand, the Bauhaus's vision, which also saw technology as the extension of the body, but inscribed within the capitalist system of production.[24] On another level, the surrealists saw in technology—represented in their dismembered automatons and fragmented mannequins—the "double logic" of the prosthesis: the machine as a "castrative trauma" and as a phallic shield against the same trauma.[25]

Even though the author of B-018 does not claim to participate in any of these theoretical ventures, the surrealist notion of the "double logic" may cast additional light on his work. The prosthetic can be seen in the articulation of the whole, where architecture appears to confront its mechanistic "other," which threatens to subsume it within its own devices: the swiveling roof, the mirrors, etc. All these fixtures attempt to assist the architectural "body" in its rehabilitation within the site of trauma. One could suggest in Khoury's operation a Constructivist approach, projecting technology as an extension of the body, but also using it in its double role as a castrative device and a protection against castration.[26] May we not surmise—in this operation that uses prosthetic devices to bury the project discreetly underground, while allowing its revelation at certain times—a desire to shield the human subject from the effects of his own self-mutilation during a war that still resists any commemoration? May we not read into it a maneuver to bury the subject and to simultaneously protect him/her from burial? This *uncanny* aspect of the work generates a double displacement: the disruption of the site and the overthrow of the classical grounding of architecture as an object normally built *above* ground.[27] In effect, B-018 *un-grounds* the architectural object on two different planes: topographically, by negating its presence as an object, and temporally, by subtracting it from its immediate history.

As Adolf Loos implied, "architecture" is only found in those specific works that transgress from the physical to the metaphysical. There are few projects that succeed in breaking through this boundary, and through this rupture suggest a particular affinity with violence, without necessarily simulating or expressing it. Khoury's project in Beirut may be one of those rare instances where architecture engages violence in a dialectical operation that in the end leads to its own overcoming through its dissolution in space and time. This, in turn, would make it a fitting monument for Lebanon's un-commemorated civil war. Perhaps it is already playing that role in a subliminal and perverse way.

Endnotes

1— Friedrich Nietzsche, "Twilight of the Idols: or How to Philosophize with a Hammer," in *The Portable Nietzsche*, (Oxford: Oxford University Press, 1998), 520.

2— Nietzsche, "Twilight of the Idols," 518.

3— Friedrich Nietzsche, *The Will to Power* (New York: Vintage, 1968), 419.

4— Nietzsche, *The Will to Power*, 422.

5— The importance of Altamira was not lost to one of Nietzsche's fervent admirers, the artist Henry van de Velde, who used Nietzschean language to describe the findings in Altamira, as a supporting argument for his own thesis on ornament. For more on the theory of ornament and van de Velde's "Manuscript on Ornament," see my article "On Henry van de Velde's Manuscript on Ornament," *Journal of Design History*, 16. 2 (2003): 139–166.

6 See Denis Hollier, *Against Architecture: The Writings of Georges Bataille* (Cambridge, MA: MIT Press, 1992).

7— Georges Bataille. *The Tears of Eros* (San Francisco: City Lights Books, 1989). Originally published as *Les larmes d'Eros*, (Paris, 1961).

8— Bataille, *The Tears of Eros*, 33.

9— Bataille, *The Tears of Eros*, 25.

10— Bataille, *The Tears of Eros*, 32–33.

11— "If we were to come across a mound in the woods, six foot long by three foot wide, with the soil piled up in a pyramid, a somber mood would come over us and a voice inside us would say, 'There is someone buried here.' *That is architecture.*" See Adolf Loos, "Architecture," in *On Architecture* (Riverside, CA: Ariadne Press, 2002), 84.

12— This photograph taken during the battle of Karantina was taken by Françoise Demulder, and made her the first woman to win the prestigious World Press Photo of the Year award in 1976.

13— This project was published in a number of international reviews such as: "B018 A La

Quarantaine," *Abitare*, 386 (1999): 44–50; "Club B018 en Beirut" in A+T 12 (1999): 126–135; Stefano Pavarini, "Quasi un altro mondo," *l'ARCA* 141 (1999): 24–31; Cynthia C. Davidson, "Dispatch from Beirut: A Project by Bernard Khoury," *ANY* 24 (1999): 8–11; Kaye Geipel, "B018, versenkt: Music-hall in Beirut," *Bauwelt* 50, (1999): 2392–7; "Heavy Metal," *Architecture* (2000): 78–85; [Untitled review], *Casabella* 65 (2000): 80; "Projet B018, club de jazz," *L'Architecture d'Aujourd'hui*, 340 (2002): 71; Anna Brichting and Federico Neder, "Nuit en Boîte–B018 music club: Architecte Bernard Khoury, Beirut, Lebanon," *Faces* 56 (2004): 42–3.

14– *L'Architecture d'Aujourd'hui* 340 (2002): 71.

15– *Bauwelt* 50 (1999): 2393.

16– Anna Grichting and Frederico Neder, "Nuit en Boîte," *Faces* 56 (2004).

17– In a lecture at the American University of Beirut in April 2002 as well as in a personal interview in June 2006, Khoury reiterated his position as an architect who does not concentrate much on these aspects, but rather on the functional and practical qualities of the projects.

18– B-018 refers to the club owner's beach resort, where he played music to a select audience of friends during the war period.

19– See Martin Jay, *Refractions of Violence* (London: Routledge, 2003), 11–24.

20– Suzanne Guerlac, "Bataille in Theory: Afterimages (Lascaux)," *Diacritics* 26. 2 (1996): 6–17.

21– For an indication of some of the polemical aspects of the project, see Omar Boustany, "J'irai danser sur vos tombes," *Revue* 127 (2001): 186–190.

22– Bataille, *The Tears of Eros*, 72.

23– This military reference was also perceived by the reviewer of the *Abitare*, who compared the project to "a piece of military hardware – an aircraft carrier flight-deck or an oversized submarine – left behind after the war." *Abitare* 386, 48. Khoury's interest in technology is also evident in his other projects, including the Centrale restaurant, a restored patrician house that dates back to the late nineteenth century. There the architect executed a radical intervention into the old house, stripping its external walls, which were then framed by an external steel frame, and created an internal concrete structure, which was wrapped by

a lattice framework of horizontal wooden strips. A barrel-cylinder was suspended precariously at the top of this empty shell, replacing traditional pitched roof. Part of the cylinder rotates to open up and offer a framed view of the city.

24– Hal Foster, *Prosthetic Gods*, (Cambridge, MA: MIT Press, 2004), 113.

25– Foster, *Prosthetic Gods*, 114.

26– Foster, *Prosthetic Gods*, 110–115.

27– This notion of the *unheimlich* comes from Martin Heidegger. Its architectural manifestations were explored by Anthony Vidler in *The Architectural Uncanny: Essays in the Modern Unhomely* (Cambridge, MA: MIT Press, 1992).

TOWARDS AN "ARCHITECTURE OF CRUELTY":

MINING THE SPATIAL SPEECH OF ANTONIN ARTAUD

DORITA HANNAH

> To speak of the unspeakable violence of space will necessarily be to
> disturb the terms of traditional discourse and make available new ways
> of talking. It is not simply a matter of addressing a different aspect of
> space. Rather it is a matter of finding a different form of address.[1]

> The problem is to make space speak, to feed and furnish it; like mines
> laid in a wall of rock which all of a sudden turns into geysers and
> bouquets of stone.[2]

In his guest editorial for the 1993 *Assemblage* issue on *Violence Space*, Mark
Wigley refers to "a loud silence," maintained in the intervals between
catastrophic world events, "that masks the more nuanced and ongoing
relationships between violence and space."[3] Insisting that this strategic
silence must be broken in order to confront the complicity between brutal
incidents and architecture, he calls our attention to "the more subterranean rhythms" that organize spaces of violence. The unspeakable nature
of violence requires a "different form of address,"[4] here found in the writing of French surrealist Antonin Artaud (1896–1948), who was often rendered speechless, despite being a poet and performer. This paradox was
reinforced in his texts, which defied language itself. Advocating a *Theater
of Cruelty*, Artaud was determined to mine spatial depths in order to reveal
and release inherent violence as a restorative force. His address took the
form of a scream so extreme it filled what Slavoj Žižek named the "hole
in reality which designates the ultimate limit where 'the word fails.'"[5]
Artaud's *Theater of Cruelty*, as both performance and architecture, sought
to activate spatial volatility in order to confront and combat cruelty. His
manifestoes revealed an *Architecture of Cruelty* as the site of recovery, constituted by a body in peril, form without a center and space in fragments.
By mining Artaud's spatial speech, this article constructs an open-ended
treatise, triggered by the specter of an explosive body at the turn of the
twenty-first century, which offers a space where his infamous scream is
encouraged to reverberate.

Violence Takes Center Stage

> *The festival must be a political act. And the act of political revolution is theatrical.*[6]

The explosive body in question is embedded in a photograph of an empty theater viewed from the stage. It could be an auditorium found in any number of performing arts venues around the world, with its plush red seats numbered in orderly rows, raking back from an orchestra pit separating the audience from the stage, and framed by a proscenium arch. The upper level of seating overhangs the stalls slightly and drops into a side balcony that gives way to a stretch of wall with clearly marked exit doors. Upon closer examination, however, there are dark forms slumped in the seats, locating the theater in a time and place of crisis. These are the dead bodies of Chechnya's infamous "black widows," strapped with bomb-belts, whose haunting presence provides a cautionary tale from the authorities that had prevented their detonation (whilst sacrificing over 120 audience members, absent from the image). The banality and passivity of the room is haunted by a specter of explosive violence.[7]

Figure 1. Television media image showing Dubrovka Theatre after the raid by Russian authorities.

On October 23, 2002, the Dubrovka Theater in Moscow was seized by Chechen rebels who infiltrated during the musical performance of *Nord-Ost*, disrupting and transforming the show into a prolonged spectacle of terror. In the midst of the second act, thirty-five armed guerrillas and eighteen "black widows" had burst into the auditorium and on to the stage, firing guns and declaring themselves Chechens at War. At this moment the audience was unsure as to what was theatrical artifice and what was real, who was a performer and who was a terrorist, who was a spectator and who was a hostage.[8] They became part of an event that shifted the stage from a site of entertainment to a site of warfare, and in this moment the space they occupied was also called into doubt. No longer an arena for fleeting acts of entertainment, the 1100-seat auditorium held captive over 800 spectators, performers, theater workers and terrorists[9] in a three-day standoff that became a significant historic event ending in tragedy, when Russia's Spetsnaz soldiers stormed the building, having filled it with a narcotic gas, which killed over 170 people. The auditorium, masquerading as a house for leisure and amusement or, in this case, a *Palace of Culture*, was revealed as a carceral space for all its occupants, emphasizing its intrinsic disciplinary nature. The violent event disclosed the architecture's inherent violence, found in its conformity rather than its radicality.

This essay considers how violence can be co-opted spatially to create a site that resists such theatricalized spectacles as the Dubrovka Theater siege, which constituted a moment of crisis, exposing the gap between architectural and theatrical realities. Akin to Foucault's "events of thought" such incidents summon something new through the unexpected, unforeseeable, singular, unique and transformative.[10] Transcending the notion of a logical sequence of actions, they are isolated in what Bernard Tschumi identifies as "the moment of erosion, collapse, questioning, or problematization of the very assumption of the setting within which a drama may take place—occasioning the chance or possibility of another, different setting."[11] Here, investigating the spatial ideas of Antonin Artaud's manifestoes for the *Theater of Cruelty*, we can suggest an alternative approach to the archetypal modernist theater that was besieged in October 2002, and which continues to proliferate internationally as a disciplinary architectural model.

Rule of Disorder

If a "rule of disorder" could be found to explain the mysterious functioning of the theatrical apparatus, it would surely be a spatial rule, a practice or policy of relating people to place.[12]

Since the turn of the twentieth century the relationship between architecture and theater has been a troubled one, with the architectural rejected by theater and the theatrical negated by architecture. Even as architectural modernism sought to industrialize, control and harmonize space, the theatrical avant-garde wished to tear it asunder, celebrating the sacrificial body dancing amidst the debris. This theatrical will to annihilation was prefigured by Friedrich Nietzsche, whose 1872 *Birth of Tragedy* embodied the violent transition into a new century. As modernism's first dramatic manifesto, it called for a return to the feverish excesses of Dionysian rites of ancient Greek performance. The Dionysian performer, as "nothing but original pain and reverberation of the image,"[13] effaced the framed distance of the *theatron*, bringing back the precedence of the *choros*, a participatory space in which it was impossible to apprehend the image as a whole. A "rule of disorder" was reintroduced to both performance and its spatiality, undermining the monumental form of the multilevel Baroque horseshoe theater with its framed proscenium stage.[14] This call for a performative return to the participatory spectacle coincided with the building of Wagner's Festspielhaus in Bayreuth (1872–1876), which revolutionized theater as both art form and built form. However, public participation became spatially controlled, crystallizing the violent gesture in architectural form, rather than embodying it as the potential to destabilize form itself. The framed distance was not effaced but reinforced, enacting a form of spatial violence.

The notion of spatial violence as a mute incorporation of power into the built environment has been voiced by a number of theorists, critiquing architecture's complicity with bureaucracy. Georges Bataille, echoing Artaud's insistence on "no more masterpieces,"[15] wished to eradicate architectural monuments, which (as static, dominant, regulated and authoritarian forms) "impose silence on the multitudes" and "inspire socially acceptable behavior, and often a very real fear."[16] This consideration of the disciplinary nature of built form was also taken up by Michel Foucault who aligned the history of powers with the history of *spaces*,[17] seeing architecture as an embodiment of abstract discursive forms of power, permeating the material realm of flesh, activity and desire by defining, regulating and limiting our quotidian practices. For Henri Lefebvre the "logic of space" conceals an authoritarian and brutal force that conditions the competence and performance of the subject, who can experience it as an obstacle of "resistant 'objectality' at times as implacably hard as a concrete wall."[18] Lefebvre's *objectality*, as a mute oppositional force, stands in contrast to Deleuze's *objectile*,[19] where the continuous and explosive phenomena of form and matter mobilize the built environment as an *object-event*, no longer framing space but overflowing its boundaries to annihilate the frame. This transformation of architecture from a disciplinary machine to an open-ended volatile form of space-in-action was what Artaud sought in his quest for a *Theater of Cruelty*, not just as art form but also as built form.

Foucault's description of the shift in nineteenth-century prison architecture,[20] from a scenic, public, collective model to a more coercive, internal model, could also be depicting the architecture of theater buildings. Since Wagner set up his Festival Theater, denouncing the persistent form of the multilevel bourgeois Italianate auditorium (often referred to as the Baroque horseshoe theater) as monumental and overdecorated, modern performance space has developed into a lifeless container. Within this passive vessel a homogeneous plane of well-organized viewers gazes transfixed at highly composed images, enacted within the technological frame of the proscenium stage. Notwithstanding claims to a democratic form, such architecture reduces the impact of audience and architecture. It disciplines behavior of the spectators, who can be likened to Plato's chained prisoners in a cave, watching shadows dancing on the walls, oblivious to the material world of light and reality outside.[21] Despite the radical reforms of the past century's avant-garde—calling for a more visceral and confrontational space between those who perform and those who watch—the enclosed, featureless auditorium that organizes viewers within an integrated, singular space, in darkened rows physically separated from the performers' realm, persists as the principle model for theater architecture.

The revolution waged against the 300-year-old model of the Baroque horseshoe theater was, paradoxically, an attack on the power of the audience encircling the room on a range of levels and communal clusters. As a dynamic force that enclosed itself and intersected with the stage-frame, the spectators merged with gilded decoration and lavish detail to form a combined spectacle of audience and architecture that effectively competed with the stage action. The assault on this distracting, dynamic and lively organism of the Baroque auditorium led to the eventual eradication of balconies, colonnades, ornamentation, promenade spaces and boxes, all in the name of a more democratic, less aristocratic and hierarchical space. However, this happened at the cost of multiple viewpoints, positions from which to assert a presence or recede out of sight, pockets of private activity within the larger collective, and the living wall of audience that energized itself as a formidable assembly, fragmented and united in its own embrace. Not unlike the prison that disciplined inmates through spatial distribution, coded activities, visibility of force and control of time, the new theater model—established in the name of reform—was a mechanism of disciplinary power that spatially regulated bodies, limiting their activities and interactions within the assumed openness of leisure, culture and entertainment.

As modernism's theater architecture became more rigid and pacifying, the avant-garde continued to call for radical spatial changes. Artaud's discourse forced built form not only to speak, but also to scream and shatter. The explosivity inherent in his manifestoes for the *Theater of Cruelty* (1930–1936) sought to liberate performance from its traditional confines, generating what Denis Hollier referred to as "a performative loosening of space."[22] Out of this volatile meeting of theater and architecture emerge possibilities for discussing spatial violence as a restorative gesture, demanding a more experiential approach to architecture, apprehended not as a homogeneous static object but as a heterogeneous dynamic event.

Constructive Abuse

> *The architectural implications of Artaud's work are obvious. If architecture was to have anything to do with unconscious mental images, it was not in the form of a representation of those images. By implication, Artaud's question was: could architecture, when seen as the necessarily painful meeting of space and life, transform the substance of its space, of reality?* [23]

In "Architecture and its Double," Bernard Tschumi questions the impact surrealism has had on the experience of "real" space. The title of his article borrows from Antonin Artaud's theatrical treatise, *Theater and its Double*, in which Artaud claims theater as the "double" of life—life as an "archetypal and dangerous reality"[24] as opposed to "sugar-coated" everyday reality served up to us. Tschumi maintains that modernist architecture "was not ready to discover the architecture of the unconscious, too busy, as it were, discovering new formal or technological breakthroughs."[25] He posits the double of formalist art and architectural discourse as a parallel stream, constantly censored by society, "an irritant: a means to reject functionalist aesthetics, to refuse the rational and to celebrate unrepressed delights."[26] However, Artaud's vision of theater was more than just an irritant. It was a way of attacking theater as the organism in question through an *architecture of gesture* and a *gesture of architecture*, setting off a reverberation, which ended in an eruption. The means of accomplishing this were both physical and spatial.

What follows is an attempt to translate the spatial speech of Artaud's writing—negotiating between written text, performing body and built environment—excavating the notion of exploding space triggered by his scream and made concrete in an architecture of performance. This acknowledges Walter Benjamin's claim that translation is a faithful form of abuse, referred to by Wigley as "constructive abuse": transformation rather than transmittal, where an act of violence is necessary. Just like a mine with its attendant action, it delves, exploits, attacks, damages, destroys and subverts the text in search of a necessary tectonic articulation. Benjamin writes of the echo of the original that lives on in what Wigley calls "a kind of spectral 'afterlife' at a different level than it had before because something buried within it has been released."[27] Translation therefore exploits the original's inner conflict, breaking open its language to liberate what has been imprisoned within. Here, a translation is offered from theory of performance to a lived spatial experience, by activating Artaud's texts to set in motion their dormant "cruel" architectures, to erupt it from the surface of the text. Like the "sounding-out" of Nietzsche's hammer, through a force that destroys, tunes and reworks, such translation makes present the haunting absence of a theatrical architecture capable of performing spatial and corporeal acts of dissolution. This "sounding-out" also reveals the unspoken divide between architectural modernism and the theatrical avant-garde: "that which would like to stay silent has to become audible."[28]

The Blind Spot of Architectural Modernism

> Unlike visual artists or theater directors, [the architectural avant-garde] had to deal with a sociopolitical and physical context that limited their freedom of movement.[29]

In her book *Architecture and Modernity*, Hilde Heynen recognizes the gap between the historical avant-garde and architecture's modern movement, maintaining that "modern architecture showed in most of its manifestations a face which was clearly distinct from the radicality and destructiveness of the artistic avant-garde."[30] Whilst she compares the early twentieth-century architectural vanguard to its radical "counterparts in art and literature,"[31] she barely mentions the theatrical avant-garde. Absence of engagement with theater is endemic to twentieth-century architectural theory, constituting a blind spot in modernism's discourse. This goes beyond architecture's rational sociopolitical and physical imperatives and owes much to theater's complicated relationship with reality, materiality and mortality.

Through its associations with mimesis, theater is considered substitutive to the real, which, as Peggy Phelan argues, it defines itself against, "even while reduplicating its effects."[32] The spatiotemporal play between theater's *that/there/then* and the lived experience of *this/here/now* calls both presence and materiality into question, challenging the spectator to negotiate issues of authenticity and virtuality. Phantasmic representations of theater also expose excesses, expressed through violence, ecstasy and death that resist rationalization and containment. Death is the economy within which performance operates because theater "becomes itself through disappearance."[33] The very substance of theater is therefore loss, its fleeting acts undermining architecture's aim to be fixed, stable and enduring. Proscenium theater, as the framed perspectival scene, also exposes the blind spot of architecture itself: the spectator's ideal view point as the vanishing point that ends in emptiness; "the imagination of annihilation and disappearance."[34]

Such annihilation is embodied in the contemporary specter of the "black widow," who simultaneously represents maternity and mortality—a powerful trope for the stage that moved from the perspectival setting to an "absolute space" of theatrical reproduction. The latter term, borrowed from Lefebvre, refers to the space of virtuality that emerged, through the Symbolists, as the dominant scenic space of twentieth-century theater, challenging traditional representational space of the nineteenth-century stage. As a dimensionless space of "invisible fullness"[35] that "consecrates" and "concentrates," it offered an empty space to be filled up and activated. The proscenium no longer provided the frame within which to construct an architectonic scene but held at bay the sublime and annihilating expanse of limitless space. Isolated and veiled by its black drapes, the stage is traditionally seen as a separate zone standing in for the void out of which forms are materialized and dematerialized. This obscure, silent and formless "empty space"—where objects and bodies appear suspended—constitutes a generic place within which events could be endlessly produced and reproduced. The blacked-out stage also reflects collective desire for the modern theater to embody a primordial space where each performance becomes an originative act born out of darkness. It is also, as Phelan suggests, linked to mourning: "a kind of mausoleum, a space designed to summon the phantasmical charge of the immaterial."[36]

The isolated and unfathomable stage-house separated from the viewing-room was prefigured[37] in Wagner's Festspielhaus, which was hailed as the triumph of rational auditorium design over the Italian Baroque tradition.[38] With the hammer of his indomitable will Wagner forged a theater that no longer permitted the audience a host of distractions afforded through elaborate decoration, multiple viewpoints and social groupings. Nothing was to encroach on the stage picture. Working first with architect Gottfried Semper, and later Otto Bruckwald in consultation with technical director Carl Brandt, Wagner developed a new model, which looked to the classical Greek amphitheater. However, by retaining and reinforcing the proscenium (the frame of which was repeated throughout the auditorium), he funneled the sweep of the amphitheater to a steeply-raked, fan-shaped wedge that concentrated the view of all spectators on the stage. Every seat in the house faced the stage with an unobstructed view of the performance, enabling audience members to filter out any distraction from one another or from the architecture itself. The fan shape, which formed its own vanishing point, reinforced the perspectival nature of the stage, containing and regimenting the public as listening viewers within the darkened auditorium (also a Wagnerian innovation). They were further separated from the illusionistic stage-world by the double proscenium and the "mystic gulf"[39] of the deep orchestra pit. The distanced *theatron* (seeing-place) triumphed over the participatory space of the *choros* (dancing-place), disappointing Nietzsche who had dedicated the *Birth of Tragedy*, in which he had demanded a return to the choric site, to Wagner. Often referred to as a "democratic plan," Wagner's space is extremely authoritarian, disciplining the audience as viewers and listeners who submit passively to the will of the producing artist[40] and the synthesis of his Gesamtkunstwerk.

This model of framed stage-house, separated from the unified and focused auditorium, became the spatial paradigm for modernist theater architecture, persisting for well over a century, despite attempts of the Bauhaus and Russian Constructivists to propose alternative mechanized auditoria, seen in Gropius's *Total Theater* for Piscator (1927), and Barkhin and Vakhtangov's scheme for Meyerhold (1932). However, one could argue that their industrialized proposals were as totalizing and controlling, and therefore, as violent, as the Wagnerian model that persists in a simplified form in theaters such as the one attacked in October 2002.

The Dubrovka Theater represents an undistinguished model for public performance that has developed and proliferated globally since the early twentieth century. It was constructed between 1968 and 1974, as the *Palace of Culture* attached to the First State Ball-Bearing Factory, in Moscow's working-class district. Soviet *Palaces of Culture* were clubhouses associated with state agencies and industry built for workers to assemble and practice their recreational activities and hobbies. The auditorium, one of many spaces within the complex, provided facilities for amateur performing arts events, lectures and meetings. These *Palaces*, designed to "enlighten, educate and entertain, while promoting revolution in daily life,"[41] were funded by taxes collected by the trade unions, which also provided elected management and staff. However, since the collapse of the Soviet Union such organizations struggled for income, renting the spaces to outside productions such as the *Nord-Ost* musical.

The most architecturally celebrated *Palace of Culture* in Moscow is situated nearby, adjacent to the Simonov Monastery and was conceived as a secular workers' temple in relation to it. Originally one of the largest and most lavishly appointed of the state clubs, it is now associated with the ZIL automobile company. Designed by the Vesnin brothers in 1930 and completed in 1937, it is recognized as a significant example of Constructivist architecture and of Alexandr Vesnin's principle of "liquid space." Referring to Le Corbusier's treatment of interpenetrating spaces, Alexandr spoke of people breathing "freely and easily" in the "open character of the space."[42] The ordered, open and unadorned auditorium stands in radical contrast to a well-known set he designed for Tairov's production of *The Man Who Was Thursday*, inserted into the proscenium arch of Moscow's Kamerny Theater in 1922–1923. Rather than open and fluid, the sceno-architecture is a multilevel structure of collaged spaces, suggestive of a layered and unstable urban machine within which the performers' bodies are integrated. As Constructivist stage "devices," such complex mobile sceneries stood in radical contrast to the auditoria that housed them. They were asymmetrical, vertiginous, and fragmented structures: epic in conception and intimate in scale. In contrast, the auditoria were passive, symmetrical, and unyielding. However, the competition designs of the Vesnins from the early 1920s reflect the dynamic structures of Constructivist stage machines in proposed architectural projects, illustrating how, as they began to build for the authorities, their work became more rigid and unified.

The guiding principle of the *Palace of Culture* to inculcate through entertainment, and the modern movement's resistance to adopt and adapt avant-garde theater constructions, throws into sharp relief a broader twentieth-century trend to codify, instruct, and manage through a commanding architecture. The theater as a disciplinary space—collecting and controlling spectacle and spectators within its severe hold—is clearly illustrated in media images of the Moscow theater siege with the hostage audience corralled into their rows of numbered seats whilst the rebels guard the limited number of visible exits, taking advantage of a clear overview from the stage and vantage points in the auditorium. This same super-visionary control worked against the rebels when the Russian authorities pumped the debilitating gas into the hermetically sealed singular space, revealing how all were incarcerated within it. The familiar, prosaic auditorium represents the static and dominant monument,[43] critiqued by Bataille for "enforcing admiration and astonishment, order and constraint."[44] Such spatial will to "command and prohibit" was what Bataille railed against and Artaud wished to literally and psychically explode, freeing the theater from its burden of representation and architecture from the weight of its monumental gravitas.

While the modernist auditorium emerged as a twentieth-century attempt to hold together a fragmentary world through the absolute space of the stage picture, following the two World Wars that had devastated Europe, neither a purely oneiric space nor the existing buildings that housed performance seemed enough for the avant-garde. Antonin Artaud and Georges Bataille observed that in the postwar condition language, the body, and space were no longer united, clean or whole, but fragmented, contaminated, and dissociated.[45] They both became obsessed with transcending the physical and conceptual limits of their art and the world around them. Theater architecture, the creation of containers for the uncontainable body in action, was considered by Artaud to be both problematic and redundant.

Enter Artaud (Flinging Bombs)

> He aims to provoke in the theatrical event, at any price, a frisson
> that shakes the spectator out of his passivity, out of the softening
> seduction that anesthetizes him by way of the pleasant, the
> picturesque and the decorative. The theater of diversion must give
> way to a corrosive theater that will gnaw away at the shell that is
> constricting it and give us back a forgotten aspect of the spectacle.
> This is the theater of cruelty.[46]

Antonin Artaud wished to undo the theater of representation and he recognized the need to dismantle it spatially in order to accomplish his goal.
However, the artist who suffered from schizophrenia (and from being
ahead of his time), never realized his theater in practice. He attempted to
perform it on three significant occasions: in a lecture on *The Theater and the
Plague* at the Sorbonne in 1933 (where he shocked the audience by enacting
his own death);[47] at a poetry reading in 1947 at Théâtre du Vieux-Colombier
(where he had to be led quietly away after three hours, having deviated into
free speech); and in his final work that same year, a radio piece entitled *To
Have Done with the Judgment of God* (which was pulled from the radio prior
to airing in 1948). On all three occasions it was Artaud's glossolalia and
screams that defined his performances. Glossolalia, described by Allen
Weiss as "a type of speech or babble characteristic of certain discourses
of infants, poets, schizophrenics, mediums, charismatics,"[48] was critical to Artaud's *Theater of Cruelty* as catharsis and exorcism "to rid himself
of God's influence and judgment."[49] But it was in his scream that Artaud
attempted to shatter theatrical and spatial conformity—the scream ultimately planned to reverberate in the sublime sound-space of the airwaves,
repudiating the built environment entirely.

In her essay "Antonin Artaud and the Impossible Theater," Helen
Finter points out that what some saw as "the unbearable exhibition of a
mental patient was for Artaud the unprecedented attempt at exploding
the boundaries of a theatrical event."[50] His "manifestation of the Real"
on the stage of the Vieux-Colombier highlighted the impossibility of
making himself heard in the theater, claiming that only bombs could
produce the desired effect.[51] The scream, like a bomb, was an attempt to
tear the fabric of representation through a cruel intrusion on the stage,
described by Alenka Zupančič as "a 'materialization' of something concealed or repressed,... the intrusion of some 'foreign reality.'"[52] This
interruption of the stage fiction by an "alien reality" disturbs the clarity

of the spectator's vision with the unexpected act that summons the *Real* into reality, momentarily rupturing the field of symbolically constructed representations with something that exceeds it. Lacan has referred to the *Real* as an impossible condition associated with the preverbal, thereby transcending language because it was lost when we entered into language. Artaud, who resisted the representational in theater and rejected the logic of language, resorted to the scream as "a fine skewer"[53] to pierce reality and theatrical space. However, his suppurations of reality were also meant to expose it.

Antonin Artaud's scream became a spatial weapon against the Aristotelian mimetic theater, actively disrupting its focus on the fictive, repetitive and imitative. The full force of its sonorous authenticity triggered his demand for a theater that utilized reality rather than representation as its principle medium, allowing architecture to play a more active role in the performance itself. As Una Chaudhuri contends, "if the real can be represented by the real itself, then representation does not have to settle for the limits and frames that constrict it in all the other media."[54] For Artaud spectacle had to act "not as reflection, but as force."[55] While his scream triggered spatial disruptions rather than literal explosions, his writing performed a complex, theatrical architecture of eruption through what Derrida referred to as his "*spacing [espacement]* ... the archi-manifestation of force, or of life."[56]

Architecture Against Architecture

> *... abandoning the architecture of present day theaters, we shall take some hangar or barn, which we shall have constructed according to the processes, which have culminated in the architecture of certain churches or holy places, and of certain temple ...*[57]

Artaud's writing resonates with the invocation of an architecture that is troubling, unsettling, resistant to representational theater and the well-established canons of its architecture. It is also more complex than that which he explicitly outlines in his first manifesto of the "Theater of Cruelty" (1932), where he calls for a ritualistic hangar/barn, with a vertiginous, layered structure eliminating the centrality of the stage within the auditorium:

So composed and so constructed, the spectacle will be extended, by
elimination of the stage, to the entire hall of the theater and will
scale the walls from the ground up on light catwalks, will physically
envelop the spectator and immerse him in a constant bath of light,
images, movement and noises.[58]

As with Nietzsche's desire for a Dionysian theater, Artaud wished to reestablish an immersive space with a more direct relationship between spectator and spectacle. This meant eradicating not only the distinction between stage and auditorium, but also the monumentality of the building, allowing it to host a "constant magic" orchestrated by the "Master of Sacred Ceremonies."[59] Such space was the product of both the theory of performance and also of the feverish mind of a diagnosed schizophrenic.

Louis Sass, in *Madness and Modernism*, saw Artaud's *Theater of Cruelty* as providing a defense against "the devitalization and derealization that pervaded his being."[60] Whilst his desire to "eclipse the mind through ecstatic sensation and fusion with the ambient world" was never realized (or materialized), he psychically occupied such a zone. The paradox of Artaud is that he wished to create *that* which he was escaping from, to hurl himself into *there*, where he feared most. He longed to immerse himself in the dissolution that haunted him. The architecture of his desire was therefore like his physical being: "this dislocated assemblage, … this ill-assembled heap of organs … like a vast landscape on the point of breaking up."[61] Spatial dis-order was a means of re-ordering the artist's own fragmented psyche and that of the greater social body. In discontinuous and disintegrating space the spectator is de-anaesthetized in order to force a cure. Therefore, theater for the tormented Artaud provided a fiercely transformative place of healing.

A Site of Recovery

In the true theater a play disturbs the senses' repose, frees the repressed
unconscious, incites a kind of virtual revolt, and imposes on the
assembled collectivity an attitude that is both difficult and heroic.[62]

Over 60 years after Antonin Artaud's treatise on the *Theater of Cruelty*, Ben Okri writes in *A Way of Being Free* that the "reality of what we are doing to one another is explosive. … There is much to scream about. … Something is needed to wake us from the frightening depths of our moral sleep."[63]

This cry of rage echoes Artaud's demand for the public to "be terrified and awaken."[64] His scream, which ricocheted through the last century, continues to hang hauntingly in the air.

While cruelty may conjure up associations with blood, pain and distress, Artaud was concerned primarily with its qualities as rigid and unrelentingly severe. For him "there [was] no cruelty without consciousness and without the application of consciousness."[65] As he wrote to Jean Paulhan in his first letter on cruelty (1932), "[it] signifies rigor, implacable intention and decision, irreversible and absolute determination."[66] He wished "to return the etymological origins of speech which in the midst of abstract concept, always evoke a concrete element."[67] This focus on concretizing the abstract illustrates the pursuit of cruelty's palpable materiality found etymologically in *cru* or "raw flesh." Hence, the body becomes the principal site in the *Theater of Cruelty*. The conflation of the concrete and the abstract posits *praxis* as the all-consuming and unfulfilled desire for Artaud. Practice was a physical manifestation of theory: "I go from the abstract to the concrete and not from the concrete toward the abstract."[68] Transforming the abstract into the concrete is also central to architecture, realized through built thought. The focus for Artaud is therefore on the act of orchestrating the body within the material space of performance.

The sleep, from which Okri and Artaud bid us wake, is the sleep of our indifference. Okri talks of the "proverbial axe to crack the ice and make the frozen blood of humanity flow again."[69] Artaud saw such cruelty in Vincent Van Gogh's brushstrokes taking to objects in a frozen world with a carver's blow, "unsealing their impenetrable trembling."[70] These maneuvers of the artist are both violent and curative. Faced with an increasingly mechanized world that was mobilizing technology for mass destruction, Artaud sought to find a restorative place, manifesting itself as a cruel and vengeful machine. By 1946 (following his confinement during WWII) cruelty for Artaud was no longer sheer necessity, but truly cruel: "the gallows, the trenches, a crematorium oven, or insane asylum. Cruelty: massacred bodies."[71] In 1947 he wrote: "there is nothing left to do but *gather the body together*, I mean PILE UP BODIES."[72]

The same year architectural historian Siegfried Giedion wrote *Mechanization Takes Command*, which documented his witnessing the assembly-line slaughter of animals. He was struck by the complete "neutrality" in the act of automated butchery, whilst for him, the inhaled odor of blood, which remained within his body, continued to rise from the walls of his stomach long after the viscera had been washed away from those of the abbattoir. In the post-war environment, Giedion considers such inurement towards mass technological killing, claiming it may be lodged deep in the roots of our time... "It did not bare itself on a large scale until the War, when whole populations, as defenseless as animals hooked head downwards on the traveling chain, were obliterated with trained neutrality."[73] This statement remains pertinent today, yet, as Artaud wrote, "only perpetual war explains a peace which is only a passing phase."[74]

Therefore, Artaud's theater becomes a site of recovery from the overwhelming cruelty of the world. This notion of a curative theater is the central premise in Hélène Cixous's essay "The Place of Crime the Place of Pardon," in which theater is affirmed as a place for revealing the wickedness and cruelty of the world. Cixous's theater is the site where we, as a collective gathering, can become more human in order to confront the quotidian nightmares of mediatized reality and the powerlessness we experience in the face of its horror. She writes:

> In truth we go as little to the theater as to our heart and what we feel
> the lack of is going to the heart, our own and that of things. We live
> exterior to ourselves in a world whose walls are replaced by television
> screens, which has lost its thickness, its depths, its treasures, and
> we take the newspaper columns for our thoughts. We are printed
> daily. We lack even walls, true walls upon which divine messages are
> written. We lack earth and flesh.[75]

The challenge then is to create a distinct location, as a world apart, where terror is evoked in order to contemplate, accept and meditate upon the act of death and therefore our own mortality. Cixous is also seeking a space of palpable materiality.

Echoing Artaud, Cixous claims that "we live under the same sun of blood" and speaks of the "naked stage," which "returns to us the living part of death or the mortal part of life."[76] She writes of the necessity for a certain theater "because it allows us to live what no genre allows us: the difficulty, the pain we have being human. Evil. What happens at the theater is the Passion, but the passion according to ... this enigmatic, tortured, criminal, innocent human being that I am, I who am thou or you."[77] We come to the theater as a place of both crime and pardon, to confront pity and terror, and have the enigma of human cruelty revealed to us. Like Artaud, Cixous sees the theater as a "temple without dogma and without doctrine ... where our torments and above all our blindnesses are played."[78] However, for her, the "curtain" remains and the spoken word retains its primacy, whereas Artaud seeks to rupture the veil of form and language—tearing down the curtain, dismantling the stage, and surrounding the audience with action.

It is the orchestration of earth (stage), flesh (participants), and true walls (built environment) that establishes an *Architecture of Cruelty*, forming the site of recovery. But what are the particular qualities of this architecture? Artaud wrote that the "secret of theater in space is dissonance, dispersion of timbres and the dialectic discontinuity of expression."[79] Not only do we have here a move away from the primacy of the visual, but also the repeated use of the prefix *dis-* (from the Latin *dis-*: apart, asunder) that operates on space by tearing it apart. Over fifty years later, Derrida referred to "strong words in [Bernard] Tschumi's lexicon," especially those beginning with de- or dis-. "These words speak of destabilization, deconstruction, dehiscence and first of all, dissociation, disjunction, disruption, difference. An architecture of heterogeneity, interruption, non-coincidence."[80] Tschumi devotes a chapter in his book *Architecture and Disjunction* to this linguistic phenomenon. In "*De-, Dis-, Ex-*" he claims that the separation of people and language has decentered the subject and society itself. Nothing, including architecture, is stable anymore.[81]

Referring to the language of gesture, Artaud saw theater as "the most effective site of passage for ... immense analogical disturbances" that formed a unity between the concrete and the abstract. This included spatial gesture here investigated through the *dis-eased body, ex-ploded space* and *de-centered architecture*.

Dis-eased Body

> *If the essential theater is like the plague, it is not because it is contagious, but because like the plague it is a revelation, the bringing forth, the exteriorization of a depth of latent cruelty by means of which all the perverse possibilities of the mind, whether of an individual or a people, are localized.*[82]

A curative space requires a body in peril: a body shaken by fever that torments it in order to restore it to perfect health; a body "convulsed and pacified."[83] Artaud likened theater to the plague, bringing to the surface the rot and filth of society as an abscess to be lanced. Like the plague, his theater was "a total crisis" that cleansed both performer and spectator in their collective experience. The body is a society and the plague a delirium, intensifying energy and allowing communication. Through his plague analogy Artaud was demanding theater become a reality rather than a representation, although in a world apart. As in spaces associated with disease, a complete, intense, and separate world is created and shared. Like many artists who suffer physically and mentally, Artaud saw disease as a visitation, a curse, and a judgment, whilst art celebrated the transcendence of mortality in the face of death.[84] Disease, which presents the ultimate threat of death, isolates, exposes, intensifies, and transforms character. Its delirium creates a lucidity that heightens consciousness, forcing the victim to see terrible truths about the nature of human existence. It deranges the senses, stimulating great passions and energies, bringing new awareness to the survivor. Nietzsche who wrote "what does not destroy me, makes me stronger"[85] saw suffering and insanity as a necessity for learning the truth.

Artaud's restorative theater offered possibilities to reconcile life with a universe out of control, working with "the underlying menace of a chaos as decisive as it is dangerous."[86] Contemporary theater had become decadent because, captivated by illusion and representation, it had broken away from gravity, "from effects that are immediate and painful – in a word from danger."[87] Acknowledging and embracing the danger and difficulty inherent in live practice, Artaud wished to create resistant work, transforming the passive spectator into an active creator. A theatrical environment that also physically resists and provokes, challenges the relationships and preconceptions of the body of its audience, which is exposed and acknowledged as a collective of individuals, physiologically affected by performance: disturbed, discomforted, and displaced... Dis-eased.

The dis-eased body in the theater is not the "black widow" co-opted into terror, nor the hostage threatened by her explosive body, nor the nervous systems overcome by toxic fumes filtering through the ventilation system. Rather, it's that of the performers who enact a resistance to containment within their own skin and the space in which they perform, transferred to the collective and individual bodies of the witnessing audience. Such performances also have the potential to infect, and therefore affect, the built environment. The dis-eased body in the theater is therefore a feverish body unleashing itself in space; a contaminated body, and body as contaminant, threatening to erupt through the borders of its own skin and refusing to be contained within the playhouse. Performance becomes a burning and active projection, storming the limits of body, audience, and building. Elaine Scarry, in her book *The Body in Pain*, writes that the human is a projecting creature and that creating may be expressed as the reversing of interior and exterior body linings in order to animate the exterior world.[88] In weakening the literal and psychological frames of the theater, definitions of inclusion and exclusion can be confounded. The dis-eased body in the theater exposes its limits, resulting in a turning inside out, which flays the body of the building, realigning it so that interior and exterior fold in on each other.

The body of the building, like the physical body it houses, doubles as the social body. Gathered for the event, this communal body is actively complicit within a culture-in-action. Dis-eased, the audience is no longer composed of passive witnesses, but, as a communal body-in-peril, becomes implicated in the force of the event. Dislocated they are made aware of their location. The dis-eased body is therefore multiple, found not only in the performer, but in the collective corpus of the audience and in the very structure that they inhabit. Architecture, as inert matter, is disturbed and thrown into convulsions. This feverish space vibrates to the point of explosion, an event triggered by the burning need to place the body at risk.

Ex-ploding Space

> The problem is to make space speak, to feed and furnish it; like mines laid in a wall of rock which all of a sudden turns into geysers and bouquets of stone.[89]

Where the silence masking spatial violence is unacceptable, the fallacy of architecture as static, solid, enduring, and mute must be detonated. Artaud forces space to speak by exploding it. He takes the established inert form of the theater auditorium and renders it a dismembered body. His scream shatters, lacerates, and eviscerates space, much the same as his magic spells waged war on the surface of the page with their scratches, tears, and burns. The reverberations ensuing from this performative scream put space into action, bringing it to the point of explosion. Writing between the World Wars, Artaud stated: "We are not free. And the sky can still fall on our heads. And the theater has been created to teach us that first of all."[90] This allusion to the sky raining danger is probably associated with the use of flight and machinery in warfare, where landscape and bodies were torn asunder by explosions. As Benjamin wrote in "The Storyteller," the shock of the First World War had shifted European perceptions and "in a field of force of destructive torrents and explosions, was the tiny, fragile human body."[91] The madness and mechanization of the war had called reality itself into question and profoundly affected the sur-

TOWARDS AN "ARCHITECTURE OF CRUELTY"

realists who took objects and brought the force of "atmosphere" concealed in them "to the point of explosion."[92] Yet, Artaud's writing on explosive space also foreshadowed the catastrophe that occurred just over 10 years after he had written *Theater and its Double*, when devouring blasts over Hiroshima and Nagasaki annihilated form, atomized bodies and incinerated space. The horror of this and its effect on "spectral conformity" haunts his later essay on Van Gogh, filled with "violent suns," landscapes of "hostile flesh"[93] erupting in "conflagration... bombardment... explosion..."[94] In a letter to André Breton, written in 1947, Artaud maintained that the only language society now understood was "bombs, machine guns, barricades and everything else that follows."[95] His calls for revolt and restoration become important demands when so much is at stake.

For Artaud violent eruptions perform a loosening of space through shock. His "supernatural explosions"[96] shatter space into spaces, creating "a living whirlwind that devours the darkness."[97] This by-product of explosive energy fragments and fills the empty spaces with movement, light and sound. Sonorous reverberations generate "possibilities for extensions beyond words, for development in space, for dissociative and vibratory action upon the sensibility."[98] The echoes that result from explosive reverberations have an immediate architectural application. Built form becomes a conductor, transferring vibrations to the "organism" that is individual body and collective public. The acoustic quality of space allows the spectacle to proceed "from the stifled silence to the headlong representation of a spasm, and from individual speech mezzo voce to the weighty and resonant storm of a chorus slowly swelling its volume."[99] Artaud's proposed industrial hangar/barn was intended to evoke "the architecture of certain churches, or holy places, and of certain temples,"[100] with their highly reverberant qualities. Defying clear articulation of language and space, they circulate, replicate, and delay sound, creating vibratory effects continuous with both the body and the building.

The volatility of Artaud's writing invokes the explosive and dynamic *Carceri* etchings of the eighteenth-century artist and architect, Giambattista Piranesi, claimed by Manfredo Tafuri as the historic precursor of the avant-garde,[101] and whose work Alberto Pérez-Gómez and Louise Pelletier celebrate as "prophetic of surrealistic juxtapositions and cubist deconstructions of Euclidean space, already indicative of different attitudes to history and an imagination no longer bound to a firm cosmology."[102] These *Prisons of the Imagination* present fragmented imagery cited by Pérez-Gómez and Pelletier as "the first deliberate use of montage in architecture to explode and destructure the homogeneous space and linear time implied in perspective."[103] In 1946, Soviet filmmaker Sergei Eisenstein wrote an essay on the fluidity of Piranesi's forms, exploring the dissolution and fragmentation of the *Carceri*.[104] By exploding the elements of an early etching *Prima Parte* (1743), Eisenstein proved Piranesi's technique in the later *Carceri Oscura* (1753), where the earlier image had flown apart. Eisenstein referred to this technique as "ecstatic transfiguration," taking the form of "dissolution," detonating and hurling architecture in all directions, to set a dynamic and multiplicitous space in motion. The viewer of these works becomes implicated in a fractured environment that proffered an architecture resistant to the domination of the absolutist enframing vision of the time. Applied to the theater, such dissolution implies not only the fragmentation of the scenic space behind the proscenium, suggesting a spatial field that extends beyond the limits of its frame, but the annihilation of the frame itself so that the unstable multilayered architecture extends into and beyond the auditorium, foreclosing on a discrete and hermetic interiority.

Diana Agrest writes, "Piranesi's 'explosive' vision compromises not just the architectural system *per se* but rather a system of relationships, of contiguity and substitution. ... This kind of explosion implies in some way the dissolution of the limits of architecture, of the ideological limits which enclose different architectural practices."[105] Piranesi's vertiginous prisons, improvised on the page, also serve to question incarceration. There is no narrative to follow and it is unclear as to the role played by the figures who seem to move freely up zigzagging staircases, across wooden galleries and bridges, through layers of arches, past festoons of rope; all seemingly mirrored to infinity, they defy containment. The images suggest a continuation of space in three dimensions, threatening to envelop the beholder. Perspective is literally shattered on the page, drawing the viewer into the frame. The vanishing point has exploded, multiplied and disappeared, taking with it the horizon that contained the body. There is no longer a commanding overview, either from the stage or of the stage.

Piranesi's carceral spaces foreshadow Artaud's spatial language. They liberate both the body and the built form through a spatial violence, deforming an architecture in which the center is constantly shifting and fracturing. Spectators are incorporated within the fractured *mise en scène*, contributing to the creation of a reality in this real-world-set-apart; what Artaud calls "the world tangential to objective reality."[106] The tangential experience is an anamorphic one where, no longer distanced from the action, the audience's peripheral vision is constantly called into play. The body that witnesses (but does not necessarily perform) is immersed in a fragmented environment, perceiving the action and space in fractured form. Derrida writes that in Artaud's participatory event "the distance of vision is no longer pure, cannot be abstracted from the totality of the sensory milieu; the infused spectator can no longer *constitute* his spectacle and provide himself with its object."[107] Not everything is directly revealed, nor is it entirely comprehensible. The controlling overview of the modern auditorium is resisted when the centrality of the stage and the performer are destabilized.

De-centering Architecture

> *The action will unfold, will extend its trajectory from level to level, point to point; paroxysms will suddenly burst forth, will flare up like fires in different spots. ... For this diffusion of action over an immense space will oblige the lighting of ... a performance to fall upon the public as much as upon the actors – and to the several simultaneous actions or several phases of identical action in which the characters, swarming over each other like bees, will endure all the onslaughts of the situations and the external assaults of the tempestuous elements, will correspond the physical means of lighting, of producing thunder or wind, whose repercussions the spectator will undergo.*[108]

Abolishing the stage and auditorium, Artaud storms the established boundaries between the viewer and the viewed, asserting a "single site" that resists passive inhabitation. Yet, as an exploded space, the site is neither singular, nor primarily visual. Architect Daniel Libeskind, in his conversation on "Theater" and "The End of Space," suggests "a space which is not a space of theater, but a space to be found, a space which has neither been colonized by either planning, architecture nor by the history of theatrical production."[109] Artaud's evocation of a hangar/barn is akin to recent "found-space" industrial sites, such the Wooster Group's *Performing Garage* in New York, Théâtre du Soleil's *Cartoucherie* outside Paris, and Sasha Waltz's *Radiale Systeme V* in Berlin. These places (originally constructed for repairing vehicles, producing weapons and pumping sewerage) are associated with mechanization and war, offering "cruel" sites of recovery, However, Libeskind continues, "Space is not one, but space is plural, space is a heterogeneity, a difference."[110] How does this fragmented and multiplicitous exploded space, house or un-house the dis-eased body?

Diana Agrest writes that the "relationship between architecture and the human body becomes particularly important at the moment in which the issue of the center, a preoccupation that filters throughout the history of art and architecture in its many symbolic roles, acquires a special meaning."[111] The explosiveness of the twentieth century signified the end of a constructed view of space: the end of a body's central position in space—the end of scenography. *Scenography* is a word that belonged to "art," "architecture," and "theater," spatially and representationally. Etymologically it means *the writing of the stage* and, since the sixteenth century, has become inscribed into our ways of seeing and experiencing theatrical space. By the end of the nineteenth century it was completely, and literally, encapsulated in the proscenium arch, as a framed perspectival construction that simultaneously distances and centralizes the viewer in the event. This was overturned by the spatiotemporal revolution that occurred during the first half of the twentieth century, through scientific revolutions and the radical imagery of the avant-garde, confronting the very way we perceive ourselves in the world and on the stage. The challenge to the domination of vision was intensified by completely disembodied technological warfare, culminating in the blinding light and atomisation of form in Japan, in August 1945. As Paul Virilio efficiently states the "masses no longer believed their eyes."[112] Such visual disenchantment enacts an enucleation that violently loosens sight from its governing position, allowing other senses to come into play. Martin Jay points out that this loss of faith in ocular proof definitively overthrew Cartesian perspectivalism,[113] thereby decentring both the "eye" of the spectator and the "I" of the performer.

Like the dis-eased and decentered body, the *Architecture of Cruelty* is neither comfortable nor yielding, neither safe nor sound. As a material embodiment of Artaud's spatial speech, it is fractured, without boundaries, discontinuous, open to fluidity of motion, and accessible to the carnality of the spectacle. The illusions of the scenographic theater have been dissipated in favor of an architecture apprehended directly for what it is rather than for what it represents.

Cruel Machine

*And just as there will be no unoccupied point in space, there will be
neither respite nor vacancy in the spectator's mind or sensibility.*[114]

As a cruel and impossible mechanism Antonin Artaud's theater was to
be "rebuilt" upon "extreme action, pushed beyond all limits"[115] with its
true and only value found in an "excruciating, magical relation to reality
and danger."[116] This *Theater of Cruelty* is not one of bloodshed or martyrdom but a cruel apparatus built to combat cruelty, through what Derrida
refers to as "the irruptive force fissuring the space of the stage."[117] And
within this opening, the *Real*, as a traumatic surplus, makes its unbearable presence felt. The invasion of the Dubrovka Theater in October 2002
staged an "irruption of the *Real*" by storming the prescribed limits of a
house of entertainment. It presented a moment when theatrical and lived
realities coincided to reveal the ultimate intrusion—that of *death*. The
stage became what Alenka Zupančič calls "A Perfect Place to Die," taking
advantage of "the public setting *par excellence*, where everything that is said
is intended for the audience."[118] The realm of this particular stage then
expanded, through international media coverage, into a phantasmatic
global platform upon which a festival of politics was played out.

Although the *Moscow Theater Hostage Crisis* is isolated as a discrete
event, its retelling defies a clear synopsis. In their analysis of the siege,
Adam Dolnik and Richard Pilch task themselves with its reconstruction
through the multiple and conflicting accounts from media, witnesses,
and participants, all which "differ significantly in their description of
virtually every aspect of the incident."[119] This highlights the impossibility
of a coherent evocation of something experienced from a range of differing perspectives. Unlike the physical space stormed by Chechen rebels
and Russian forces, there is no totalizing overview to the event that also
resists a discrete spatiotemporal containment. Dolnik and Pilch cite it
as an "expressive act" which, like a theatrical production, was planned,
rehearsed, and enacted. But unlike the conventions of the traditional theatrical "show," any pre-arranged scripting of action was always err to the
unpredictabilities of reaction, despite the number of possible scenarios
that may have been taken into account and practiced.

The selection of the site by the rebels was highly strategic, not only
for its centrality and proximity to the Kremlin, but because it guaranteed
a large number of people within a space ideal for "barricade hostage-
taking".[120] As a well-planned and rehearsed event, it revealed the overt

theatricality inherent in such terrorist stagings, seen in the affective timing, combat uniforms, and conspicuous incorporation of the apparatus of weaponry. This was reinforced by the powerful presence of the "black widows" as spectral forms of terror-in-mourning with their veils and bomb-belts. The rebels also utilized the performers from the show, placing those wearing military uniforms in strategic positions to confuse the distinction between real and costumed militia. They exploited the familiar space of the proscenium theater to present body and building as explosive and deadly weapons; wiring the architecture with charges and planting two conspicuous bombs in seats within the auditorium. As living bombs the women also took up tactical positions, including guarding the orchestra where the first hostage was shot and which was utilized as a toilet for lines of waiting people who helped each other in and out of its stinking pit—a tragic spin on Wagner's "mystic abyss" with its "vapors arising from the primeval womb of Gaia."[121] Observation points were set up throughout the auditorium, aided by the self-surveying quality of the space itself, and the clearly marked exits were wired with explosives. Therefore, the hermetically sealed auditorium and its immediate environs became a container for the deadly narcotic gas that drugged and eventually killed many of its inhabitants, allowing the armed forces to raid the theater and execute the rebels who detonated neither the bodies nor the building.

The deadly raid that concluded the siege was enacted because the authorities were faced with enemies who were prepared to sacrifice themselves and others for their cause: "those who ... staged their operation with the ultimate goal of their own dramatic demise."[122] Zupančič explains how suicide, as a "borderline act," is "something completely different from 'doing' or 'action'. It incorporates some radical no! to the universe which surrounds it and involves an irreducible moment of risk."[123] She points out that Lacan's model of the act came from the act of suicide, where every real act is a "suicide of the subject," allowing the subject to be born again as a new subject. This is aligned to Phelan's ontological unrepeatability of performance and Artaud's desire to erase repetition, which "separates force, presence, and life from themselves."[124]

As a political act, the Moscow Theater Siege co-opted the inherent violence of theater architecture, revealing its complicity in controlling public space, and was cruel in the most obvious sense of the word. Violent in its very conformity, the building took audience, terrorists, and authorities hostage. In its role to control and discipline both performance and public, it facilitated the spectacle of horror, resulting in a tragedy that was neither truly theatrical nor constructive. The distanced frame, ordered seating, and carefully controlled exits also enabled the political spectacle to be played out by both sides to tragic effect. Within less than four months, the theater was renovated for a remounting of the musical production Nord-Ost:

> Mr. Vasilyev [Nord-Ost producer] said there was nothing in the theater that would remind people of the dreadful day when the rebels struck as the interior had been completely redesigned. ... But security guards will be present at the theater and audiences will have to pass through metal detectors before entering. ... The seats – previously dark red – are now light blue. The orchestra pit, which the hostages had to use as a toilet, is now level with the audience.[125]

This restoration, which maintained the auditorium's original layout, was limited to technical improvements, a change in color scheme, and increased surveillance. The orchestra pit that was previously sunk below the stalls was raised to floor level to literally bury an excremental site where the rebels killed the first of four hostages. The pit continues to operate as a spatial divide, now bound by a moveable wall for the security of the musicians. The violence was quickly covered over and the moment of rupture, when real terror entered the theater, failed to open up a debate regarding the problematic role played in this event by the existing architecture. Instead the increased presence of security systems reinforces the perpetual state of crisis, in which terror remains an ever-present spectre, further instrumentalizing violence in the built environment.

Measures taken in the name of security continue to ignore the subterranean rhythms that evade architectural discourse, barricading in both building and thought. Other solutions have to be sought to the confinement of body and psyche that tends to prevail as a solution against incursions of violence. Artaud, highlighting that the performing body is an inherently uncontainable entity, revealed architecture's impossible task to provide secure containment. Out of his writing an Architecture of Cruelty emerges that suggests alternative strategies, not only for theatre architecture specifically, but public space generally. The Architecture of Cruelty is both discrete and permeable. It disallows a unified overview and demands an active engagement of the observer to comprehend its complexity. By destabilizing the body in a three-dimensional layering of movement systems, voids, and interstitial zones, it rejects the notion of a fixed and controlled center. Its alternating and overlapping realities bring the slow time of built form into play with the varying temporalities of performance and fictive space. As a performative force, architecture's spatial volatility provides potential resistance to invasion and attack.

Endnotes

1— Mark Wigley, "Editorial," *Assemblage (Violence Space)* 20 (1993): 7.

2— Antonin Artaud, *Theater and Its Double*, trans. C.M Richards (New York: Grove Press, 1958), 98.

3— Wigley, "Editorial," *Assemblage*: 7.

4— Ibid.

5— Slavoj Žižek, "In his Bold Gaze My Ruin is Writ Large," in *Everything You Always Wanted to Know about Lacan (But Were Afraid to Ask Hitchcock)*, ed. Slavoj Žižek (London: Verso, 1992), 239.

6— Jacques Derrida, "The Theater of Cruelty and the Closure of Representation," in *Mimesis, Masochism and Mime: the Politics of Theatricality in Contemporary French Thought*, ed. Timothy Murray (Ann Arbor: University of Michigan Press, 1997), 53.

7— This photograph is one of many that can be found on the internet, staged for the camera by the Russian authorities, who emptied the auditorium of the dead bodies of the citizens. The explosive body simultaneously represents a threat and a cautionary tale.

8— For several long seconds the audience assumed the gunmen in ski masks were part of the show. A woman in the audience, who was interviewed on the television documentary "Terror in Moscow," recalls thinking "what a clever theatrical concept." "Terror in Moscow," HBO, *America Undercover*, dir. Dan Reed, 2003.

9— The rebels themselves had become captive in the space; unable to escape once they had entered (many as members of the audience) and taken it over.

10— Michel Foucault, *Archaeology of Knowledge and Discourse on Language*, trans. A. M. Sheridan (New York: Pantheon Books, 1972), 215–237.

11— Bernard Tschumi, *Architecture and Disjunction* (Cambridge, MA: MIT Press, 1998), citing John Rajchman on Foucault, 256.

12— Una Chaudhuri, *Staging Place: The Geography of Modern Drama* (Ann Arbor: University of Michigan Press, 1997), 21.

13— Friedrich Nietzsche, *The Birth of Tragedy and the Genealogy of Morals*, trans. Francis Golffing (New York: Doubleday Press, 1956), 39.

14— This is pointed out by Chaudhuri who is referring to Peter Brook's suggestion in his 1968 treatise, *The Empty Space*, that "the science of

theater-building" may be "better served by asymmetry, even by disorder," 21.

15— Artaud, *Theater and Its Double*, 74.

16— Georges Bataille, "Architecture," in *Rethinking Architecture*, ed. Neil Leach (London: Routledge, 1997), 21.

17— Michel Foucault, *Power/Knowledge: Selected Interviews and Other Writings: 1972–1977*, ed. Colin Gordon (New York: Pantheon Books), 149.

18— Henri Lefebvre, *The Production of Space*, trans. Donald Nicholson-Smith (Oxford: Blackwell, 1991), 57.

19— Gilles Deleuze, *The Fold: Leibniz and the Baroque*, trans. Tom Conley (Minneapolis and London: University of Minnesota Press, 1993), 19.

20— Michel Foucault, *Discipline and Punish: The Birth of the Prison* (New York: Vintage Books, 1995).

21— Plato, "The Allegory of the Cave," in *The Republic*, ed. Desmond Lee (New York: Penguin Classics, 1997).

22— Denis Hollier, *Against Architecture: The Writings of Georges Bataille* (Cambridge, MA: MIT Press, 1998), xi.

23— Bernard Tschumi, *Questions of Space: Lectures on Architecture* (London: AA Publications, 1995), 71.

24— Artaud, *Theater and its Double*, 48.

25— Ibid.

26— Tschumi, *Questions of Space*, 77.

27— Mark Wigley, *The Architecture of Deconstruction: Derrida's Haunt* (Cambridge, MA: MIT Press, 1993), 4.

28— Friedrich Nietzsche, *Twilight of the Idols and the Anti-Christ*, trans. R.J. Hollingdale (Toronto: Penguin, 2003), 31.

29— Hilde Heynen, *Architecture and Modernity* (Cambridge, MA: MIT Press, 1999), 66.

30— Ibid., 29.

31— Ibid., 28.

32— Peggy Phelan, *Unmarked: the Politics of Performance* (London: Routledge, 1993), 146.

33— Ibid., 3.

34— Ibid., 25.

35— Lefebvre, *The Production of Space*, 49.

36— Peggy Phelan, *Mourning Sex: Performing Public Memories* (London: Routledge, 1997), 2.

37— Wagner had not formulated the scenic revolution of absolute space, deferring to existing modes of scenery. However, it was his grandsons, Wolfgang and Weland Wagner, who established a more abstracted environment on the Festspielhaus stage in the 1950s and 1960s.

38– George C. Izenour, *Theater Design* (New York: McGraw-Hill, 1977), 75.

39– Richard Wagner, "Bayreuth (the Playhouse)," in *Prose Works: Volume 5*, trans. William Ashton Ellis (London, 1873), 335.

40– Donald C. Mullin, *The Development of the Playhouse* (Berkeley: University of California Press, 1970), 148.

41– Joy Ziegeweid, "Faded Dreams," *Moscow Times*, August 5, 2005.

42– Vesnin cited by S.O. Khan-Magomedov, *Alexandr Vesnin and Russian Constructivism* (New York: Rizzoli, 1986), 173.

43– It is worth noting that Wagner aimed to resist architectural monumentalization by building his festival theater as a temporary structure. However, the monumental nature of the artwork it housed, and the Wagnerian legacy, led to its recognition as a timeless masterpiece.

44– Bataille, "Architecture," 21.

45– Although Georges Bataille wrote sparingly on the theater and only knew Artaud peripherally, he was haunted by the scream he witnessed in Artaud's Sorbonne lecture and was affected by his Letters from Rodez with "their shock, the violent shaking of ordinary boundaries." See Georges Bataille, "Surrealism from Day to Day," in *Antonin Artaud: A Critical Reader*, ed. Edward Scheer (London: Routledge Press, 2004), 19.

46– Andre Green, "The Psycho-analytic Reading of Tragedy," in *Mimesis, Masochism and Mime: the Politics of Theatricality in Contemporary French Thought*, ed. Timothy Murray (Ann Arbor: University of Michigan Press, 1997), 145.

47– Anais Nin, *The Diary, 1931–1934* (New York: Harcourt, Brace and World, 1996), 191–2. "He was in agony. He was screaming. He was delirious. He was enacting his own death, his own crucifixion."

48– Allen S. Weiss, "'K,'" in *Antonin Artaud: A Critical Reader*, ed. Edward Scheer (London and New York: Routledge, 2004), 152.

49– Ibid., 153.

50– Helen Finter, "Antonin Artaud and the Impossible Theater: the legacy of the theater of cruelty," in *Antonin Artaud: A Critical Reader*, ed. Edward Scheer (London: Routledge, 2004), 48.

51– Ibid.

52– Alenka Zupančič, "A Perfect Place to Die: Theater in Hitchcock's Films," in *Everything You Always Wanted to Know about Lacan (But Were Afraid to Ask Hitchcock)*, ed. Slavoj Žižek (London and New York: Verso, 1992), 79.

53– Artaud, cited by Weiss, "'K,'" 158.

54– Chaudhuri, *Staging Place*, 23.

55– Cited by Derrida and found in Artaud, *Ouevres Completes*, Vol. 4 (Paris, Gallimard, 1970), 297.

56– Jacques Derrida, "The Theater of Cruelty and the Closure of Representation," in *Mimesis, Masochism and Mime: The Politics of Theatricality in Contemporary French Thought*, ed. Timothy Murray (Ann Arbor: University of Michigan Press, 1997), 46.

57– Artaud, *Theater and its Double*, 96.

58– Ibid., 124–5.

59– Stephen Barber, *Blows and Bombs: Antonin Artaud: The Biography* (London and Boston: Faber and Faber, 1993).

60– Louis A. Sass, *Madness and Modernism: Insanity in the Light of Modern Art, Literature & Thought* (Cambridge, MA: Harvard University Press, 1992), 238.

61– Ibid., 240.

62– Artaud, *Theater and its Double*, 28.

63– Ben Okri, *A Way of Being Free* (London: Phoenix House, 1997), 52.

64– Anais Nin, *The Diary: 1933*, 192.

65– Artaud, *Theater and Its Double*, 102.

66– Ibid., 101.

67– Ibid.

68– *Antonin Artaud: Selected Writings*, ed. Susan Sontag (Berkeley and Los Angles: University of California Press, 1976), 362.

69– Okri, *A Way of Being Free*, 52.

70– Artaud, *Selected Writings*, 495.

71– Antonin Artaud, *Oeuvres Completes, Vol. 1, Part 1* (Paris: Gallimard, 1976/1984), 11.

72– Artaud, *Selected Writings*, 494.

73– Siegfried Giedion, *Mechanization Takes Command: a Contribution to Anonymous History* (New York: Oxford University Press, 1948), 245.

74– Artaud, *Selected Writings*, 507.

75– Helene Cixous, "The Place of Crime, The Place of Pardon" in *20th Century Theater Reader*, ed. Richard Drain (London and New York: Routledge, 1995), 341.

76– Ibid., 340.

77– Ibid., 340–1.

78– Ibid., 342.

79– Artaud, *Theater and its Double*, 113.

80– Jacques Derrida, "Point de Folie – Maintenant l'Architecture," in Bernard Tschumi, *La Case Vide – La Villette* (London: Architectural Association, 1986), 15.

81– Tschumi, *Architecture & Disjunction*, 85.

82– Antonin Artaud, *Theater and its Double*, 30.

83– Artaud, *Selected Writings*, 507.

84– This is discussed at length by Jeffery Meyers in *Disease and the Novel: 1886–1969* (New York: St Martins Press, 1985).

85– Friedrich Nietzsche, "Twilight of the Idols," in *The Portable Nietzsche*, trans/ed. Walter Kaufmann (New York: Penguin Books, 1954), 467.

86– Artaud, *Theater and Its Double*, 51.

87– Ibid., 42.

88– Elaine Scarry, *The Body in Pain: the making and unmaking of the world* (New York: Oxford University Press, 1985), 284.

89– Artaud, *Theater and Its Double*, 98.

90– Ibid., 79.

91– Walter Benjamin, *Illuminations* (New York: Schocken Books, 1968), 84.

92– Walter Benjamin, *Reflections* (New York: Schocken Books, 1978), 182.

93– Artaud, *Selected Writings*, 488.

94– Ibid., 504.

95– Cited by Ronald Hayman, *Artaud and After* (Oxford England and New York: Oxford University Press, 1977), 58.

96– Artaud, *Theater and Its Double*, 130.

97– Ibid., 102.

98– Ibid., 89.

99– Ibid., 112–3.

100– Ibid., 96.

101– Manfredo Tafuri, *The Sphere and the Labyrinth: Avant-Gardes in Architecture from Piranesi to the 1970s* (Cambridge, MA: MIT Press, 1987).

102– Alberto Pérez-Gómez and Louise Pelletier, *Architectural Representation and the Perspective Hinge* (Cambridge, MA: MIT Press, 1997), 77.

103– Ibid.

104– Sergei Eisenstein: "Piranesi, or the Fluidity of Forms," in Tafuri, *The Sphere and the Labyrinth*, 65–90.

105– Diana Agrest, *Architecture From Without: Theoretical Framings for a Critical Practice* (Cambridge, MA: MIT Press, 1991), 52.

106– Artaud, *Selected Writings*, 155.

107– Derrida, "The Theater of Cruelty and the Closure of Representation," 53.

108– Antonin Artaud, *Theater and its Double*, 97.

109– Daniel Libeskind, "The End of Space," *Transition* 44/45 (1992): 86–91.

110– Ibid.

111– Agrest, *Architecture From Without*, 177.

112– Cited by Martin Jay, "The Disenchantment of the Eye: Surrealism and the Crisis of Ocularcentricism," in *Visualizing Theory: Selected Essays from V.A.R.*, ed. Lucien Taylor (New York: Routledge, 1994), 193.

113– Jay, "The Disenchantment of the Eye," 212–3.

114– Artaud, *Theater and Its Double*, 126.

115– Ibid., 85.

116– Ibid., 89.

117– Derrida, "The Theater of Cruelty and the Closure of Representation," 53.

118– Alenka Zupančič, "A Perfect Place to Die: Theater in Hitchcock's Films," in *Everything You Always Wanted to Know about Lacan (But Were Afraid to Ask Hitchcock)*, ed. Slavoj Žižek (London, New York: Verso, 1992), 81.

119– A. Dolnik and R. Pilch, "The Moscow Theater Hostage Crisis: the Perpetrators, their Tactics and the Russian Response," *International Negotiation*, Martinus Nijhoff Publishers, 8. 3 (2003): 578.

120– Ibid., 589. Dolnik and Pilch argue that in staging a successful nationalistic musical, the theater was also a place that guaranteed middle- to upper-class hostages, reinforcing the perception that any citizen can become a target.

121– Richard Wagner, "Bayreuth (The Playhouse)," in *Richard Wagner's Prose Works*, Vol. 5, trans. William Ashton Ellis, (New York: Broude Brothers, 1896), 335.

122– Ibid., 604.

123– Zupančič, "A Perfect Place to Die," 93.

124– In "The Theater of Cruelty and the Closure of Representation," Derrida writes that this is "the profound essence of Artaud's project," 51

125– BBC News, "Moscow Musical Fights Back," February 6, 2003, 14:17 GMT.

FROM TARGET TO WITNESS:

ARCHITECTURE, SATELLITE SURVEILLANCE, HUMAN RIGHTS

ANDREW HERSCHER

"Properties From Afar": The Forensics of Architecture

Only a few years after satellite images became commercially available in 1999, human rights organizations began to use those images, as well as the products of other remote sensing technologies, to represent a proliferating array of human rights issues. If, as many have argued, the central operation of human rights organizations is "mobilizing shame" for rights violations, and if this mobilization relies upon the exposure of purportedly hidden or unseen violations, then the use of remote sensing by these organizations might be understood to only extend their current practice.[1] Yet, for its proponents, remote sensing comprises a powerful technology of exposure, a means to visualize spaces and events that are seemingly off-limits to the on-the-ground scrutiny of rights advocates. According to a typical claim, "satellites are allowing non-governmental organizations the ability to detect and respond to human rights violations as never before."[2] Emerging after often-assumed links between revelation, shame and political action came under question in the wake of catastrophes in Bosnia and Rwanda, remote sensing has offered human rights organizations a new means of revelation, a revitalization of the epistemology of exposure, and a reinvestment in the political possibilities accorded the representation of rights violations. It has promised a dramatic extension of the proximal, on-the-ground sensing of those violations and so a concomitant expansion of knowledge about them and of opportunities to assist their victims and persecute their perpetrators.

"Remote sensing means examining properties from afar, by satellite-based sensors, aerial photography, radar systems, sonar, lasers, radio frequency receivers, thermal devices, seismographs, magnetometers, gravimeters, scintillometers, and other sensing instruments."[3] While this definition of remote sensing explicitly details the technical equipment by means of which this sensing is facilitated, it also implicitly suggests the new cultural and political status of its objects—"properties" examined from afar, in many cases, architecture. At a historical moment when human rights abuses are increasingly visualized through satellite surveillance and other remote sensing technologies, architecture has assumed the status of a privileged representation of a humanity in distress—a humanity whose representation, both visual and political, is otherwise ostensibly fugitive or non-existent. Satellite images of damaged and destroyed architecture allow a distressed humanity to be at once visualized and endowed with political significance; therefore, in recent years, images of damaged or destroyed buildings have been used to document a series of human rights abuses across the globe, from ethnic cleansing in

Kosovo, through the destruction of improvised settlements in the guise of slum clearance in Zimbabwe, to the destruction of villages in the guise of counter-insurgency in Burma. Such documentation has taken the form of legal evidence, as in the case of Zimbabwe's slum clearance; publicity to raise interest in human rights issues, as in projects like *Crisis in Darfur*, produced by the United States Holocaust Memorial Museum in collaboration with Google Earth; or a generalized form of information directed at "private citizens, policy makers, and international courts," as is claimed in the project, *Eyes on Darfur*, produced by Amnesty International in collaboration with Google Earth.[4]

The link between architectural destruction and the violation of human beings established by human rights satellite surveillance is now so constituted as not to need gloss or mediation. *Crisis in Darfur* was thus launched with the explanation that,

> *Typically, perpetrators of genocide operate under a cloud of denial and deception. The Sudanese government maintains that fewer than 9,000 civilians have been killed in the "civil war" in Darfur. Claims like these are easily refuted when any citizen worldwide can view high-resolution satellite imagery and other critical evidence which was previously accessible only to a limited few. Now, any user of Google Earth can zoom down to Darfur and see the extent of the destruction, village after village.*[5]

This staging of satellite images of destroyed buildings as immediate representations of genocide suggests the new visibility of architecture in the age of remote sensing. In the mid-1930s, Walter Benjamin famously claimed that "architecture ... always represented the prototype of a work of art the reception of which is consummated by a collectivity in a state of distraction."[6] Today, if architecture is the object of a distracted gaze, then this is a gaze positioned in a time and place of perceived order—the time and place in which the emergency is elsewhere. In satellite images rendering evidence of human rights emergencies, architecture becomes the object of a highly-focused attention, a visible nexus between an audience of observers and a community of suffering.[7] The work of architectural destruction in the age of remote sensing is, therefore, nothing short of a human rights spectacle, mediating between and interpellating two publics: one in the privileged position of humanitarian viewer and the other in the subaltern position of victim in presumed need of humanitarian relief.[8]

As such, architecture is transformed from a target of violence to a witness to violence. Damage and destruction become forms of evidence, testifying to the violence that caused them. Following the emergence of forensic anthropology and forensic archaeology, the possibility of utilizing architectural evidence in legal processes has thus fostered the development of forensic architecture, a body of expertise in which damaged and destroyed buildings are translated into evidence, admissible in legal processes as well as salient in more general contexts of describing and protesting human rights violations.[9] Architectural forensics is often centered on the first-hand inspection of buildings damaged or destroyed in political violence; however, the commercial accessibility of satellite images beginning in 1999 has expanded the forensic gaze to the inspection of images of architecture obtained by remote sensing. This expansion has allowed a previously privileged gaze on architecture, only available to institutions in states with remote sensing technologies, to be available to a wide range of communities, organizations and institutions critical of governmental activities and policies. In this sense, human rights forensic architecture is a protocol of reading newly accessible images of architecture, ostensibly deformed by a state's illegal or unethical actions.

Recorded by remote sensing technologies and framed in human rights discourse, damaged or destroyed properties examined from afar are traces of otherwise invisible human beings whose human rights are understood to be threatened or violated—traces that are less "detected" by remote sensing than produced by it. Yet the production of this trace has a more complex relationship to human rights work and thought than noted by practitioners of and commentators on human rights remote sensing. At the least, human rights advocates present remote sensing as a complement to existing documentation practices, a component of an "incremental accumulation of painstaking fact-checking of data points and verification of independently derived conclusions."[10] At the most, advocates present remote sensing as itself a means of preventing human rights abuses: "by using satellite imagery and other information technologies to create a virtual panopticon in regions at risk of genocide, it may be possible to deter acts of violence against civilian populations."[11]

In both cases, to be seen is to be dominated; human rights advocates thereby appropriate and extend the imperial gaze of the surveillance state.[12] But the *prospective domination* of violent others that human rights remote sensing is often thought to bring about occurs along with an *enacted domination* of violated victims. The perceived value of human rights remote sensing comes from its capacity to extend the ability of human witnesses to testify to or visualize rights violations. Yet remote sensing transforms what it extends. According to the logic of the supplement as analyzed by Jacques Derrida, remote sensing has not simply added to the witnessing, or on-the-ground sensing, that has hitherto comprised the central form of human rights documentation.[13] The supplement, writes Derrida, "adds only to replace ... if it represents and makes an image, it is by the anterior default of a presence ... it is not simply added to the positivity of a presence ... its place is assigned in the structure by the mark of an emptiness."[14] The emptiness that remote sensing has to produce in order to supplement is in the sensing conducted by human beings, the labor of witnessing. Thus, what advocates of human rights remote sensing have neglected to recognize is that remote sensing has rendered the testimony of human witnesses incomplete and inadequate on its own terms, and now necessary to "corroborate" or "verify" from the satellite's privileged position.

In the context of military remote sensing, no crisis ensues from the delegitimization of testimony. The satellite's supplementation of a human witness is simply an enhancement of "intelligence."[15] But even though human rights remote sensing ostensibly serves to bear witness to the violation of humanity, it throws into crisis the capacity of the very human beings it serves. Posed as the "proof" of testimony and other forms of witnessing, remote sensing does not only *substantiate* human witnesses to human rights violations, but also *supplants* those witnesses as authoritative sources. Human rights remote sensing thus bears a paradoxical relationship to the human subject of human rights: the subject loses authority to decisively testify to violations of its rights since this authority is assigned to non-human objects whose images "corroborate" and "verify" the testimony of subjects.

The representation of human rights violations via remotely-sensed imagery thereby marks or even initiates a series of transformations, some tendentious and others poignant, in human rights documentation and publicity: the reliance on a highly technologized and fully corporatized mode of vision as a means of corroborating embodied words and images; the establishment of remote sensing's temporal delay and visual abstraction as marks of heightened objectivity; the use of remotely-sensed architecture as decisive representations of human rights violations; the imbrications of human rights advocacy in the techniques and practices of bio-power; and, most importantly, the withholding of authority from the human subject to decisively prove the violation of his or her human rights.

Remote Sensing as Human Rights Documentation

Prior to the launch of privately owned imaging satellites beginning in the 1990s and the subsequent commercialization of remote sensing, this sensing could only be carried out by governmental agencies in highly technologized states, first the United States and Soviet Union, and then others in North America and Europe.[16] The remote sensing of human rights abuses first became topical when these states enmeshed human rights issues in legitimizations of interstate violence, one instance of the more general recalibration of global politics around moral narratives of human rights after 1989. For example, in August 1995, the United States Department of State released before-and-after satellite images of areas near Srebrenica in order to document mass graves of Muslim refugees killed by Bosnian Serb forces; obtained from US surveillance satellites, these images supported the US argument for NATO military action against Serbia.[17] Similarly, in the 1999 NATO bombing campaign against Serbia, NATO spokesmen were supplied with images from US surveillance satellites in order to represent human rights abuses carried out by the Serb forces that comprised NATO's adversary at the time.[18]

As with many other practices understood to be the province of the liberal state, the neoliberal state outsourced remote sensing to private corporations that were ostensibly able to develop it more intensively and efficiently.[19] The first of these corporations were licensed in the United States; at present, satellite imagery is also produced and sold by corporations licensed in France, the United Kingdom, and jointly in Taiwan and the United States.[20] Shortly after the Kosovo War, once tightly controlled satellite images became commodities available for purchase in the "free market." In October 1999, the first commercial satellite image was released, from GeoEye Corporation's IKONOS satellite; by 2003, commercial companies were the principal suppliers of satellite imagery to the US government.

Human rights organizations quickly began to avail themselves of satellite imagery, as well. Among the first NGOs to use remote sensing for human rights work was Human Rights Watch, which used satellite images, among other data, to investigate the number and cause of civilian deaths during the US invasion of Iraq and to document the destruction of houses by the Israeli Defense Forces in Gaza, both in 2003.[21] Similarly, the Committee for Human Rights in North Korea, a US-based NGO, used satellite images in conjunction with interviews and other data to report on the system of camps for political prisoners in North Korea, also in 2003.[22]

Remote sensing was formalized as a means of human rights advocacy with the foundation of the Geospatial Technologies and Human Rights initiative by the Science and Human Rights Program of the American Association for the Advancement of Science (AAAS) in 2005.[23] Since 2006, within the frame of this initiative, the Science and Human Rights Program has collaborated with several national and international human rights organizations to employ satellite imagery in human rights documentation. Among the cases that this imagery was used to document were the forced dislocation of civilians in Zimbabwe by government forces in 2005; the forced dislocation of civilians in Burma's Karen Province by government forces in 2006 and 2007; attacks on civilians by Janjaweed forces in Chad and Darfur, Sudan, in 2005 and 2006; and the effects on Lebanese civilians of the 2006 Israel—Hezbollah conflict.

More recently, the advent of Web 2.0 has further broadened the intersection between satellite imagery and human rights advocacy. The most prominent examples of this intersection occur on Google Earth, in which users can create "placemarks" to mark any location for any reason. Through "placemarking," a range of individuals and institutions have become, in effect, human rights entrepreneurs, correlating texts and images of reported human rights violations with sites depicted on Google Earth; *Crisis in Darfur* and *Eyes on Darfur* both comprise examples of this sort of entrepreneurship.

In this range of geographical settings and political contexts, there have been a number of prominent similarities in the way that satellite imagery has been employed and understood, as well as in the effects that its use and understanding have generated.[24] As David Campbell has pointed out, human rights advocates have used remote sensing imagery in exactly the same way as surveillance states, even those criticized for human rights abuses—as evidence of an "unsurpassed objectivity."[25] This "objectivity," however, has a history.[26] One dimension of this history lies in the recruitment of photography, and, in particular, surveillance photography, as an immediate, direct and objective transcription of reality by what John Tagg has termed "privileged apparatuses within the given social formation."[27] Thus, although remote sensing images are currently *authored* by private corporations, the *authority* of these images has been established by and drawn upon by the surveillance state, for which remote sensing is a primary device of power and knowledge.

Another dimension of this history lies in aesthetics. As Roman Jakobson observed, any realist aesthetic is, to a large degree, a recoding of prior realist aesthetics.[28] The aesthetics of remote sensing relies upon documentary photography, whose codes and conventions have established parameters for the "objective" depiction of reality. In particular, it draws upon what Mark Dorrian has called the "vertical image" that became technically possible with the advent of aerial photography.[29] After its emergence in military reconnaissance in World War I, the vertical image was associated with an objectifying and distancing gaze on wartime violence and destruction.[30] As Bernd Hüppauf describes, the aerial perspective offered a point of view from which "scenes of destruction may be seen as grandiose spectacles or places of pure horror, but they no longer arouse feelings of empathy, pity or sorrow."[31] The circulation of these images by states involved in the war could thus assist in the production and reproduction of public support for the war—a war whose violence was rendered invisible in vertical images.[32]

In the context of the history of aerial photography, the mobilization of remote sensing imagery in human rights advocacy represents a recuperation of this photography towards explicitly humanitarian or ethical ends.[33] In human rights advocacy, the vertical image is repurposed as a visualization of hidden or unknown violence, or a defamiliarization of legitimized or authorized violence "to demilitarize military perspectives," in the words of Lisa Parks.[34] Hence, in human rights remote sensing, the visual abstraction and dehumanized perspective of the vertical image no longer signify a loss of information or a reduction of knowledge, but precisely the opposite—a reconstituted model of objectivity, now dedicated to acknowledging the suffering other, located in the mechanized vision of the extra-terrestrial camera.

Violated Architecture

Commercially available satellite imagery now possesses resolutions ranging from forty centimeters to one meter.[35] Combined with a satellite's intermittent overpass of sites, ranging from once every two or three days to once a week, satellites are endowed with a capacity to depict the architecture of human beings, but not individual human beings themselves.[36] As described by AAAS's Science and Human Rights Program, "violations that effect infrastructure and housing, in particular, or that require large build-ups of military, paramilitary forces are especially visible to … satellites."[37] In each case—infrastructure, housing, build-up—the object of the satellite's gaze is architectural or at least of architectural scale. Therefore, human rights violations must be documented in terms of the architectural traces those violations leave. Human rights remote sensing thus represents violations *by* architecture and violations *of* architecture.

An example of a violation *by* architecture includes the system of prisons, forced-labor camps, and detention facilities in North Korea used to repress political prisoners (figure 1). Testimonies of former prisoners who defected to South Korea have documented this system in great detail and satellite images have depicted the sites that such testimonies describe. While these sites appear in abstract or generic form (the roofs of buildings, the empty spaces around buildings), annotations from testimonies identify the uses of buildings and spaces (prisoner housing, confinement cell, public execution site, burial site, and so on). These annotated images provide what is then framed as corroborating evidence to testimonies representing a repressive and violent regime—a regime that targets victims for imprisonment and often-extreme punishment without judicial process, and that also denies all reports of the same.

Examples of the violation *of* architecture include housing demolitions in Zimbabwe and Burma. In each case, satellite images documented the presence of structures at one moment in time and the very absence of the same structures at a later moment, with these before-and-after moments bracketing the unrepresented violation, itself the object of scrutiny. In Zimbabwe, satellite images showed informal settlements one or two years before and a few months after they were destroyed in the course of a forced dislocation of impoverished communities in and around Harare in April 2005 (figure 2). This dislocation, termed "Operation Murambatsvina" or "Operation Drive Out Trash" by the government, was, on its own terms, a slum clearance program that commenced just after widely disputed parliamentary elections in Zimbabwe. Though the operation itself was invisible in remote sensing imagery, the images of informal settlements before it had begun and of the remains of these settlements after it had been completed suggested the status of the operation as causal in the settlements' destruction. In Burma, satellite images showed Eastern Burmese villages in 2000, six years before the Burmese Army set out on a violent counter-insurgency, and then, the remains of those villages in 2006 and 2007, following that counter-insurgency, similarly suggesting the status of the counter-insurgency as causal in the villages' destruction (figures 3a and 3b).

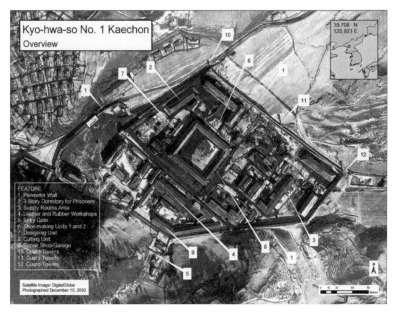

Figure 1. Kyo-hwa-so No. 1 Prison Camp, Kaechon, South Pyong-an Province, North Korea. Image from David Hawk, The Hidden Gulag: Exposing North Korea's Prison Camps. Prisoners' Testimonies and Satellite Photographs (Washington: U.S. Committee for Human Rights in North Korea, 2003). Image courtesy U.S. Committee for Human Rights in North Korea.

Figure 2. Porta Farm settlement, Zimbabwe, with destroyed structures marked in red. Image from Amnesty International, "Shattered Lives: The Case of Porta Farm" (2006).

Figure 3a (top) and Figure 3b (bottom). Before and after images of a removed village, Papun District, Burma. Images from American Association for the Advancement of Science, Science and Human Rights Program, "High Resolution Satellite Imagery and the Conflict in Eastern Burma: Summary Report" (2007). Before image courtesy GeoEye, Inc; after image courtesy DigitalGlobe, Inc.

Architectural Evidence as Supplemental Evidence

As the preceding already indicates, satellite imagery is sought and emplotted as human rights evidence in order to corroborate other evidence, obtained from or produced by on-the-ground sources. In the words of the AAAS's Science and Human Rights Program,

> Geospatial technologies can broaden the ability of non-governmental organizations to rapidly gather, analyze, and disseminate authoritative information, especially during times of crisis. They can also provide compelling, visual proof to corroborate on-the-ground reporting of conflicts and natural disasters affecting human rights.[38]

Here, remote sensing imagery is staged explicitly as a supplement to other evidence ("on-the-ground reporting"): to supplement this other evidence is to "corroborate" it and render it proven.

In other contexts, remote sensing is understood not only to "prove" on-the-ground reporting, but also to heighten its emotional impact. Thus, the following staging of *Crisis in Darfur*, by one the project's authors:

> [High-resolution satellite] images of the charred remains of village after village provided undeniable proof of the extent of destruction and its aftermath, with hundreds of thousands of tents in refugee camps dotted across the region. By bringing together geo-referenced photos and videos from Museum staff and acclaimed international photographers, as well as testimonies from Amnesty International, the stories of what happened to these villages became more personal and compelling.[39]

Yet, with the supplementation of on-the-ground reporting and other information on human rights violations by evidence obtained from remote sensing, the field of human rights evidence and the practice of witnessing are fundamentally transformed.

Satellite imagery covers much of the entire globe, and images must be found or produced of sites whose locations are closely defined and circumscribed. The evidence that defines and circumscribes these sites comes from on-the-ground sources—testimonies of witnesses, reportage and photography by human rights organizations, and so on. This is evidence in which the presence of the human being, both as author of evidence and as subject of evidence, is registered in a number of ways: in the signing of reports; the naming of perpetrators and victims of violations; and the making of testimonies by individual victims. Assigned to "corroborate" or "prove" this evidence, however, remote sensing renders the evidence uncorroborated and unproven on its own terms.

Thus, in the case of Zimbabwe, Amnesty International commissioned the AAAS to obtain satellite images documenting Operation Murambatsvina. Yet, in the months after the operation had begun, human rights organizations in Zimbabwe reported on its violence and devastation in numerous formats.[40] In July 2005, the UN Special Envoy on Human Settlements Issues in Zimbabwe, Anna Kajumulo Tibaijuka, synthesized and expanded on these accounts in a comprehensive report on the first months of the operation, with testimony from affected people, photographs of destroyed communities and displaced people, and data on the number of families affected by the operation, the number of houses and other structures demolished, and the number of people made homeless.[41] Nevertheless, the satellite images of before-and-after views of the operation commissioned by Amnesty were framed as decisive proof. In the words of Kolawole Olaniyan, director of Amnesty's Africa Program, "these satellite images are irrefutable evidence—*if further evidence is even needed*—that the Zimbabwean government has obliterated entire communities."[42] Olaniyan's ambivalence about the necessity of "further evidence" to prove the already-documented effects of the operation points precisely to remote sensing's ambiguous status as a supplement, simultaneously verifying existing evidence and also rendering that evidence unverified without the substantiation of satellite imagery.

Similarly, the authors of the AAAS report on Burma write they used satellite imagery "to corroborate reporting gathered by organizations already active in the region."[43] These organizations, both national and international (the Free Burma Rangers, the Karen Human Rights Group, the Thailand Burma Border Consortium, Human Rights Watch, Amnesty International, and others) reported thoroughly and extensively on forced dislocations of villagers in eastern Myanmar. These reports were posted on the Web sometimes only days after a dislocation and often included extremely precise information on the perpetrators of the dislocation, identifying the army unit and commanders in question; the victims of the dislocation, enumerating displaced villagers; and the nature of the dislocation, naming the number of houses destroyed, and the current status and location of displaced villagers. At times, these reports also included maps of displacement by district; photographs of destroyed houses and displaced villagers; and testimony from displaced villagers. Nevertheless, supplemented by satellite imagery offered as "corroboration," these reports became uncorroborated themselves.

Closed Territories, Open Skies

The expanded exposure of human rights violations ostensibly made possible by remote sensing assumes a topography of closed territories and open skies. In the words of Larry Cox, executive director of Amnesty International USA, "what this satellite technology does, it makes it possible to break down those walls of secrecy. Not only to get information, but to get information in a way that's irrefutable."[44] The release of satellite imagery of sites in repressive states like Burma and North Korea thus occasioned vivid descriptions of a topography of secrecy and a technology of exposure. "Burma is a black hole ... it's totally off limits," one article quoted a human rights advocate asserting, setting up the expanded visual field made possible by remote sensing technology.[45] "While the junta can control the street, the monasteries and even the Web, they can't control the sky," the author of another article claimed.[46] In the case of North Korea, a human rights advocate analogously stated that "satellite images ... will be used to understand and expose the human rights and humanitarian situation in this still-closed society, formerly known as the 'hermit kingdom.'"[47]

The binary opposition that underlies such accounts—closed territory/open sky—reasserts simplistic tropes on both sides. On one side, this binary ignores the local and transnational human rights organizations whose reports provide the basis for satellite examination in the first place. These reports reveal and expose human rights abuses, revelations and exposures that satellites imagery is recruited to corroborate. Satellite images themselves, then, do not reveal or expose secret spaces so much as they visualize and reconfigure a topography of secrecy.[48] That is, through the very gesture of revelation, the satellite image asserts a prior secrecy that has become exposed—but a secrecy that is, in fact, partial or fragmented, if it even exists at all. Here, human rights satellite surveillance conforms to a paradigm of "spectacular secrecy" that has become generalized in contemporary visual culture.[49]

On the other side, this binary ignores the status of remote sensing technology as at once corporate property and the subject of a dense constellation of national laws and policies. In the United States, the government has attempted to maintain control of commercial satellite imagery by reserving a right to "shutter control," or to restrict imagery, in order to protect "national security" or "foreign policy interests"; by instituting various time restrictions determining the release of imagery; by denying commercial licenses for certain sorts of high resolution imagery; and by maintaining the right to "censorship by contract," or the purchase of all output from a satellite for a specified period of time. The supposition of a topography of closed territories and open skies represses both the openings to repressive states made by on-the-ground actors and the closures of the sky structured by corporate practice and national law and policy; both repressions, however, serve to stage the satellite as the privileged witness of human rights issues.

(Remote) Seeing as/and Believing

While most human rights advocacy has been predicated on the axiom that "seeing is believing"—that to visualize a phenomenon is to make it immediately available to knowledge—the predominant use of satellite imagery suggests that it is only *remote seeing* that offers fully believable representation and that sight on the ground is subject to distortions, biases and obstacles that render it inherently unreliable. When remote seeing is believing, seeing up close and personal becomes an undependable and only preliminary form of vision.

The prosthetic expansion of the human sensorium offered by remote sensing, then, comes with a concomitant violence to that sensorium. With the advent of remote sensing, the presumed authenticity of human experience, upon which human rights witnessing and testimony rest, is replaced by new theories of experience and truth. The capacity to truthfully represent an act of violation passes from the witness who "directly" experiences that act to the satellite that depicts its architectural aftermath. The truth of the witness is replaced by the truth of remote sensing, whose images are narrated as offering an immediate representation of reality. This replacement transforms the epistemological value of witnessing, as well as the ontological status of the human itself. It establishes a continuum between witnessing and verifying, leaving witnessing itself only able to yield unverified evidence. This is not to make a humanist critique of the violence done to the human sensorium by inhuman technology; rather, it is to register the status of that sensorium as always a product or effect of inhuman forces and techniques. Seen in this way, remote sensing serves to make visible not only its explicit subject matter, but also the inherent imbrications of the human and inhuman. The shift in the technical mediation of humanity that remote sensing institutes thereby involves a shift in what it is to be human.

In his discussion of capitalist globalization, Pheng Cheah has described the same dynamic, which, he writes, forces us "to acknowledge that what we know as human has always been given to us by an inhuman temporality and spacing that we cannot fully grasp or control."[50]

Cheah has explicated the technologies of bio-power that allow humanity to be manifested through economic development, but also necessitate and legitimize an inhuman structure of competition and inequality. For Cheah, the latter comprise a general inhumanity, "a form of inhuman production that cannot be regulated and transcended because it is the condition of possibility of humanity ... [forming] the concrete human being and all its capacities at the most material level."[51] Cheah argues that human rights discourse, in its normative form, cannot comprehend the constitutive enmeshment of the inhuman and the human. The career of remote sensing in that discourse reveals that human rights advocacy is not only engaged in the *comprehension* of inhumanity, but also in the *mediation* of it. The capacity of satellite images to represent the truth of human rights violations emerges only with a concomitant incapacitation of human witnesses to represent that truth. This incapacitation disallows human beings from testifying to violations of their own humanity; it is an inhuman evacuation of dignity and authority from the human that proceeds in the very process of advocating for human rights.

"No-One Was There..."

In the beginning of 2009, Sri Lankan military forces launched an offensive against Tamil militants, the Liberation Tigers of Tamil Eelam (LTTE), with the intention of ending the decades-long war between the LTTE and the government. Tens of thousands of Tamil civilians were caught within this offensive. By April 2009, the LTTE had been forced to retreat to a small section of land in Northeast Sri Lanka, where all civilians were prevented from fleeing. At the same time, Sri Lankan forces launched a series of violent attacks on the LTTE, which, according to the testimony of survivors as well as UN representatives and human rights organizations, inflicted many casualties on civilians.

According to the LTTE, these civilians were targeted by government forces; according to the Sri Lankan government, they were forcibly conscripted as human shields. The Sri Lankan government prevented independent journalists from accessing the war zone, leaving the warring parties and their respective advocates as primary authors of representations of the catastrophe that Tamil civilians were engulfed within. Reports from human rights organizations documented cases of the LTTE forcing civilians to testify in accordance with its narrative of the war; hence, the Sri Lankan government discounted all civilian testimony as contaminated. Both the LTTE and Sri Lankan government thus shared an identical refusal to allow victims of this catastrophe to testify to their condition; both arrogated the right to speak about victims of the war from those victims themselves. When Brigadier Udaya Nanayakkara, the Sri Lankan military spokesman, proclaimed that "there can't be any civilians killed by government forces ... How can the UN know about this? It had no people on the ground," he implicitly practiced precisely the dehumanization that his forces were accused of, an accounting of "people" that excluded those people vulnerable to violence.[52]

This arrogation of the capacity to testify may be regarded as a restricted inhumanity, the outcome of contingent circumstances—an inhumanity that it is possible to overcome. And yet, this arrogation was repeated by those parties who became involved in the war precisely in order to advocate on behalf of its victims: the international mass media, human rights organizations and the United Nations alike. Thus, according to John Holmes, the UN Under-Secretary for Humanitarian Affairs, an investigation into what took place in the Sri Lankan war zone was warranted because "no-one was there, no-one knows and we may never know. And that's why an investigation would be a good idea."[53]

It is possible to state that "no-one was there," that no-one was in the war zone, only if those who *were* there, those who were the objects of both violence and of human rights protection, do not count as ones. Violence, from both the LTTE and the Sri Lankan forces, was the first denomination of human beings, the first reduction of ones into no-ones. Withholding from these ones the ability to testify to their own fate, however, human rights advocacy confirmed this denomination.

As has become routine in the age of remote sensing, satellites were called upon to testify in this seeming breach of testimony.[54] This call, made through the AAAS Science and Human Rights Program, was made by Human Rights Watch and Amnesty International. As the AAAS report on Sri Lanka described, "as no outside parties were allowed access to the time frame in question, these reports [of international news sources and the UN Office for the Co-Ordination of Humanitarian Affairs] were largely unverified."[55] Remote sensing provided this verification by means of images of the damage that the Sri Lankan military wrought in what that same military termed a civilian "safe zone": shell impact craters around houses, shelled buildings, burned buildings, and building debris (figure 4). At the same time, the damaged architecture captured by remote sensing reinscribed the displacement of those who lived and who died in that architecture, those whose own testimony could not be credited until it was "verified" by remote sensing's supplement.

Yet, even the verification of the testimony of human beings is not to credit the humanity of its authors or to return to these authors a previously evacuated humanity. Indeed, this verification may represent another stage of inhumanity—a recognition of humanity that has to be processed through an inhuman apparatus of bio-power. Derrida, among others, has insisted on the maintenance of a distinction between the testimony of the witness and the evidence of proof:

> If there is bearing witness and if it answers properly, incontestably,
> to the name and the sense intended by this name in our "culture," in
> the world that we think we can, precisely, inherit and to which we can
> bear witness, then this bearing witness must not essentially consist in
> proving, in confirming a knowledge, in ensuring a theoretical certitude,
> a determinant judgment. It can only appeal to an act of faith.[56]

For Derrida, the faith that testimony solicits is not a function of its unverified status but of its irreducible difference from what it represents. This difference requires that testimony be interpreted not in terms of its relation to the putative object of representation but on its own terms. The testimony of a witness, then, should not require supplementary verification, either within or beyond juridical settings, because there is nothing inherently incomplete, inadequate, or uncorroborated about it. It is the emergence of supplements to testimony, such as remote sensing imagery, that ineluctably renders testimony partial, incomplete, and uncorroborated. Before testimony could be supplemented, it served as corroborative; after testimony could be supplemented, it needed to be corroborated. Therefore, the status of testimony as unproven and satellite imagery as proof are not determined by substantive qualities of either category of evidence, but rather by the nature of their relationship.

Human rights claims are claims made for recognition and remedy on the basis of the claimant's humanity. What the recourse to remote sensing in human rights work signifies, however, is an absence of faith in the human—an absence enacted precisely in the act of advocating for human rights. This absence ought to be marked and mourned. For whom or what can human rights advocacy protect when it is predicated on an inability to believe (in) human beings?

Figure 4. "Crater formation within the CSZ (Civilian Safety Zone) between May 6 and May 10, 2009," Sri Lanka. Image from American Association for the Advancement of Science, Science and Human Rights Program, "High-Resolution Satellite Imagery and the Conflict in Sri Lanka" (2009). Image courtesy DigitalGlobe, Inc.

Endnotes

1— On the mobilization of shame in human rights work, see Thomas Keenan, "The Mobilization of Shame," *South Atlantic Quarterly* 103:2/3 (2004).

2— Science and Human Rights Program, American Association for the Advancement of Science, "Geospatial Technologies and Human Rights," http://shr.aaas.org/geotech.

3— "Geospatial Technologies and Human Rights."

4— See *Crisis in Darfur*, http://www.ushmm.org/maps/projects/darfur/ and *Eyes on Darfur*, http://www.eyesondarfur.org/about.html.

5— Michael Graham, "United States Holocaust Memorial Museum *Crisis in Darfur*," http://www.google.com/earth/outreach/cs_darfur.html.

6— Walter Benjamin, "The Work of Art in the Age of Mechanical Reproduction," in *Illuminations*, trans. Harry Zohn (New York: Schocken, 1969), 217-252.

7— On the witnessing public constituted by human rights publicity, see Meg McLagan, "Principles, Politics and Publicity: Notes on Human Rights Media," *American Anthropologist* 105:3 (2003).

8— On the "human rights spectacle," see Kathleen Erwin, "The Circulatory System: Blood Procurement, AIDS, and the Social Body in China," *Medical Anthropology Quarterly* 20:2 (2006).

9— See Eyal Weizman, "Forensic Architecture: Only the Criminal Can Solve the Crime," *Radical Philosophy* 164 (2010).

10— S. Aday and S. Livingston, "NGOs as Intelligence Agencies: The Empowerment of Transnational Advocacy Networks and the Media by Commercial Remote Sensing in the Case of the Iranian Nuclear Program," *Geoforum* 40:4 (2009).

11— Matthew Levinger, "Geographical Information Systems Technology as a Tool for Genocide Prevention: The Case of Darfur," *Space and Polity* 13:1 (2009): 74.

12— On this gaze, see Chad Harris, "The Omniscient Eye: Satellite Imagery, 'Battlespace Awareness,' and the Structures of the Imperial Gaze," *Surveillance and Society*, 41:1/2 (2006).

13— On witnessing and human rights advocacy, see Meg McLagan, "Human Rights, Testimony and Transnational Publicity," *The Scholar and Feminist Online* 2:1 (Summer 2003), http://www.barnard.columbia.edu/sfonline/ps/mclagan.htmhttp.

14— Jacques Derrida, *Of Grammatology*, trans. Gayatri Chakravorti Spivak (Baltimore: Johns Hopkins University Press, 1986), 145.

15— A vivid example of this enhancement came in Colin Powell's famous presentation of satellite surveillance imagery of Iraq to the United Nations in 2003, when Powell compared the omniscient perspective of the satellite with the perspective of UN weapons inspectors "under constant surveillance by an army of Iraqi intelligence operatives." See http://www.washingtonpost.com/wp-srv/nation/transcripts/powelltext_020503.html. On the militarization of technologically enhanced vision, see Rey Chow, *The Age of the World Target: Self-Referentiality in War, Theory and Comparative Work* (Durham: Duke University Press, 2006).

16— On the history of remote sensing, see Pamela Mack, *Viewing the Earth: The Social Construction of the Landsat Satellite System* (Cambridge, MA: MIT Press, 1990) and Dwayne Day, John M. Logsdon and Brian Latell, eds., *Eye in the Sky: The Story of the Corona Spy Satellites* (Washington: Smithsonian Institution Press, 1998).

17— On the satellite imagery of the Srebrenica massacre, see Lisa Parks, *Cultures in Orbit: Satellites and the Televisual* (Durham: Duke University Press, 2005), 77–108.

18— On the satellite imagery of human rights abuses in Kosovo, see Andrew Herscher, *Violence Taking Place: The Architecture of the Kosovo Conflict* (Stanford: Stanford University Press, 2010), 75–83.

19— The remote sensing industry in the United States was privatized by President Bill Clinton in 1994; see Parks, *Cultures in Orbit: Satellites and the Televisual*, 80.

20— See W. E. Stoney, *ASPRS Guide to Land Imaging Satellites*, American Society for Photogrammetry and Remote Sensing (2008), http://www.asprs.org/news/satellites/.

21— Human Rights Watch, *Off Target* (2003), http://www.hrw.org/en/reports/2003/12/11/target

and Human Rights Watch, *Razing Rafah*, http://www.hrw.org/en/reports/2004/10/17/razing-rafah.

22– David Hawk, *The Hidden Gulag: Exposing North Korea's Prison Camps. Prisoners' Testimonies and Satellite Photographs* (Washington: U.S. Committee for Human Rights in North Korea, 2003).

23– The initiative was funded by a $110,000 grant from the John D. and Catherine T. MacArthur Foundation in December 2005.

24– See Chris Perkins and Martin Dodge, "The 'View From Nowhere?' Spatial Politics and Cultural Significance of High-Resolution Satellite Imagery," *Geoforum* 40:4 (2009).

25– David Campbell, "Tele-Vision: Satellite Images and Security," *Source* 56 (Autumn 2008).

26– On the history of objectivity, see Lorraine Daston and Peter Galison, eds., *Objectivity* (New York: Zone Books, 2007).

27– John Tagg, *The Burden of Representation: Essays on Photographies and Histories* (Amherst, MA: University of Massachusetts Press, 1988), 189.

28– Roman Jakobson, "On Realism in Art," in *Language in Literature* (Cambridge, MA: Harvard University Press, 1990).

29– On *documentary photography*, see Tagg, *The Burden of Representation: Essays on Photographies and Histories*; Abigail Solomon-Godeau, *Photography at the Dock: Essays on Photographic History, Institutions and Practices* (Minneapolis: University of Minnesota Press, 1991); and Robin Kelsey, *Archive Style: Photographs and Illustrations for U.S. Surveys, 1850–1950* (Berkeley: University of California Press, 2007). On the aerial view, see Mark Dorrian, "The Aerial View: Notes for a Cultural History," *Strates* 13 (2007), http://strates.revues.org/document5573.html and Davide Deriu, "Picturing Ruinscapes: The Aerial Photograph as Image of Historical Trauma," in *The Image and the Witness: Trauma, Memory and Visual Culture*, eds. Frances Guerin and Roger Hallas (London: Wallflower Press, 2007).

30– An early and important theorist of this gaze was Ernst Jünger; see, for example, "War and Photography," *New German Critique* 59 (1993).

31– Bernd Hüppauf, "Experiences of Modern Warfare and the Crisis of Representation," *New German Critique* 59 (1993): 57.

32– See Caroline Brothers, *War and Photography: A Cultural History* (London: Routledge, 1997).

The objectification of violence in the vertical image of wartime destruction was noted by Walter x7xxxx7 in the epilogue to "The Work of Art" essay: "Mankind, which in Homer's time was an object of contemplation for the Olympian gods, is now one for itself. Its self-alienation has reached such a degree that it can experience its own destruction as an aesthetic pleasure of the first order." See Benjamin, "The Work of Art in the Age of Mechanical Reproduction," 235.

33– Some theorists of military reconnaissance photography pose this recuperation as a recovery of this photography's "latent agency"; see, for example, Deriu, "Picturing Ruinscapes: The Aerial Photograph as Image of Historical Trauma."

34– Parks, *Cultures in Orbit: Satellites and the Televisual, 83.*

35– For example, GeoEye's Ikonos-2, in operation since 1999, has one meter panchromatic resolution and 4m multispectral resolution; Digital Globe's QickBird-2, in operation since 2001, has 60cm panchromatic resolution and 3m multispectral resolution; Spot Image's Spot-5, in operation since 2002, has 2.5m panchromatic resolution and 10m multispectral resolution; ImageSat International's EROS-B, in operation since 2006, has 70cm panchromatic resolution. See Stoney, *ASPRS Guide to Land Imaging Satellites.*

36– For example, Ikonos-2 can revisit a site every 2.9 days at 1m resolution and 1.5 days at 1.5m resolution; QuickBird-2 can revisit a site every three to seven days, depending on latitude; Spot-5 can revisit a site every three to seven days, depending on latitude; OrbView-3 can revisit a site approximately every three days. See Stoney, *ASPRS Guide to Land Imaging Satellites.*

37– "Geospatial Technologies and Human Rights."

38– "Geospatial Technologies and Human Rights."

39– Graham, "United States Holocaust Memorial Museum *Crisis in Darfur*."

40– See, for example, Forum, "Order Out of Chaos, or Chaos Out of Order? A Preliminary Report on Operation 'Murambatsvina'" (June 2005), http://www.swradioafrica.com/Documents/ZHRNGOFOrderoutofchaos.htm.

41– Anna Kajumulo Tibaijuka, "Report of the Fact-Finding Mission to Zimbabwe to Assess the Scope and Impact of Operation Murambatsvina by the UN Special Envoy on Human Settlements Issues in Zimbabwe" (2005), http://ocha-gwapps1.unog.ch/rw/rwb.nsf/db900SID/HMYT-6EJM2G?OpenDocument.

42– Amnesty International, "Zimbabwe: Satellite Images Provide Shocking Evidence of the Obliteration of a Community" (2006), http://www.amnesty.org/library/info/AFR46/008/2006.

43– Science and Human Rights Program, American Association for the Advancement of Science, "High-Resolution Satellite Imagery and the Conflict in Eastern Burma: Summary Report" (2007), http://shr.aaas.org/www/aaas_burmareport_28sept2007.pdf.

44– Robin Mejia, "These Satellite Images Document an Atrocity," Washington Post, June 10, 2007, http://www.washingtonpost.com/wp-dyn/content/article/2007/06/05/AR2007060501701.html.

45– Peter N. Spotts, "Monitoring Human Rights? Get a Satellite," Christian Science Monitor, June 23, 2006, http://www.burmanet.org/news/2006/06/23/the-christian-science-monitor-monitoring-human-rights-get-a-satellite-peter-n-spotts/.

46– Bryan Walsh, "An Eye in the Sky on Burma," Time, September 28, 2007, http://www.time.com/time/world/article/0,8599,1666734,00.html.

47– Hawk, The Hidden Gulag: Exposing North Korea's Prison Camps. Prisoners' Testimonies and Satellite Photographs.

48– See Chris Perkins and Martin Dodge, "Satellite Imagery and the Spectacle of Secret Spaces," Geoforum 40:4 (2009).

49– See Jack Bratich, "Public Secrecy and Immanent Security," Cultural Studies 20:4/5 (2006).

50– Pheng Cheah, "Humanity within the Field of Instrumentality," in Inhuman Conditions: On Cosmopolitanism and Human Rights (Cambridge, MA: Harvard University Press, 2006), 230.

51– Cheah, "Humanity within the Field of Instrumentality," 231.

52– Times Online, "Calls for War Crimes Inquiry Over 20,000 Civilian Deaths in Sri Lanka," May 29, 2009), http://www.timesonline.co.uk/tol/news/world/asia/article6387782.ece.

53– BBC News Service, "Calls Mount for Sri Lanka Probe," May 31, 2009, h ttp://news.bbc.co.uk/2/hi/south_asia/8075277.stm.

54– AAAS Science and Human Rights Program, "High Resolution Satellite Imagery and the Conflict in Sri Lanka," 12 May 12, 2009, http://shr.aaas.org/geotech/srilanka/srilanka.shtml.

55– AAAS Science and Human Rights Program, "High Resolution Satellite Imagery and the Conflict in Sri Lanka."

56– Jacques Derrida, "Poetics and Politics of Witnessing," trans. Outi Pasanen, in Sovereignties in Question: The Poetics of Paul Celan, eds. Thomas Dutoit and Outi Pasanen (New York: Fordham University Press, 2005), 79.

CONSTRUCTION RITES, MIMETIC RIVALRY, VIOLENCE

BECHIR KENZARI

If violence constantly looms at the horizon of the construction industry, it is because the act of building is centered around conflicts and expectations that involve several competing actors. Architects, engineers, contractors, developers, politicians all partake in the formation of an institution of mimetic desirability, inside of which violence is cultivated. Rooted in a distant antiquity, the unfair treatment of an architect/builder adapts itself to different settings and takes on a multitude of forms, from cold-blooded accusations to cancellations of projects. Whether through public reprimand, blackmail, withdrawal of commissions, professional suspension, or a host of other penalties, the common portrayal of the architect as the ultimate guilty party reveals inherent institutional biases, which cannot be understood without evoking the archaic history of construction rites and the underlying mechanism of rivalry. The notion of the *other*, the rival, is pivotal here as the limit of the architect's powers. As a member of the same building community, the other—politician, engineer, contractor, developer—possesses powers and capacities essentially similar to the architect's. Hence, the other represents a threat.

Therefore, my challenge is to identify the mechanism of rivalry and acknowledge the nature of its architectural origins, with the stress on the victimary supplement. If we are accustomed to thinking about architecture in terms of its coherent, constructive, and technical nature, it is because we have ignored the violent foundation of the profession. Yet, structures of exclusion are defining practices of disciplinary formation. Although the fact of violence against the architect has long been repressed, it can be deduced from myths and rituals once their structures have been unraveled. In particular, the distinct scenario of the surrogate victim, which I will follow throughout the article, can be discerned from texts that offer distorted, fragmentary, or indirect testimony.

I hope that with my effort various contemporary tensions and puzzling questions related to the exercise of architectural profession will receive preliminary, but satisfying explanations. Even though in the last section of this essay I attempt to link some of my findings to contemporary architectural cases, my general intention is to provide a background that could be used as a foundation for future studies on the subject.

1. Rites of Construction and Violence

A reflection upon the reality of violence in relation to architecture must first take into account and come to terms with the history of the rites of construction. According to traditional theories of sacrifice, societies and groups that performed rites of construction originally immolated human beings and buried them in the foundations of buildings. These rites were performed either to propitiate the spirit of the soil that the building operations were about to harm or to guarantee the stability and safety of the future construction. With time, human offerings were substituted by animals and objects.

This practice is confirmed in several places. In analyzing the origins of the habit of burying shadows in the foundations of buildings, James Frazer notes that in modern Greece, when the foundation of a new building is being laid, it is the custom to kill a cock, a ram, or a lamb, and to let its blood flow on the foundation stone, under which the animal is afterwards buried. The object of the sacrifice is to give strength and stability to the edifice. Sometimes, however, instead of killing an animal, the builder entices a man to the foundation stone, secretly measures his body, a part of it, or his shadow, and then buries the measure under the foundation stone. It is believed that the man will die within a year. This custom is evidently a substitute for the old practice of immuring a living person in the walls or under the foundation stone of a new building in order to give it strength and durability, and guard it against the intrusion of ghosts and enemies that may otherwise haunt the place.[1]

In much the same way, in *Sacrifice: Its Nature and Functions*, Henri Hubert and Marcel Mauss note that in the building sacrifice, one sets out to create a spirit who will be the guardian of the house, altar, or town. Therefore, rites of attribution are developed. The importance of the victim (whose skull is walled up) depends on whether the building is to be a temple, a town, or a simple house. The object of the sacrifice is either to conjure up a protecting spirit or to propitiate the spirit of the soil that the building operations are about to disturb. Depending on the situation, the color of the victim varies: it is, for example, black, if the spirit of the earth has to be propitiated, or white, if a favorable spirit is to be created.[2]

In the article "The Rites of Construction According to the Popular Poetry of Eastern Europe," Lazar Sainéan writes that immuring a human being inside the foundation of a city, a bridge, a tower, or any other edifice was a widespread practice in the ancient world and a ritual that has survived from even more remote times.[3] Sainéan notes that for a long time, it was believed that to reinforce any building, a living human being had to be walled up inside its foundations. This notion was most likely generated by the irresistible tendency to bestow an own life and sensibility upon nature, based on the rationale that all physical phenomena and things of this world were endowed with a soul of their own. The earth, for example, is not an inert and raw mass. It is the residence of auspicious and malicious spirits, which either protect or destroy the deeds and works of the mortals. Any building on this earth is, therefore, an infringement upon the domain of the spirits. A compensation and expiation are due if their territory is violated. It is to appease the spirits' resentment that a human would be offered. The victim serves to bridge the gap between nature and culture.[4]

Such a point of view raises a question relatively ignored in the anthropology of construction rites—namely, whether such sacrificial acts might not have been disguised forms of criminal violence. Also: were the sacrificers themselves aware of a violent dimension in the performance of their rituals? To answer this question, it might be useful to take a few examples. In sacrificial practices involving the immolation of human beings, the Greek *Bouphonia* (the festival of killing the ox), as presented by Hubert and Mauss, all those who had taken part in the sacrifice were called to the Prytaneion, where religious ceremonies were held. There, they threw the blame upon each other, and the knife used to kill the victim was condemned and thrown into the sea. The purification resembled the expiation of a criminal act.[5] As George Hersey maintains, whether or not animal sacrifices reenacted human ones, there was clearly the sense among the worshippers that blood sacrifice was a crime of some sort. "Priests who sacrificed animals could be tried for doing so, even though, presumably, they had simply fulfilled their religious duties. Sometimes even the murder weapon itself was convicted. This explains why an early Christian convert from Paganism like Clement of Alexandria could claim that pagan religion consisted of 'disguised murders and burials.'"[6] The fact that some rituals prescribed libations and expiations while the victim was being led to the place of slaughter and that excuses were being made for the act that was about to be carried out, suggests that violence did play a role in sacrifices. The reconstruction of the victim on the alter could be seen as a refutation of the murder, "or better still could suggest that, thus reconstituted and set in a holy place, it was reborn as an immortal."[7] Hence, the cruelty depicted by architectural shaping and ornament as a mimetic abandonment of the original myth of sacrificial practices is also to be stressed. Like Greek tragedies, architectural ornaments tend to restore architectural violence to its mythological origins. The example of the Condor Sacrificial Stone in Machu Picchu is a pertinent case. Not only does the sacrificial stone contain groves for draining a victim's blood, but the chamber that is located between the "wings of the condor" has carved groves too, presumably, in order to direct the flowing blood of the victim into the pit (figure 1).

Of course, there are rare cases where the sacrifice is not concealed, but celebrated in the open. As Denis Hollier—commenting on Bataille's article "L'Amérique disparue" ("Extinct America")—reports, the world of the Aztecs is the model of a society that does not restrain the sacrifice that shapes its life. Transient, and at the peak of its glory and power, this society disregarded the need to put in place the institutional structures that would have sheltered its future, but offered itself to extinction as carelessly as it sacrificed its victims, when Cortez's army landed in Mexico. "It presents the only image of society based upon death and faithful to this basis to such an extent that it was somehow powerless and died out. The pyramids it left behind were not used to disguise death but to exhibit before the eyes of its people the spectacle of the death of the sacrificial victim ... Inca imperialism, on the contrary, was a civilization of *hidden* death. Victims were strangled deep within the temples, whereas the Aztecs turned their sacrifice into a bloody spectacle."[8]

If we add all this up, we can state that as a rule, the city is a dissimulated graveyard. Lying underneath the perceptible layers of urban consciousness, the city's double (the original sacrifices) is a reminder of an anxiety that must have been constantly appeased by the continuous offering of scapegoats, as it was the case, for example, in ancient

Figure 1. Machu Picchu, Condor Sacrificial Stone. Photo by the author.

Carthage where infants were presumably offered to Moloch.[9] Built on top of this buried and repressed reality, cities function as places in which the originary violence has been carefully concealed. In the poetic language of the great tenth-century poet Al-Maārri, the whole earth is nothing, but a graveyard: "Friend, behold, this earth is nothing but the bodies of our ancestors on which we should carefully tread!"

2. Rivalry, Violence and the Built Environment

> Let us also review these sacrificial stones, which constitute the foundational site of the ancient city. These stones point to lynching stories badly dissimulated.
> R. Girard, *Des Choses Cachées Depuis la Fondation du Monde*, 231

There are also several legends and anecdotes involving violence, related to the foundation of cities, that point to an underlying mechanism of rivalry and revenge. In these stories, the following pattern can be identified: two parties involved in the construction process compete to assert one design or building's supremacy over the other. The competition eventually leads to the death of one party: an architect, master mason, or city founder. As a consequence of the antagonistic relationships that characterize the shaping of the built environment, the architect, the builder becomes a scapegoat—that is, an innocent victim who is blamed for a specific accident/misfortune to divert attention from real causes.

This pattern is in line with René Girard's victimary anthropology, and, especially, his thesis on the relation of violence to mimetic desire. As set out in *Violence and the Sacred*, the subject and the rival desire the very same object, and the struggle for primacy leads to violence. The rivalry does not arise from the fortuitous convergence of two desires on a single object, though: the subject desires the object because the rival desires it. By desiring an object, the rival alerts the subject to the desirability of the object. Thus, the rival serves as a model for the subject, not only regarding such secondary matters as style and opinions, but also, more essentially, regarding desires. The mimetic confluence of desires on the same object makes the object dangerous to appropriate.[10]

Conflictual implications of the ancient notion of mimesis have not yet been clearly analyzed in architectural terms. Yet, architectural desire is essentially mimetic, in the sense that by desiring a project, an architectural rival alerts the competing subject (a contractor, developer, ruler) to the desirability of that project. Because of the competitive nature of the building industry, architects, contractors, developers, planners, and politicians participate in the formation of the institution of mimetic desirability inside of which violence is nurtured. The exclusion of the architectural other, the rival, is a natural consequence of the appetite that takes on several manifestations and uses different pretexts to legitimatize itself through the scapegoating mechanism.

It is possible to examine the notion of rivalry and present it as a source of an essential philosophical concern with otherness and finitude. Since rivalry is typical of a way of life characterized by awareness of competition and the ever-present possibility of violence, it has also been articulated in philosophical categories, notably in the thought of Descartes and Hobbes.

In Descartes's philosophy of doubt, the existence of the other manifests itself primarily as a frightening devil (*malin génie*), whose power is beyond the reach of all powers. The prospect of a violent struggle with this other suppresses any pressing desire to increase one's influence and suspends all illusory thinking associated with that impulse. The evil demon is depicted as clever and deceitful as he is powerful, and has directed all his efforts to deception and falsehood.[11] As Piotr Hoffman has noted, Descartes's evil demon, whose threatening presence casts into doubt all of one's beliefs and certainties, is, in fact, "the personification of the human threats confronting an individual in an environment of violence."[12]

The same could be said of Hobbes's thesis on the state of war, when a man's power involves an essential comparison with the power of others. Hobbes holds that all individuals are by nature equal, and this equality produces a hope of attaining one's goals. Since every individual seeks his/her own conservation and pleasure, the result is competition and mistrust of others. "[T]herefore, if any two men desire the same thing, which nevertheless they cannot both enjoy, they become enemies; and in the way to their end, which is principally their own conservation, and sometimes their delectation only, endeavor to destroy or subdue one another."[13] As expounded in the *Leviathan*, the state of nature is fraught with divisive struggle. Hence, until all individuals live under a common power, they remain in a state of war with one another.[14]

To sum up, occlusions, aggressions, and exclusions to which architects are subjected correspond to the destiny of a generic victim—any figure whose fate is determined by the aggressive conduct of a competing other. In what follows, I attempt to manifest this thesis in a few iconic cases, significance of which resides in their applicability that extends far beyond episodic, and which, therefore, can be defined as types.

2.1 Fratricide/Filicide

The first founder of the earthly city, then, was a fratricide.
Augustine, *The City of God*

To read architecture through the prism of mimetic rivalry and all its violent consequences is to unearth aspects of architectural discourse that are often kept in the background. Such unearthing should be first undertaken in the foundational violence, which brings into play essential forms of human rivalry, such as sibling rivalry. Although fraternal relationship is instinctively regarded as affectionate, mythological, historical, and literary examples tell a different story. In the famous legend of Romulus and Remus, Remus is killed by his brother, Romulus, under the pretext that the first mocked the second when they were constructing the city walls. Yet, a deeper motive can be detected: since Romulus desired to be the sole ruler of the new city, he had to eliminate his brother under some pretext. Rivalry was thus overshadowed by an insult. The story of Romulus and Remus is a typical instance of the mythical struggle between brothers, like the one between Cain and Abel, noted by Augustine in the *City of God*.[15] Following Augustine, Girard also states that the first city was the outcome of a fratricide because it was Cain's son Enoch who built the first city and gave it the name of Enoch.[16]

The frequency of this pattern gives it a ritualized dimension. To account for the relation between the foundation of cities and fratricide is to stress that desire, precisely because it is mimetic, does not spare even fraternal relations from turning into the most violent encounters. The foundation of Rome, like the foundation of many other cities, revolves around the conception of a space of desire, the setting that is ideal for the emergence of struggles and conflicts. As Jean-Pierre Chevillot pointed out in *Le désir bouc émissaire*, "since desire is mimetic, the city becomes the site of power struggles and, therefore, the site of violence."[17] Although it is possible to speak of the foundation of Rome clearly in terms of rivalry, other cases do not warrant the same degree of clarity because sacrificial success implies an intentional shifting, slippage, and dissimulation. The ethos of rivalry assumed by a violent program is often obscured in a multiplicity of ways, so that in the end, several sacrificial motifs can intermingle in a single story.

Such multilayering can be found in the Biblical story of Abraham's would-be sacrifice of his son. On the one hand, the Bible records the rivalry between Abraham's wives Sarah and Hagar, and alludes to a potential rivalry between Abraham's two sons, Isaac and Ishmael (*Genesis* 21–22).[18] Then, it mentions the episode of Abraham's would-be sacrifice of his son Isaac (*Genesis* 22). The Koran refers to the same story, but does not specify whether it was Isaac or Ishmael who was to be sacrificed (*The Ranks* 100–107). Yet, the Koran also mentions that the *Kaaba* ("House of Abraham," the cube-shaped building in Mecca, which is the most sacred site of Islam) was built by Ishmael and his father Abraham in the Becca (Mecca) valley (*The Cow Chapter* 127).[19] Drawing upon these facts, the rivalry between Isaac and Ishmael could be interpreted anthropologically in several ways. It is either a simple extension of the rivalry between two competing wives, Sarah and Hagar; from this perspective, Abraham would have tried to sacrifice Ishmael to satisfy Sarah's desire, which was to secure the supremacy of her son, Isaac. Or, it could read as the result of a cultural influence: Abraham, who lived for sometime in Haran, was perhaps following the Phoenician custom of offering the first born to Moloch. In the latter account, the building of the *Kaaba* and the story of Abraham's sacrifice of his son would have included the appeasement of the spirit of the site and hence, a human offering.[20] Such interpretation could perhaps shed the light on the habit of the sacrifice of a ram during the yearly *Hajj* (pilgrimage to Mecca). Besides being crucial for the formation of the paternal complex in Islam (where the renunciation of the murder of the son is continuously staged and reenacted), this ritual, performed in Mecca on the third day of the *Hajj*, seems to function as a reminder that the originary would-be sacrifice took place near the "House of Abraham." What the pilgrimage ritual highlights is an original reclamation and communion which consists—among other things—of organizing the recollection of father and son in the same sacred site where the child was almost sacrificed, and which would later become the ultimate seat of holiness in Islam.[21]

2.2 The Fate of Dido, or Self-sacrifice of the Builder

Phoenician Dido rules the growing state,
Who fled from Tyre, to shun her brother's hate.
Great were her wrongs, her story full of fate.
Vergil, *The Aeneid*

The ambivalence regarding the real intentions behind sacrificial acts is characteristic of narratives where the founder of a city is forced to sacrifice himself/herself. The quasi-suicidal death of Queen Dido, the founder of

Carthage, stands as another version of the foundational sacrifice motif. After Dido founded Carthage, Hiarbas, the King of the North African Maxitani, desired to marry her so badly that he threatened to sack the young city if the Queen refused. To make his point clear, he summoned ten Carthaginian deputies to convey his intentions. However, when the deputies met the queen, they lied to her: they informed her that all Hiarbas wanted was to receive a few learned Carthaginians who would be willing to teach the native North Africans the art of writing. In case his demand was refused, he would sack Carthage. On hearing this, Dido reproached them for not sacrificing themselves for the good of their city. The deputies retorted that she too had to put her words into action: they disclosed the real intention of the North African king and encouraged Dido to marry him and sacrifice *herself* for the sake of Carthage. The surprised queen declared that she would venture to where the fate of Carthage resided: she erected a funeral pyre at the gate of the city and immolated several victims, supposedly to appease the spirit of her dead husband before she could entertain a new conjugal union with Hiarbas. Then, however, she climbed the funeral pyre, and before stabbing herself and perishing in the flames, she turned to her people and said, "I now am going to join the soul of my husband."[22] Her act was thus turned into a typical renewal rite as opposed to an organized political plot. The dethronement could be seen as a sort of coronation performed in reverse, as Girard would call it.[23] The queen, a widow and builder of a powerful emerging city, feeling betrayed by her subjects, acted as her own sacrificer, transforming herself through a quasi-religious act into a double of all her enemies.[24]

Such conduct is not dissimilar from architects "sacrificing" themselves in response to injuries inflicted on them by the public, other professionals, or politicians. The urge to avoid the worst violence leads to injuring one's own self instead. Because the builder cannot defend himself/herself and because there can be no denunciation of institutional violence without a minimal payback to the injured party, the only way to resist violence is to choose a less violent violence. Self-injury (rather than institutional violence) is what this peculiar economy of violence demands. To prove its innocence, the institution turns the sacrifice into the expression of the victim's guilt, depression, and his/her professional incapacity.

The story of Dido is a typical illustration of this pattern, but the history of architecture abounds with other, more recent examples. The case of Francesco Borromini (1599–1667) is particularly interesting. Although historians recount the rivalry between him and Bernini (1598–1680), the rivalry exacerbated by difficulties at St. Peter's Basilica and the Palazzo

Barberini in Rome, where Borromini worked under Bernini from 1629 to 1632, they have not called our attention to the *real* cause(s) that led to Borromini's death. Yet, the way Borromini died is quite known: in a fit of personal and professional despair, he committed suicide in 1667 by throwing himself on a ceremonial sword, and lingered in excruciating pain for twenty-four hours before dying. To tentatively explain the possible causes of this desperate act, historians have stressed the architect's frustration with not getting enough work, his difficult temperament, his constant arguments with patrons, his melancholy, and so on. A typical account is provided by Jake Morrissey in *The Genius in the Design: Bernini, Borromini, and the Rivalry That Transformed Rome*:

> It was in his sestiere, in the house where he lived, soberly and alone, that Borromini died early on the morning of August 3, 1667. His suicide seemed sudden – impetuous and unpremeditated. But Borromini had taken the first steps toward it years before, during the final, dispiriting phase of his career. A frustrating series of unfinished projects had bedeviled his for nearly a decade. In 1657, as Bernini was working on the breathtaking colonnades in St. Peter's Square and creating the Cathedra Petri, Borromini was embroiled in increasingly heated arguments with his patrons. He quarreled with the Pamphili, one of Rome's preeminent papal families, over the church of Sant'Agnese in Agone, which was to be the centerpiece of the clan's ambitious rebuilding campaign for the Piazza Navona. The conflict became so acrimonious that Borromini quit the building site in a misguided attempt to force the family to see things his way. The tactic backfired. Rather than compelling Prince Camillo Pamphili, the nephew of Pope Innocent X, Borromini's former papal patron, to see his error and apologize, it incited his dismissal."[25]

By seeking psychological and individual motives of the suicide, historians—intentionally or not—have overlooked the possibility that it had been effected by social and professional forces, and that without these forces the architect's death could have been avoided. The suggestion that Borromini's self-murder was essentially a personal decision brushes off the fact that his act could have been the immediate response to injuries inflicted by his rivals (Bernini and/or the patrons.) Since conceivably Borromini was unable to defend himself against institutional violence, he chose self-sacrifice. My explanation adheres to a coherent logic: the incapacity to face institutional violence can lead to fatal self-injury. Suicide becomes a form of self-sacrifice, the purpose of which is not to destroy the self, as much as to denounce institutional violence and to point to the reasons that affected the desire to die. The self-immolation of Mohamed Bouazizi in the recent Tunisian uprising confirms such reading: in protest against the harassment and humiliation that had been continuously inflicted on him by a municipal official and her aides, Bouazizi set himself on fire.[26]

2.3 The Reward of the Builder

The Lakhmites tribe rewarded me in the same way they rewarded
Sinimmar; and Sinimmar was an innocent man.
Al-Mutalammis (Pre-Islamic poet)

The fragile relation between a ruler and an architect is loaden with contradictions. The strategy of the ruler is to keep the architect both included and excluded, both present and absent, both recognized and ignored. The ruler may sometimes need to violently eliminate the architect as a preventive measure, particularly when the latter's design mission is completed. Within the strategic logic of authority, such extreme scenario prevents the architect's expertise from being used by other rival rulers. The ruler aims to silence and dissolve the ultimate seat of the architect's ingenuity: the body. By inflicting pain on the body of the builder, the ruler tries to violate the victim's creative talents.

Such a scenario is played out in many legends. As narrated by Arab chroniclers, the proverbial "Reward of Sinimmar" stands for the ill fate of the Greek architect Sinimmar (or Simeon) who, upon the completion of the building of the Khaournaq Palace in Hira in Southern Iraq in the sixth century CE, was killed by his patron Noman Ben Imroul'Qais.[27] In one version of the legend, Noman pushed Sinimmar from the top of the palace to make sure that the latter would not offer his expertise to other rival kings. Other versions give different reasons for this gross ingratitude. Supposedly, when Sinimmar completed his masterpiece, he commented: "Had I been paid generously and treated nicely, I would have been able to build a better palace, a palace which would follow the movement of the sun in its gravitation!" The king then asked: "So you were capable of building a better structure, but you didn't?" When the architect replied affirmatively, the king gave the order to his guards to push Sinimmar from the top of the palace.[28]

The same pattern is found in the legend of Manole, also known as the story of the *Monastery of Arges*. A wealthy Wallachian prince, *Negrou Voda* (Black Prince), decided to build a monastery. Once the site was selected, the masons, led by the master builder Manole, started erecting the walls. However, whenever they approached the top, the walls collapsed. Trying to solve this mystery, they decided to offer a sacrifice to appease the spirit of the land. They agreed that the first human who appeared in the morning would be immolated. It happened that it was Manole's wife, who brought breakfast to her husband. The heart-broken Manole had to keep his vow, and so immured his own wife alive within the monastery walls. The spirit of the site was thus appeased. Once the project was completed, the prince asked the master builder whether he was capable of building a better monastery. Manole replied positively. Feeling betrayed, the prince ordered the murder of the master builder and his assistants. In another version, the prince, who did not wish to see Manole build monasteries for rival princes, ordered the scaffolding to be removed while the masons were still working on the roof. Stranded at the top, master builder made a pair of wings in order to escape, but he crashed to the ground and perished instantly.[29]

René Basset tells of a similar legend in Russia and in Romania. Ivan III Vasilievitch plucked the eyes of the Polish architect who built the Ivangorod Fortress in Livonia around 1492, so that no similar structure would be built. The same legend was later applied to Ivan IV the Terrible, who in a similar way punished the architect who built the Vasili Blajennyi church when Kazan was taken in 1554. In one version of the story, the king plucked the eyes of the Italian architect. In the second, the architect was asked if he was able to design a more beautiful church than the one he had just completed. When he replied yes, the king ordered his head chopped off.[30] The legend became so popular that it inspired authors, such as Ismail Kadare and Marguerite Yourcenar, to compose fictional interpretations of it.[31]

The ruler often assumes the architect's role and behaves as his/her double. As a surrogate "builder," the ruler appropriates the essence of the architect's creative prerogatives, which is perhaps why the entire history of architecture is crowded with names of kings and princes who assumed credit for buildings as their due. Inscriptions commemorate primarily the patron or the official who commissioned or supervised the work, and only secondarily the architect. Hence, the names of architects who conceived some of the most celebrated structures (from the Ziggurat of Ur, to the Temple of Jerusalem, to the great mosque of Cordoba) are unknown.

When the role of the architect is assumed by the ruler, both parties enter into a relation that puts the issue of authorship into question. The architect, the one who actually designs and conducts the building operation, is bound from the start to a fate that denies him/her the possibility of expressing anything, but the commissioner's architectural fantasies. Inevitably, any transgression is to trigger a vindictive mechanism. The story of Apollodorous of Damascus is revealing.[32] In his *Roman History*, Dio tells that Apollodorous, who had built a lot for Trajan, was involved in a dispute with the young Hadrian, who was an amateur architect. Hadrian was told by Apollodorous to "go away and draw [his] pumpkins. For [he did]n't understand these matters." Hadrian vowed revenge. When he became an emperor and started building the great temple of Venus, he sent Apollodorous the plans to show him that the latter's services were not necessary. Renowned for his free speech, Apollodorous stated bluntly and with a sneer that: (1) the temple should have been built on high ground and that the earth should have been excavated beneath it to make it stand out on the Via Sacra. In this way, the basement cavities could house the machines for the theatre (apparently the Coliseum), which could be "assembled and observed" and brought on stage "unforeseen." (2) The statues of the goddesses were too high for their cellae. As designed by Hadrian, the goddesses could not "get up and go out." When the emperor became aware of his mistakes reading these critical remarks and realized that they could no longer be fixed, he let out his anger and grief by putting Apollodorous to death.[33]

Like a modern immigrant with a constant drive to succeed, Apollodorous was both a foreigner in Rome and a pioneer in the most up-to-date disciplines. He devoted his entire life to work and achievement, and had therefore become the ideal type of man who could be expulsed from the city or killed whenever his services were no longer needed.

3. Contemporary Examples

Sacrifice begins with work.
Julia Kriesteva, *Strangers to Ourselves*

The ambiguous relation between architects and rulers (politicians, patrons, or clients) is always concerned with the supremacy of the latter over the former. This is clear also in contemporary examples. On Sunday, May 23, 2004, a portion of the roof of the new Terminal 2E at the Charles de Gaulle International Airport gave way, killing four people. For several weeks newspapers in France speculated on the reasons of the collapse and the person(s) responsible for it. In their descriptions of the elliptical shell made of concrete, glass, and steel that was the main feature of the terminal's "ultramodern" and "futuristic" design, many journalists implied that the designer, the French architect Paul Andreu, was the primary culprit.[34] The architect was categorical, however, and declared: "I don't think I made a mistake."[35] Le Monde then wrote, "L'architecte ne pense pas avoir fait d'erreur." (The architect doesn't think he made a mistake.)[36] A few days later, in fact, French officials speculated that the contractors were to blame.[37]

While facing institutional injustice, architects often act individually and withdraw from the work arena altogether. Such reaction, which is not completely non-violent, involves—to use Walter Benjamin's expression—an "estrangement" from the sphere of the employer.[38] It is both an avoidance of service and an escape from the violence indirectly exercised by the client. Although this does not constitute a strike in the proper sense of the word, it is still a reaction to abuse. Architects are organized in professional unions, but these unions rarely consider activism as a way to defend the profession against exploitation. When, for example, the conservative Australian Liberal and Country Party decided in 1965 to stoke controversy around the Sydney Opera House, the architect Joern Utzon withdrew from the project after he had been blamed for just about everything: from cost increases to delays and construction problems. As Bent Flyvbjerg argues, Utzon fell victim to a politically lowballed construction budget, which eventually resulted in a cost overrun of 1,400 percent. According to Flyvbjerg, the real cost of the Sydney Opera House has more than just a monetary value, as "[t]he real loss in the Sydney Opera House project is not the huge cost overrun in itself. It is that the overrun and the controversy it created kept Utzon from building more masterpieces."[39] A similar scenario repeated itself when Johan Otto von Spreckelsen backed out of the Grande Arche de la Défense project in Paris before its completion, apparently depressed by red tape and bureaucratic pressure. The architect resigned on July 1986 and ratified the transfer of all his architectural responsibilities to his French associate. La Grande Arche was eventually inaugurated in 1989, two years after von Spreckelsen's premature death.

The tendency to blame the architect whenever something goes wrong in the shaping of the built environment is an old custom. With roots in a distant antiquity, the unfair treatment of the builder can adapt itself to different settings and be carried out under a multitude of pretexts, from cold-blooded accusations to cancellation of an architectural project itself. Whether through public reprimand, blackmail, cancellation of commissions, professional suspension, or a host of other penalties, the portrayal of an architect as the ultimate guilty party works against any sustained image of justice and reveals inherent institutional biases. As Girard pointed out, despite its appearance, the judicial system remains inherently violent and vengeful. "As soon the judicial system gains supremacy, its machinery disappears from sight. Like sacrifice, it conceals—even as it also reveals—its resemblance to vengeance, differing only in that it is not self-perpetuating and its decisions discourage reprisals."[40] While acknowledging the differences—both functional and mythical—between vengeance, sacrifice, and legal punishment, it is important—Girard stresses—to recognize their fundamental identity. Because these three institutions are essentially the same, they tend to adopt the same types of violent responses in times of crisis. Simultaneously, as shown below, the strategies adopted to stigmatize the architect are paralleled by an effort to elevate the institutional party above all suspicions of violence and endow it with a tranquil serenity.

> On September 8, 1962, at 8.30 a.m., I was standing on the eaves of the mansard between the bedroom window and the bathroom. I had tied a double rope to the radiator near the sink. I had woven it myself, and then smeared it to make its color match that of the roof tiles, but the rope proved not to be long enough, because of the knots that had reduced its length. We often think of all the details, and then, at the last moment we discover some basic oversights... The intertwined strips stretched between the radiator and the balcony allowed me to drop the main part of the rope straight down onto the drainpipe. A man was whistling to himself down below in the garden. I was calm. I was weighing less than fifty kilograms at that time, clothes included. The maneuver would have been acrobatic. "I am occupying a high position," I thought, and a smile came spontaneously to my lips. I suddenly felt exhausted, after so many days of waiting and so many injections. I had spent seventeen months of immobility, moving only from my bed to my sofa and from my sofa to the bathroom, walking on crutches.
> F. Pouillon, Mémoires[41]

Figure 2. Point-du-Jour: view of the courtyard with the pool and the sculpture by François Stahly. Courtesy Mary Johnson.

Figure 3. Point-du-Jour: courtyard with pool. Courtesy Mary Johnson.

These words, describing the escape from a clinic where he was admitted in 1962, begin the *Mémoires* of Fernand Pouillon (1912–1986), an architect whose considerable architectural gifts have been clouded by the myth of a scandal. For a long time, Pouillon's name was known to the French public in connection to the bankruptcy of the CNL (Comptoir National du Logement), a housing development firm set up by the architect in 1955 to design and market housing operations in the Parisian region. Among the major projects designed was the Point-du-Jour residential complex (2,500 housing units), at Boulogne-Billancourt, in the affluent western part of Paris. During the marketing of the Point-du-Jour, the CNL was declared insolvent (figures 2 and 3). Pouillon, in an effort to save the operation, sold all his properties, and generously and willingly paid his creditors back. However, 1,700 would-be owners, encouraged by rumors and a fierce press campaign, took the case to court. The descriptions of Pouillon as "the man with a white tuxedo and lace cuffs" and "the man nicely dressed [who] is in fact an opulent crook," began to appear in the newspapers.[42] The court estimated that the deficit of the operation at the time of the bankruptcy, at the beginning of 1961, was around one and a half billion francs. According to the accusation, these sums were lost in the disastrous and felonious operations that deviated from the elementary rules of commercial ethics. Pouillon, the major actor, was accused of having violated the principles governing the architectural profession. On March 5, 1961, he was arrested and incarcerated in La Santé jail. On September 23, 1961, his name was crossed off the list of the Architects' Union, apparently under pressure from the Construction Minister.[43]

Suffering from lung problems, Pouillon was next sent to the Fresnes infirmary. On April 29, 1961, he was committed to a clinic on Rue d'Alleray and transferred to a psychiatric clinic in Ville-d'Avray in July. He was locked in a room on the third floor, a space usually reserved for patients suffering from agitated confusion. From this clinic, after he had lost hope for a fair trial, he escaped on the night of September 8/9, 1962. He secretly moved to Italy/Switzerland where he sojourned for some time. The case opened on May 2, 1963, before the Criminal Court of La Seine in the absence of the main accused, who was still on the run. However, on May 14, 1963, Pouillon returned to Paris and made a dramatic appearance at a second trial involving him and his business associates. In the court he declared that he came to apologize and to explain to the "victims" of the ruined CNL that it was to them that he wished to offer his own self-critique. He explained that he was ruined, in bad health, and that he feared for his life. He gave his speech, depicting the whole story as

Figures 4 and 5. Climat de France, Oued Koreiche, Algiers. Courtesy Seif Khiati.

"an affair of men" that had nothing to do with commercial law. He also stated that he truly believed in the role of the architect and admitted that he made enemies only because of his successes as both an architect and developer. He strongly argued that the French architectural code of practice was unfair because it kept architects away from their traditional role as builders and acknowledged that he had challenged this code and run the risk of turning into an outlaw. He also claimed that, as far as he was concerned, he was an innocent man, a victim who gave up his fortune to save the CNL even before the investigation began.

The 11th Criminal Court made its ruling on July 13, 1963 (*Le Monde* commented that none of the defense's arguments was taken into account). Fernand Pouillon, sick and frail, was brought to court lying on his stretcher. Like all the other accused, the only thing that was mentioned in his favor was the huge sums of money he paid back after the bankruptcy, a fact that helped to reduce the four-year jail sentence to three. Months passed. In February 1964, doctors declared that the architect's health was not compatible with a penitentiary regime. At first the Paris investigating magistrate rejected the request that the architect be placed on parole, but it was granted on February 20, 1964. Pouillon had already served seven months of the three-year sentence and had written two books in jail: *Pierres Sauvages* and *Mémoires*. When he was finally freed on February 25, 1965, he moved to Algiers, familiar to him since he had spent some time there in the early 1950s, where he designed three major projects: Diar-Es-Saada, Diar-el-Mahçoul, and Climat-de-France (figures 4 and 5). From 1965 to 1985 the newly independent government entrusted him with the construction of more than thirty hotels for the Ministry of Tourism.

Pouillon was eventually granted amnesty in June 1971 under the government of Georges Pompidou, according to Article 12 of the June 1969 law, related to persons who distinguished themselves in the cultural and scientific fields. The first international recognition of the architect's talent and significance came late in 1982, when the Venice Biennale paid him homage on the occasion of the second international architecture exhibition (*Architettura nei paesi islamici*). Pouillon eventually returned to France in 1985, where he died on July 24, 1986, at the age of 74.[44]

Today we know the reasons behind the incarceration of the unfortunate architect: the fear of politicians and businessmen to see the housing development business fall into the hands of architects. The violence against Pouillon, from media bias to political tactics, from professional disloyalty to physical suffering of the architect, is structured around the rivalry between two sides: architect (*maître d'œuvre*) and developer (*maître d'ouvrage*). As both an architect and adventurous entrepreneur, Pouillon challenged the status quo and wished to reconcile the antagonistic factions of the building act—namely, design, finance, and construction. In his mind, he had the picture of the medieval *maître d'œuvre* who was at the same time designer, entrepreneur, and master builder. As Bernard Marrey noted, Pouillon was "the man who wanted to become three."[45]

Pouillon's frequent reference to this golden age of the *maître d'œuvre* is manifest in his written work. When he reedited *Les pierres sauvages*,[46] he subtitled it *Journal du maître d'œuvre Guillaume Blaz*. Years later in 1973, he even proposed setting up a National Institute of Maîtres d'Œuvre (IMO) and suggested the following idea: "Why don't we set up an Institute where *the maître d'œuvre* would have the chance to have access to more resources, to become alert and to acquire a deeper mind and a finer taste, to have a better control over his work? The *maître d'œuvre* should understand and assimilate everything; he should be able to contribute to the composition of the whole work and its construction details."[47]

Having in mind this ideal of uniting in one single authority both *maître d'œuvre* and *maître d'ouvrage*, Pouillon challenged the very essence of what he judged to be the problem of architecture in France at that time, namely the Architects' Code of Practice, also known as the Guadet Code. Up until the Second World War, the architectural profession had been ruled by the Guadet Code, adopted by the Congrés des Architectes of Bordeaux in 1895. This code defines the activities to which the architect should limit himself/herself—namely, the study and execution of an architectural project. The code stresses, in Article 2, that the architect practices a liberal and not a commercial profession, and that his/her role is incompatible with that of an entrepreneur, industrialist, or provider of building materials. His/her compensation should be limited to honoraria. To avoid any ambiguity, Article 21 of the same code threatens to withdraw the title "architect" from any designer who practices also as an entrepreneur, quantity surveyor, or auditor. Later versions of the code, including Louis Hautecœur's, prohibit the architect from making any profit from his/her involvement in the building industry. Again, his/her only remuneration should be limited to the honorarium (s)he receives from the client.[48]

Pouillon did not see anything wrong with the transgression of the architectural code, however. During his trial, he stressed that Auguste Perret, who enjoyed a great fame, found himself acting both as an architect and contractor, and that everybody found this combination to be a good idea: "Like him, I took some risks in order to lower the building costs. Had I been a crook, I could have been a bit more prudent, and that could have left me with something better than the destitution which I am presently going through."[49] In an article "Architecture et promotion," dedicated to the CNL affair (*Le Monde*, December 13, 1963), Guillaume Gillet analyzed the relation between building and finance. This document is not well known, but it is a valid testimony of architects' feelings at the beginning of the 1960s on the fact that a traditional role was taken away from them by a newcomer: a developer. Gillet writes:

> Since the end of the reconstruction and the consequent depletion of the budgets allocated to it, the architect in France has lived under the regime of the developer, defined as a physical or moral character who raises funds and capitals with the aim of purchasing land and investing in its development. So many mediocrities we deplore today have their roots in this almost-forgotten truth. And yet, we are unfairly blaming architects en bloc for this state of things. In many foreign countries today, architecture and building industry work in tandem, as the case used to be in this country. I therefore understand and agree with the demarche of Pouillon; for it is becoming a habit in France that contractors and property developers organize and sponsor business parties, tend to own expensive cars, yachts and castles. They invite and entertain the same people who are supposed to give them orders. Pouillon wanted to upset this new setting and to show clear signs to the public that the architect could and should be as sumptuous as a general-in-chief.[50]

Beyond the tropes of legal interpretations associated with the case, the imprisonment of Pouillon is a strong reminder that a thorough understanding of the profession of architecture cannot be grasped without an understanding of its origins in the history of construction rites and without an analysis of the mechanism of rivalry that seems to govern its functioning. The story of Pouillon and the painful experiences he went through, from incarceration to exile, prove one more time that the architect remains a vulnerable element within the matrix of the construction industry. Taken in isolation, the story of Pouillon is nothing but a personal drama, but when seen against the backdrop of the continuous relation between architecture and violence, each detail starts to acquire greater significance.

Acknowledgements

I thank the following people for their support and assistance: Marie-Odile Masson, in charge of the Copyrights Department of *Le Monde*, for searching, copying, and sending me the relevant articles published by *Le Monde* in relation to the Pouillon affair; Rachel Méhaignerie, producer at the Kerala Films for facilitating the purchase of the film "Fernand Pouillon, le roman d'un architecte;" Mary Johnson and Seif Khaiti for having taken the photos, respectively, of the Point-du-Jour project in Paris and the Climat de France in Algiers.

Endnotes

1— James George Frazer, *The Golden Bough: A Study in Magic and Religion*. Volume 1, abridged edition (New York: The Macmillan Company, 1923), 191.

2— Henri Hubert and Marcel Mauss, *Sacrifice: Its Nature and Functions* (Chicago: The University of Chicago Press, 1964), 65.

3— Lazare Sainéan, "Les rites de la construction d'après la poésie populaire de l'Europe Orientale," *Revue de l'Histoire des Religions* (Mai/Juin 1902): 371–378.

4— Sainéan notes that the ritual of immuring humans alive was briefly studied by Grimm, Tylor, Liebrecht, Andree, and Sartori.

5— Hubert and Mauss, *Sacrifice, Its Nature and Functions*, 33.

6— George Hersey, *The Lost Meaning of Architecture* (Cambridge, MA: MIT Press, 1992), 18.

7— Hersey, *The Lost Meaning of Architecture*, 18–19.

8— Denis Hollier, *Against Architecture* (Cambridge, MA: MIT Press, 1992), 47–48.

9— In psychoanalysis, the theme of the double has been thoroughly treated by Otto Rank in his essay "The double: A Psychoanalytic Study" (1914) and, of course, by Sigmund Freud in *The Uncanny* (1919).

10— René Girard, *Violence and the Sacred* (Baltimore: The Johns Hopkins University Press, 1979).

11— René Descartes, *Meditations On First Philosophy* (New Jersey: Prentice Hall, 1960), 17–23.

12— Piotr Hoffman, *Violence in Modern Philosophy* (Chicago: The University of Chicago Press, 1989), vii. On the idea that Descartes' "evil demon" is grounded in the notion of complete vulnerability to an "other," see Piotr Hoffman, *Doubt, Time, Violence* (Chicago: The University of Chicago Press, 1987).

13— Thomas Hobbes, *Leviathan: With Selected Variants from the Latin Edition of 1668* (Indianapolis: Hackett Publishing Company, 1994), 75.

14— Frederick Copleston, *A History of Philosophy*, Volume 5 (New York: Image Books, 1959), 32.

15— "The first founder of the earthly city, then, was a fratricide; for overcome by envy, he slew his brother, who was a citizen of the Eternal City and a pilgrim on this earth. It is not to be wondered at, then, that, long afterwards, at the foundation of that city which was to be the capital of the earthly city of which we are speaking, and which was to rule over so many nations, this first example – or, as the Greeks call it, archetype – of crime was mirrored by a kind of image itself. For there also, as one of the Roman poets says in telling of the crime, 'The first walls were wet with a brother's blood.'" Augustine, *The City of God* (Cambridge, UK: Cambridge University Press, 1998), 639–640.

16— *Genesis* 4: "And Cain knew his wife; and she conceived, and bare Enoch; and he built a city, and called the name of the city, after the name of his son, Enoch." See René Girard, *Des Choses Cachées Depuis La Fondation du Monde* (Paris: Adage, 2004), 209. For further details, see also Alain Meurant, "Romulus, un Caïn Romain?" in *La Violence: Représentations et Ritualisations*, ed. Myriam Watthee-Delmotte (Paris: L'Harmattan, 2002), 182–188.

17– Jean-Pierre Chevillot, *Le Désir Bouc Emissaire* (Paris : L'Harmattan, 2004), 55.

18– "And Sarah saw the son of Hagar the Egyptian, which she had born unto Abraham, mocking. Wherefore she said unto Abraham, Cast out this bondwoman and her son; for the son of this bondwoman shall not be heir with my son, even with Isaac. And the thing was very grievous in Abraham's sight because of his son." (*Genesis* 21–22)

19– See Al-Imam Ibn Katheer, *Tafsir Al-Quran* (Commentary of the Koran), volume 4 (Saida and Beirut: Al-Maktaba Al-Asriya, 2002), 3–18. Also note that most Islamic scholars would like to argue that it was Ishmael, the eldest, and not Isaac, who was sacrificed.

20– This ambivalence could partly explain the grief of Abraham and his inability to explain to his son the sacrificial call. In the Bible, the father withheld from his son the real intention of the divine call: "And Isaac spoke unto Abraham his father, and said, My father: and he said, Here am I, my son. And he said, Behold the fire and the wood: but where is the lamb for a burnt offering? And Abraham said, My son, God will provide himself a lamb for a brunt offering" (*Genesis* 22). In the Koran, the intention is conveyed allegorically through a dream: "My son, I dreamt that I was sacrificing you. Tell me what you think. He replied: Father, do as you are bidden. Allah willing, you shall find me faithful" (*The Ranks*).

21– For a psychoanalytic reading of the sacrifice ritual in Islam, see Fethi Benslama, *Psychoanalysis and the Challenge of Islam* (Minneapolis: University of Minnesota Press, 2009). Benslama does not make a direct link between sacrifice and temple-building, however!

22– There are many readings to this story, but what concerns us here is the nature of the sacrificial act itself. See, for example, François Decret, *Carthage ou l'empire de la mer* (Paris: Editions du Seuil, 1995), 50.

23– Girard, *Violence and the Sacred*, 304.

24– On this point, see Serge Lancel, *Carthage* (Tunis: Cérès Editions, 1992), 39–42. It is also legitimate to read in the myth of Dido perishing in the flames the religious obligation of self-sacrifice that the king/queen had to perform, particularly, in times of crisis. This myth apparently preserved its full force until the spring of 146 BCE. When Carthage was assaulted by Scipio Emilianus in 146 BCE,

the wife of the defeated general Hasdrubal and her children jumped from the roof the Esculape (Eschmoun) Temple into the flames (Appian, *Libyca*, 131). With a feminine figure sacrificing herself to protect the city, myth and history converged in order to close the loop.

25– Jake Morrissey, *The Genius in the Design: Bernini, Borromini, and the Rivalry That Transformed Rome* (New York: Harper Perennial, 2006), 4–5.

26– Although this is not a place to analyze the detailed significance of this self-immolation, it is worth-noting that this death has caused controversy among Muslim scholars. Since suicide is forbidden in Islam, some clerics regarded the self-immolation act as a suicide, while others saw in it a heroic sacrifice. While Al-Azhar, the most prestigious religious institution of the Sunni Islam, issued a fatwa (edict) stating that suicide violates Islam even when it is carried out as a social or political protest, the influential Egyptian cleric Yusuf al-Qaradawi spoke sympathetically of Bouazizi. The Arab public in general regards Bouazizi as a heroic martyr who didn't mean to kill himself as much as to protest against injustice and humiliation.

27– René Basset, "Les Alixares de Grenade, et le Chateau de Khaournaq," *Revue Africaine* (1906): 22–36.

28– El Isbahani, *Kitàb el Aghani*, Book 2 (Beirut: Dar Ihya Etturath el Arabi, no date), 423.

29– Sainéan, "Les rites de la construction d'après la poésie populaire de l'Europe Orientale," 371–376.

30– Basset, "Les Alixares de Grenade, et le Chateau de Khaournaq."

31– See Ismail Kadare, *The Three-Arched Bridge* (New York: Arcade Publishing, 2005) and Marguerite Yourcenar, *Oriental Tales* (New York: Farrar Straus Giroux, 1986), 37–51.

32– For a detailed discussion of the story, see Ronald T. Ridley, "The Fate of an architect: Apollodoros of Damascus." *Athenaeum.* Fasc. I-II-1989 (Como: Litographia New Press, 1989): 551–565.

33– Cassius Dio, *Roman History* (London: William Heinemann, 1925-7), 429–433.

34– Christopher Hawthorne, "The Architectural Blame Game," *New York Times*, May 27, 2004, http://www.nytimes.com/2004/05/27/garden/design-notebook-the-architectural-blame-game.html.

35– Andreu declared on TF1 that he did not think he made mistakes in the design of the building, of which one section collapsed on Sunday, May 23. He added he was saddened by the death of the four people.

36– *Le Monde*, May 27, 2004.

37– Hawthorne, "The Architectural Blame Game."

38– Walter Benjamin, "Critique of Violence," in *Reflections* (New York: Scocken Books, 1986), 281.

39– Bent Flyvbjerg, "Design by Deception: The Politics of Megaproject Approval," Harvard Design Magazine 22 (Spring/Summer 2005): 50–59.

40– Girard, *Violence and the Sacred*, 22.

41– See Fernand Pouillon, *Mémoires d'un architecte* (Paris: Editions du Seuil, 1968), 9. Unless otherwise specified, all translations from French to English in this article are the author's.

42– Ibid., 407.

43– Pouillon writes in his Mémoires: "After some reluctance, the Architects' Union crossed my name off on September 23, 1961... I have to salute the president of the Union's Seine Chapter, Gutton, who suggested to the High Court that my name should be only suspended. It was the right time for all these gentlemen from the Union to take their revenge, then they left it to [the minister] Sudreau to carefully take care of my ruin." See Fernand Pouillon, *Mémoires d'un architecte*, 439.

44– The first monograph of Pouillon's work appeared in 1986, the same year the architect died. This book was written by Bernard Félix Dubor, with an avant-propos by Bernard Huet and a preface by Jacques Lucan; see Bernard Félix Dubor, *Fernand Pouillon* (Paris: Electa Moniteur, 1986). In 1996 a conference was organized in Marseille to honor the architect's legacy. Jean-Lucien Bonillo edited a second book highlighting the scope of the architect's oeuvre; see *Fernand Pouillon, architecte méditerranéen*, ed. Jean-Lucien Bonillo (Marseille: Imbernon, 2001). A third book was written by Jacques Lucan; see Jacques Lucan, *Fernand Pouillon, architecte: Pantin, Montrouge, Boulogne-Billancourt, Meudon-la-Forêt* (Paris: Picard/ Editions du Pavillon de l'Arsenal, 2003).

45– Bernard Marrey, "L'Homme qui voulait être trois," in *Les Bâtisseurs de la modernité*, ed. Olivia Barbet-Massin (Paris: Le Moniteur, 2000), 88–95.

46– This book, which won the prix des Deux-Magots and the prix Médicis, was first published in 1964 by the Editions du Seuil.

47– Catherine Sayen, "Maître d'œuvre et maître d'ouvrage," in *Fernand Pouillon: architecte méditerranéen*, 164.

48– On this subject, see Michel Raynaud, "Le métier d'architecte autrement," in *Fernand Pouillon, architecte méditerranéen*, 152–159.

49– François Chaslin, "Le procés Pouillon," in *Fernand Pouillon: architecte méditerranéen*, 189.

50– Chaslin, "Le procés Pouillon," 189.

THE TOPOGRAPHY OF FEAR:

ARCHITECTURE'S FOURTH WALLS AND INSIDE FRAMES

DONALD KUNZE

The late Italian architect and theorist Aldo Rossi famously described the horror of architectural destruction, brought home through the personal witness of the wartime violence:

> Anyone who remembers European cities after the bombings of the last war retains an image of disemboweled houses where, amid the rubble, fragments of familiar places remained standing, with their colors of faded wallpaper, laundry hanging suspended in the air, barking dogs—the untidy intimacy of places. And always we could see the house of our childhood, strangely aged, present in the flux of the city.[1]

The image of a half-room, with doors opening onto canyons and interiors exposed to the unforgiving elements, as well as an equally callous public view, is even more tragic for its comic resemblance to the classic "cut-away" room of a movie set, whose missing fourth wall is occupied by the crew and production equipment, invisible stand-ins for the audience, which will later occupy this torn-away space. The differences are obvious and not so funny. The family of the bombed apartment cannot reoccupy it. They do not act out their lives to a paying public. In contrast, the fourth wall is essential to the happy domestic life of fantasy. The violent tear initiates the most delicate dream. Even when the camera is inserted into the midst of the set, the fourth wall is still present, in the form of the audience's psyche at an imaginary edge, which is also a kind of center.[2]

In a real and geometric sense, the audience is a scandal. The fourth wall is an "inside frame," which converts the inside to the outside. The eye's invasion of the private interior inverts visibility, space, time, and causality; however, the real violence is not of this exception made to "normal" rules, but the revelation that the rupture was there "all the time," a fragile fracture waiting to give way. Such violent ruptures reveal a secret about architectural fear. Fear is not just the breakdown of homeliness; it is a return to a "primal condition." As in the account of the Tower of Babel in *Genesis*, destruction was built in from the start by the presumed ambition of the builders to penetrate the heavens. Doesn't architecture in *general* insure its ruin, when the very actions it takes to defend itself from external threat are run in reverse?[3] This was the clever point of Piranesi's *Carceri*—a prison is perfected the more it becomes a general condition of space itself.[4] The external threat appears at the center, the heart/hearth. In Pascal's infinite sphere, the circumference is nowhere and the center, everywhere. In the prism of architecture, the wall is recursive; the uncanny is inscribed within homeliness. The violence of war and the apparatus of cinema do no more than amplify an original and pervasive "obverse."

The issue of the obverse requires some introduction. In Einstein's First Theory of Relativity, space kept to its Newtonian role. Massive objects could "warp it," allowing light to bend around stars, and so forth. As Slavoj Žižek points out, however, Einstein's breakthrough came when he advanced a stronger position: that "matter itself is nothing but curved space."[5] Einstein's transition from a weak to a strong theory was based not on empirical observation, on a quality of matter that had been previously overlooked—it was an internal reference to meaning itself.

When we consider architecture as experience, we can see that it takes inside framing into account *in advance of* the event that seems to reveal it as a scandal. This is most clearly the case with the issue of security, perhaps the most time-honored component of the architectural formula. Security would seem be the *sine qua non* that makes architecture essential for human life. In the guise of devising a positive solution to "security problems," architecture creates an undoing double.[6] Isn't architecture simply the positive version of the violent response to some central anxiety *provoked* by building? And, isn't this anxiety based on the suspicion that building is taking place *on top* of something that was unlawfully seized?

I will take up these questions in relation to a case where, first of all, building seems unnecessary (although architecture, as "form," is at a maximum); and where, second, the issue of prior occupancy would seem not to apply—the Garden of Eden.

The Biblical Garden of Eden, shown in Athenasius Kircher's version (figure 1), keeps building to a minimum—a wall. Hence, we can regard Eden's situation as a controlled experiment. "Wild nature" extends beyond, but inside God establishes a covenant with Adam and his partner, Eve. Because of this minimal architectural feature, the couple's needs are met; they are secure, at home. Wilderness is held at bay. In a formula written in the style of the British mathematician George Spencer-Brown, the wall may be symbolized as an enclosing distinction.

EDEN | WILDERNESS

In this calculus, Eden could be seen as a special case, a defining intensification of the Wilderness, preserved in its "special-case-ness" by the wall.[7] The wall does not put Eden and the Wilderness at opposite ends of the same line, but rather shows distinction itself to be radically perverse. The exterior is inscribed into the middle through the device of the serpent. The position of the serpent could not be clearer—it occupies the tree of Knowledge of Good and Evil.

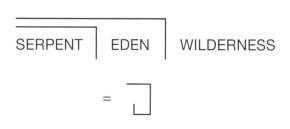

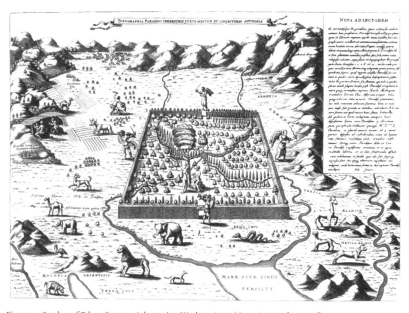

Figure 1. Garden of Eden. Source: Athenasius Kircher, Arca Noe, Amsterdam, 1765. Reproduced with the permission of Rare Books and Manuscripts, Special Collections, the Pennsylvania State University Libraries.

THE TOPOGRAPHY OF FEAR

The serpent did not slip in accidentally or get overlooked during the construction phase. He (?) is the *central defining feature* of paradise, as well as its central exception. Like the Einstein example, the serpent is not how space is bent when you put a man/woman into it but, rather, the "tell" that reveals that space was "man/woman" all along.[8] In the Eden story, the serpent plays the role of the knowledgeable outsider who is in the position to show Eve what the world was like *before* God sheltered Adam! True to multiple ethnological interpretations, the serpent embodies the *form* of distinction, here set up to separate and define Eden and the Wilderness. He is a prototypical Uroboros, both container and contained.

Eden would seem to be new construction, but the presence of the serpent suggests a case of repurposing. God has not successfully evicted his troublesome tenant. The wizened serpent lingers behind, regaling the newlyweds with stories of life in the old days. He invites Eve to admire the tree that he had tended so well before God moved in. Isn't this serpent the prototype of all the subsequent popular culture door-slamming demons in Stephen King novels? Doesn't he remind us that, before God built this subdivision, this was *his* garden? From Eden to Amityville, the matter has involved a failure to recognize and a clear disdain for some significant prior condition. Eden reminds us that gated communities—and space itself—are forgetful by nature. However, the forgetting comes at a price: the fourth wall, obversion.

In Nan Ellin's *Architecture of Fear*, as in most treatments of the subject, the problem of fear is considered to be primarily historical and social.[9] Concentration of capital engenders crimes against property, the discomfort of ethnic minorities, the distinctions that are built into the walls of ghettos. The authors accept the threat-value of what is feared—that our fear is justified. We don't have to, or can't, understand fear as such. Fear is simple: a threat to the good life. In other words, *Carthago delenda est!*— get rid of fear by overpowering its sources. But, when U. S. President Franklin D. Roosevelt asserted that we have nothing to fear but fear itself, he was suggesting that human fear is a self-referential vector of the human condition. Fear finds its objects, and we can easily study these objects with a view to neutralizing them, but fear's power lies in its durable system of circular causality. Thus, fear may be created *ex nihilo* to establish a basis for decisive action; it may begin as an effect and end as a cause. One might say that fear's capacity to move from appearance to reality, predicate to essence, is the consumable by product of fear's self-constructing form.

This is the general case of "self-identity" (A=A), about which Hegel employed his proverbially sharp tongue. "If anyone opens his mouth and promises to state what God is, namely God is—God, expectation is cheated, for what was expected was a *different determination* ... Since only the same thing is repeated, the opposite has happened, *nothing* has emerged ... Identity, instead of being in its own self truth and absolute truth, is consequently the very opposite ... it is the passage beyond itself into the dissolution of itself."[10]

Fear is the reverse of self-destructing identity: it comes out of nowhere and is resilient. Yet, both fear and self-identity involve a *double negation*. For those readers allergic to philosophy, double negation is luckily also the stuff of slapstick. In *City Lights* (1931), a tramp avoids the police by taking a shortcut through a parked limousine. A blind flower girl takes him to be the limo's wealthy owner when he emerges from the limo's door. He plays this part to amuse her, thinking that she must be daft, until he realizes that she is blind. He continues the role of the wealthy patron by, miraculously, finding money for the operation needed to restore her sight. The operation is a success, but the tramp isn't. His friendship with the alcoholic, bipolar millionaire who was his means of philanthropy ends in imprisonment. When the flower girl ultimately sees her benefactor, just released from jail and shabbier than ever, she's repulsed. Acting the part of an "empty signifier," the hard-working tramp has been negated not just as the rich patron he unintentionally impersonated, but as the truly self-sacrificing philanthropist he had become! One doesn't need Hegel to explain Chaplin here; Hegel's point belonged to comedy in the first place.[11] Double negation is the lock of comedy's logic.[12]

Double negation can scare as easily as amuse when architecture shows its obverse as pure violence. In Edgar Allan Poe's "The Masque of the Red Death," the pains taken to insulate the rich revelers from the plague insure the plague's swift revenge, as the refuge turns into an incubator. This economy of inversion points to the legal principle of usufruct: you are allowed to use something without owning it (privation) as long as you don't abuse the privilege (prohibition). Privation (the wall around Eden) involves prohibition (don't eat the fruit). The privation of Poe's castle results in not just death but punishment.[13] The applications of the privation-to-prohibition rule of usufruct to popular culture are based on fear's use of the "inside frame" technique—and are therefore intrinsically architectural. The inside frame is the backed-up toilet, the gushing oil well, the bomb-packed SUV in Times Square. Hell is distributed from the inside out. Disaster is a matter of the short circuit inside the dimensionality that has held apart two antipodes. The entertainment value of the inside frame should not blind us to its technical achievement: the conversion of *distinction* into *content*. Eden's serpent, a glyph of pure distinction, a cipher of the unconscious, speaks. The surplus element, some externality, is inscribed at the heart(h).[14] Its voice is not just acoustic but *acousmatic*: filled with puzzles and contradictions, but also omens and enigmas.[15]

The inside frame materializes what Slavoj Žižek has described as "master signification."[16] A master signifier is a concept established not by empirical observation or social custom but by an inner "logic" that, itself irrational, cannot be refuted. The meaning that results is resistant to criticism because it sustains its identity internally. It comes from nowhere (*hapax legomenon*) and has no logical basis, but is capable of structuring related meanings. For example, the shark of the Stephen Spielberg film, *Jaws* (1975), functions as a Deleuzian "demark," or negative mark, something that stands outside of the natural order. It appears when swimmers are exposed to danger through the selfishness of the local businessmen, who know the risk, but wish to keep the beaches open to sustain their profits. The shark can be read as nature fighting back against humans who encroach on its oceanic domain, also as moral-theological retribution for teenagers having sex in the water. Or, it can be counted as just one more "illegal immigrant" arriving onshore. First, the master signifier appears to summarize/condense a "cluster of effective properties." Second, the process is reversed, and the signifier is the *result of* the properties that call it into being. Third, the process is reversed again so that the effective properties exist, as Fredric Jameson puts it, *because of* the master signifier.[17] The shark "must be destroyed," not just to remove the obvious threat, but to break the tight constellation of meanings that resist penetration. Yet, even this destruction is a part of the impenetrable logic that affirms and sustains the shark as a master signifier.

The Unhomely Home

Anthony Vidler's seminal work on the architectural uncanny argues that the uncanny is central to the entire experience of architecture—not just the fringe cases. Vidler follows Freud's essay closely and brings to bear important contextual elements (the Great War, disruption of the idea of Europe as home), but he underplays Freud's surprisingly Hegelian observation that the *unheimlich* is not simply the conversion of something familiar into something unfamiliar, but a conversion that *retains* the sense of the familiar.[18] This is comparable to Einstein's argument in his Second Theory of Relativity, where curvature is shown to be built in to space itself, not an exception to a naturally uncurved space. As Freud says of the *unheimlich*, something that *ought to have remained a secret* is discovered. It was there all the time. Thanks to a secret agreement to let sleeping dogs lie, it was harmless until we violated the "no trespassing" sign, converting privation to prohibition.

Here, we can go further with the insights of psychoanalysis. Freud identified two additional elements that are key to the uncanny: the themes of optics and the double. It's easy to see how the double is related to Hegel's crisis of self-identity. Inspired by E. T. A. Hoffman's tale "The Sandman," Freud refers the theme of the *Doppelgänger* to a "crisis of the ego." How is the theme of optics related to this? The case at first seems circumstantial. The child Nathanael in "The Sandman" is frightened by night visits made by a lawyer, Coppelius, to his father. Nathanael conceals himself behind a curtain to spy on them as they conduct alchemical experiments using a small hearth concealed in a cabinet. Spying and Coppelius's fluid, mysterious identity are linked from then on. Nathanael connects Coppelius, whose name is Latin for "eye socket," to the story told by his nurse about a Sandman who throws sand in children's eyes to make their eyeballs fall out of their heads to feed the voracious children of the half-moon. Years later, Nathanael is accosted by an itinerate salesman of optical goods, the Italian Coppola, who resembles the sinister lawyer. Coppola has conspired with Professor Spalanzani to construct an automaton, Olimpia. Nathanael catches a glimpse of the beautiful Olimpia sitting at the window of the Professor's apartment and, enchanted, seeks out her company. Olimpia's conversation gets its charm from its empty inconclusiveness; her deep soul is born in her beautiful blank eyes. This effect is akin to the Turing Test's method of proving consciousness. The blank eyes work like Turing's curtain: in their very blankness they appear to embody spiritual depth.[19] When Nathanael witnesses Spalanzani and Coppola dismantle the doll during a violent argument, he suffers a nervous breakdown and must be nursed back to health by his former fiancée and her brother. Just when it seems that he is cured of his obsessions, the trio goes on an outing to the town-hall tower. Nathanael looks out through a telescope and thinks he sees Coppelius in the crowd below. Maddened, he jumps to his death.

The story's combination of optics and the (crisis of) identity is a matter of topology rather than logic. In its rubber-sheet spaces, we can catch a glimpse of Eden, serpent at the center, negating the negation, framing from the inside out. Details return us to the boy behind the curtain, silent witness of hearthside rituals, fearful of losing his sight for stealing such a view—blindness as the cost of knowledge; blindness converted to invisibility; invisibility as the means of dislocation into an everywhere; everywhere reincarnated as nowhere. The sequence of negations and conversions defies Cartesian space and time, but cultivates a more universalizing order based on topology and recursion.

This is enough to turn any cozy retreat into a tomb–trap. Moral: hiding from the gaze of envy never works, because envy is the stuff of invisibility to begin with; the optics of the uncanny works *inside* concealment; and every wall, margin, and hiding place is also (an acousmatic) center. In the famous postwar film anthology of Gingrich stories, *Dead of Night* (1945), directors working with Arturo Cavalcanti constructed what might be regarded as an encyclopedia of uncanny optics and identity issues in cinema.[20] The anthology format of the film not only effects an uncanny Möbius band linkage of dream and reality—the main character has "seen everyone before"—but the country house parodies its own fate by being a place of *unheimlich* storytelling, an "acousmatron."

An architect, Walter Craig, is called out to discuss renovation plans with the owner of a decaying country house, Pilgrim's Farm. His *déja-vu* experience begins as soon as he meets the guests gathered for a weekend house party. He also vaguely recollects that he has done something awful. One of the guests is a psychiatrist, Dr. Van Straaten, a European refugee who refuses to accept the supernatural implications of the guests' stories. Van Straaten tries to correct Craig, but the other guests side with the architect and supply their own personal experiences.[21] Van Straaten parries with psychiatric explanations. Craig realizes his feared catastrophe when he strangles Van Straaten with his necktie.

The guests' tales, true to the Freudian uncanny, involve optics and identity in support of the general themes of the undead, doubles, and time travel. The first is told by a former race-car driver, Hugh Grainger. Recovering from a racing accident in hospital, Grainger rose from his bed at night to uncurtain his window onto an inexplicably day-lit scene. In the courtyard below, he saw a hearse whose carriage-driver nodded to the coffin behind him and advised, "Just room for one inside, sir." After his release from hospital, he was about to board a bus for home, but the conductor was a twin of the hearse-driver. When the conductor also said, "Just room for one inside, sir," its "acousmatic" meaning was clear. Grainger declined. Seconds later, the bus and its passengers crashed down a culvert.

A socialite recounts how she gave her fiancé a mirror that turned out to be haunted by its nineteenth century owner, who, paralyzed and confined to his bedroom after a riding accident, had gone mad and murdered his wife on suspicion of her infidelity. The bedroom's mirror remained faithful to the powerful emotions of this drama and continued to reflect the space where the murder had taken place, transmitting the original owner's jealousy to the new owner until the mirror was smashed.

The psychiatrist is cajoled into telling about his own strange experience, in which the automaton theme of "The Sandman" comes into play. A ventriloquist performing at Chez Beulah, a Paris nightclub, had seemingly lost control of his act. The dummy had "gotten the upper hand" and psychically overcome his master, driven to shoot a colleague in fear that the dummy would abandon him for the more talented rival. Van Straaten reunited the jailed ventriloquist with his dummy to induce a mental cure, but the "dummy personality" again emerged and taunted the ventriloquist to the point when he destroyed the dummy and suffered a complete nervous breakdown. When he "recovered" his first words were, spookily, the acousmatic voice of the dummy.

Dead of Night's coupling of optics and acousmatics is instructive. The haunted mirror works like a magic fourth wall; this fourth wall makes the new owner a dummy of the first, who begins to speak in the voice of the paralyzed jealous husband. The race-car driver's hospital window opens onto a future; but it is the acousmatic meaning of "just room for one inside, sir" that prophecizes death. The ventriloquist's dummy is like a shadow or mirror image asserting a will of its own; but the reversal of egos ends ultimately in a full exchange of voices.

The country house itself combines the optics of its central function, the hearth—whose Latin name is *focus*—and the idea that the Gingrich tales told in succession constitute a *skolion* to invoke dark gods. Throughout the film, the psychiatrist uses his glasses to switch on his critical interventions. So, when his glasses break in the final scene, the architect's nightmare begins in earnest and the *skolion*'s prophecy becomes real. Craig takes off his tie. Van Straaten must be strangled, the streets must be tangled (labyrinth); the sacrifice, made (*templum*); fate's Möbius twist.

Lacan emphasizes that *jouissance* is a "useless margin." And so, we see the essential architecture of the country house, as a setting of ghost storytelling, is the essential center of Craig's circular return to the same nightmare. The country house's displays of stuffed trophies remind us of the Eden theme. The house's marginality is double: its synecdoche of the countryside, a margin of a margin. Its centrality is also doubled by the hearth, a center of a center. The camera pans to the fire to transition the separate episodes, making the center into a margin, a hinge for the voice that is passed from guest to guest. In the practice of the *skolia*, songs sung by the guests in turn around the tables of ancient banquets, each new song was initiated by passing a harp or laurel branch. In *Dead of Night*, the guests offer each other cigarettes to open up their anthology gallery and call ghosts back from Hades. The monogram of this gallery is a labyrinth or, more simply, a circle that returns to the same "empty" gap of *jouissance*, asymbolic in its fictional status, traumatic in its dramatic structure, acousmatic and anamorphic in its techniques and effects. How appropriate that this circle with a gap is also the Cartesian model of the eye, whose breach affords inversion and whose chiasm(s) afford a "transportation," a placelessness, a parallax view (figure 2).

This coupling of optics and motility puts the *unheimlich* into the center of the theory of architecture, just as it should be rightfully restored to the center of Freud's and Lacan's theories of the clinic.[22] Architecture is "permanently uncanny," the building site is still warm from the previous occupant, as household gods (*manes*) or thin serpent, who may be fed at

Figure 2. Odilon Redon (French, 1840–1916), Eye–Balloon, 1878. Charcoal and chalk on colored paper, 16 5/8 x 13 1/8" (42.2 x 33.3 cm). Reproduction courtesy the Museum of Modern Art, New York.

the hearth. The uncanny's secret of "what ought to have remained hidden" is, of course, precisely what we opened the novel to read or came to the cinema to see, set in motion by the chiastic flip that re-temporalizes space in three steps: a gap created by desire; *partial objects* of desire that resist meaning and symbolization; and a reformulation of the infra-thin gap between demand and desire. In the Lacanian "formula" desire = desire of the *Other*, we cannot afford to forget how the Other gets on stage, or by what perversely folded spaces He sustains His voice. He is also It: the Thing that is singular and plural at the same time (since its double both exists and doesn't exist): James Joyce's "twone" (*Finnegans Wake*, also a Möbius band story), the object visible only to the blind, the acousmatic word comprehensible only when whispered, muffled, sung, or screamed.

As in *Dead of Night's* haunted mirror tale, the inside-out, remote-vision eye is anthropologically and theologically tied to the idea of a "previous occupant," where blindness and/or invisibility are frequently involved. In ancient Greek households, ancestral spirits were believed to reside in the family hearth, which had to be shielded from the view of strangers; but it may also have been that it was actually the sight of the ancestors that had to be blinded—to make them speak? The case of Eden is no less complex. The theology of the *Zohar* holds that in order to make room for creation, God contracted, leaving behind a divinely charged negative space.[23] Hence, Eden occupies the ground of a "previous occupant" in the same sense that, in Vergil's *Georgics*, humans are exhorted to take good care of what the gods have left behind in their retreat to Olympus. The space vacated by a prior occupant is still haunted, because the departing gods actually do not know that their emigration has left them neither alive nor dead, but "undead." In other words, the worst case of atheism is realized: God is not dead, He is unconscious.[24] In *Genesis*, there are two undead characters haunting the couple. The usually all-seeing God seems like an anxious ghost when he asks, "Adam, where are you?" Stranger still is the serpent, reduced to a cipher or glyph of the function of the boundary, a talking *temenos*, and his weird, self-fulfilling prophecy.

Beyond the Purloined Letter

The theological idea of a gnostic dimensionality opened up inside ordinary time-space, as *Dead of Night* demonstrates, loses none of its richness when secularized within popular culture. Thus, when Jacques Lacan wished to affirm the scriptures of the Freudian clinic, he turned with profit to Edgar Allan Poe's detective tale, "The Purloined Letter."[25] Lacan personified the stages by which the visible breaks out of its own polarities (visibility/invisibility and sight/blindness) by analyzing the famous story of a stolen letter, found only by the detective who realizes that the letter has been hidden by being left out in the open. Poe is not simply showing how easy it is to overlook the obvious; he sets up a demonstration of how invisibility works within visibility within his own text as well as within his story about a royal intrigue.

In Poe's story, set in Paris, the King, Queen, and Minister find themselves together in a chamber in the palace when a letter potentially compromising to the Queen is delivered. The Queen and Minister recognize the author of the handwritten address, and hence the potential scandal, but the King notices nothing. The Queen would like to retrieve the letter and destroy it; the Minister would like to use it to blackmail the Queen; but neither can act without giving away the very advantage that possession would bestow. At an appropriate moment, however, the Minister is able to remove the letter. The police, working for the Queen, expect it to be expertly hidden and so do not notice that the Minister has left the letter out in the open. The ingenious detective Dupin coolly deduces that the Minister will do just this, visits the Minister, and secures the letter by staging a fake distraction.

This account retells the story of Eden and helps us come to terms with the paradoxical inscription of an inside frame. The letter is concealed by being a radically external object placed in a radically internal spot. If the letter is opened and read, its revelation about external scandals will disrupt the internal order. The letter is the snake that threatens to turn Eden into a wilderness. The letter is so external, in fact, that it cannot be admitted into the field of things that are ordinarily visible. Its hiding place is so internal that it, too, defies visibility by being maximally visible. This crisscross of radical externality and radical internality is, Poe demonstrates, a permanent feature of space: a built-in curvature; not something that, as Einstein would say, is created by the special warping of a powerful gravitational attraction, but a part of the field itself. In this sense, it shows how the fourth wall works by obversion. The letter is a radical outside set into the middle of visibility, but it remains durably invisible. This is not just a magician's trick, the creation of a temporary pocket space, a poché. The letter as an object in the story is a prototype of the way Poe constructed the entire story. In addition to Lacan's analysis of the three kinds of visibility, we may add the literary discovery of Richard Kopley: that Poe saw in the letter a prototype for ciphers that transfer the story's mystery to the unconscious of the reader.[26]

The roles of the King, Queen and Minister, and Dupin can be formalized as three kinds of visibility. Initially, the casual glance (exemplified by the King) incorporates invisibility in a conditioned way. The figure is distinguished from its contextual ground; in this way the King fails to notice the letter. His attention is cultivated disdain: why should he notice this letter or that? The Queen and Minister employ a more sophisticated kind of glance and can see into spaces created by folds and warps, but they themselves must play by the rules of theatrical illusion making, used to surprise audiences through time-honored tricks. This second visibility employs two kinds of reality: what could be called "type one Real," R_1, a commonsense notion of reality as that which metaphorically surrounds/encloses some illusory set-up (as in the "real-world" city streets that surround the theater); and "type two Real," R_2, an internal defect or a breakdown in the middle of visibility, such as paradox or inconsistency, provoking a revision in the idea of what's happening, such as the pocket spaces created by the close-up magician.[27] The relation of R_2 to R_1 is clear in the story of the purloined letter. The letter is a "demark:" out of place, disruptive, an "anxious object"—an R_2 wrinkle in the smooth fabric of reality that has created a trap for the Queen and a compulsory intrigue for the Minister. Understandably, R_2 becomes also the perfect place to hide the damaging letter: a pocket of space invisible even though technically exposed.

The letter that lies at the center of the Queen's anxieties is also the key to her "escape" to R_1, the outside world where she is still the unchallenged, unruffled Queen—but how? R_2, the EXIT sign to the freedom of R_1, runs between Scylla and Charybdis—the King and Minister—and functions as a password required for escape to safety. Dupin guesses that this password has to do with estimating his opponent's mentality, a ploy he describes as key to the popular street game of "odds and evens," also known as Morra. Odds and evens, deployed extensively in Poe's text, becomes the inside frame, the password that is the silent term of the third form of the glance, Dupin's glance. It is an R_2 working at the level of the plot, the space of the story, and the logic of reading itself.

Richard Kopley has shown how Poe inserted this game into the middle of the story by first selecting a central point of exchange—conveniently, the point at which the reward check is handed over to Dupin. From here, the text is divided literally into two parts. The "even" half echoes the "odd" half. Kopley has no interest in Lacan's theory of three glances, nor does he employ any versions of anamorphosis or the inside frame.[28] Nonetheless, his analysis provides the missing link that connects the anxiety management of this Poe story with the issues of architectural fear and violence. It is also the key allowing Lacan's important analysis to return to the cornerstone, the Mirror Stage, where the uncanny of optics and identity are restored to their key roles in critical theory. How?

Poe was a natural-born cipher expert who could work out most substitution codes ("m" for "a" "h" for "b," etc.) in his head.[29] For Poe, the real story occurred in a space created between matching terms. Some pairs are simple echoes ("scrutinized each individual square inch" is mirrored by "scrutinizing with the microscope") and placed as markers to align the two sides of the narrative. Other coordinates are established to reveal a chiasmus ("the poet is one remove from a fool" and "all fools are poets"). Once calibrated, a line-by-line comparison of the two "sides" reveals more provocative pairings. Reference to the classical story of Atreus and Thyestes matches the opening phrase that gives away the construction secret, "It was *an odd evening*" [emphasis mine]. This makes the reader think, in retrospect, about the story's recursive logic in the context of the gruesome menu of the Thyestean Feast.[30] This ancient cannibal dinner seems to be the perfect analog for a self-consuming text.

Kopley has identified the central anamorph, the phonetic palindrome, "card-rack," within whose *poché* the letter was hidden. Poe's reference to Morra and recommendation of a winning strategy (distinguish between the choices of a smart *versus* dumb adversary) constitutes an R_2-style escape for the Queen, Dupin, and the reader. The key phrase, "an odd evening," is both about the literally unusual events and the odd-even mechanism that creates, between two separated pairs, the primary achievement of this fold in space: the creation of a "third eye" in the text, an "organ without a body," shared by Dupin, Poe, and the astute reader—the third eye capable of mobilizing blindness in relation to invisibility.[31]

Despite Kopley's resistance to Lacan as a literary critic, Lacan would have enjoyed Kopley's analysis, since it returns "The Purloined Letter" to the radical center of Lacan's theory of the subject, the Mirror Stage.[32] When the police inspect the Minister's apartment "with a microscope," they are assuming that the trick of concealment casts the letter beyond the margins of visibility. Lacan's point about the gaze being inscribed as the blind spot *inside* visibility suggests that the police should have considered the nature of the gaze itself. Unlike Foucault's idea of the gaze as a magic ray of power, the relation of the gaze to visibility is anamorphic, a function of finding a point of view that is not simply a manipulation of geometric positions, as in the second, Queen-Minister kind of visibility.

Poe aligns this third kind of seeing with a use of the text as an "automaton," a literary computer that thinks for the reader. Whether or not the reader notices the symmetrical placement of twinned phrases and references, the story opens up a dimension of exchange, a light-beam shining between R_2, the internal defect, and R_1, the external escape. The purloined letter is thus both literally and structurally a case of the Lacanian *extimité*—an intimate externality, able to function as a master signifier because of its central dysfunctionality: an inside frame.

The purloined eye, outside of the body, joining the ambiguous emptiness/blindness of the eye with the tradition of the wandering finder of truths, is nothing less than the *psyche*, the soul, and in particular the soul in "the journey within that collapsed dimensionality of Hades, the invisible, the interval 'between the two deaths.'"[33] As in all such journeys, architecture built into the impossible task is required: an extimate connection, outside to inside, the R_2 defect to R_1, escape.[34]

Automaton, *Mon Amour*

The program of the *heimlich*/*unheimlich* is optical and existential. In the crises self-materialized by confrontations with one's double, travel through time, and other devices of the fantastic, the *psyche*-soul wanders, a disembodied eye, between the two deaths. But, what about the figure of the automaton? Was Hoffman's Olimpia just a diversionary episode, something the author could well have done without? Or, is there a telling role played by the automaton in the very formula of optics-identity that constitutes the *unheimlich*? Hoffman's Olimpia plays the part of the Lacanian *objet petit a*, the "object–cause of desire," which refuses to be assimilated by the networks of symbolic order. What is owed within symbolic networks is what can be (th)ought. In contrast, the object of desire is what cannot be given. *Chez* the Turin Test, behind the beautiful blank eyes of Olimpia, a mind is present thanks to the "curtain" that conceals it.

The Aristotelian efficient cause in this case is clearly that Nathanael has projected his thoughts into the blank space behind Olimpia's limpid eyes. However, the matter is not so simple. These are not thoughts Nathanael once had but suppressed until the opportunity arose to credit them to Olimpia. They were "suppressed" retroactively; they had not been lost into the unconscious at some past moment, because they were not possessed in the first place. They were remembered and imagined simultaneously, a case of a *déjà-vu* short circuit or, more philosophically, Platonic *anamnesis*, the view that knowledge is really memory. This is not a simplistic idealism where the perceiver projects content into some objective situation, but an uncovering of the unconscious through anamorphic parallax. In other words, the automaton involves, in place of epistemology, a theory of reception and collective memory that is summarized most effectively in the idea of ventriloquism. The perceiver's/audience's mind is interior-framed into the space veiled by the eyes of the automaton. To be more precise, this inside frame establishes itself at a point *psychically* antipodal to the subject who animates it. This, in my mind, justifies restoring the antique Stoic distinction between *animus* and *anima*.[35] The feminine *anima* is a matrix or screen, a net of relations that, as it widens, loosens the normally tight bonds of causality and temporality.[36] The *animus* is a wedge, a gap, an inside frame whose contents are presented in the negative—at points opposite, in forms mirrored, at times far removed.

The subject-as-audience, *anima*, and the antipodal subject-as-animator, *animus*, of the enigmatic automaton are mediated by "eyes," formed as gaps in a screen/curtain. Yet, once the *unheimlich* is triggered through one of the devices of the fantastic, the screen centralizes an anamorphic-acousmatic object-encounter.[37] As a crisscross of both symbolic and unsymbolizable structures, the screen reproduces the internal acousmatic anamorphosis of the word and idea of the *unheimlich*. The *unheimlich* is not just central to uncanny experiences; it is the key to the inside-out logic of the master signifier, replicated in turn by the three-part visibility defined by Jacques Lacan. In these terms, architecture, defined as "always and already" on top of a site of eviction or retreat, is permanently and radically anamorphic: a screen, an inside frame, the mouth of an uncanny voice.

Carthago Delenda Est!

There are three possible positions for architecture to take *vis à vis* violence. The first is to consider violence as a separate phenomenon and regard architecture as external to it, either promoting violence or providing protection from it. This traditional view, which gives rise to the question of what is architecture's relation to violence, applies to cases such as Sarajevo, where hills surrounding the city's public spaces provided snipers with lines of fire, causing residents to carefully calculate their paths and meeting places according to the risks of being shot. Occupants of the World Trade Center Towers, after the first terrorist attack led by Sheik Omar Abdel Rahman in 1993, took on the liability of the buildings' role as a symbol of U. S. capitalism. In both cases, architecture is dominated by contexts that radically alter the use and significance of elements originally designed to serve other purposes.

The second possible relationship is a generic one, where the kinds of violence created by conditions of overcrowding, exposure to natural disasters (hurricanes, floods, earthquakes), or vulnerability to crime, war, disease, or terror affect the nature of space in general without attaching to specific architectural qualities or elements. When in 2002 the sniper team of Lee Boyd Malvo and John Allen Muhammed struck down, seemingly at random, exposed victims in the Washington D. C. area, it was the space itself that seemed to carry the potential of murder. Such is the case also with airborne disease or toxin, where a threat has indefinite or unpredictable boundaries. In *White Noise*, for example, author Don DeLillo describes a toxic cloud that terrorizes residents of a small college town, Blacksmith.[38] Residents evacuating in long lines of cars pass by towns whose residents are being advised to stay inside. The real fear of poisoned air is eclipsed by the residents' disappointment that the news media are not giving the event enough airtime.

Architecture's move, from seeing fear as "external" (cf. Nan Ellin's anthology, *Architecture of Fear*) to assimilating it as an "intrinsic" quality of all space, mirrors the move from Einstein's first Theory of Relativity to the second, stronger version. Normative space is warped by large masses ("danger") in the first case; in the second, space itself, architectural space included, is rendered dangerous as the boundaries of a threat or actual violence disappear. These two positions correspond to the first two of Lacan's three visibilities and the two concepts of the Real—internal defect, R_2, and escape to some higher-order reality, R_1. The King is easily duped by the boundaries between visible and invisible; his relation to R_2 is manipulated. The Queen and Minister take in everything, but—like the residents of Blacksmith—are limited in their ability to act effectively. They can manipulate visibility/invisibility but do not hold the key to the cipher that links them. The Minister makes use of the indefinite (perceiver-generated) boundaries of visibility/invisibility and exposes the letter so that it is not noticed, but the "escape option," R_1, rests with Dupin's realization of the "anamorphic condition" lying between the two versions of the letter, the letter as visible/visible and the letter as exposed/invisible. This is the same logic that Poe uses to structure the literal letters of the story, matched by line counts and theme references. It is indeed an "odd evening."

In keeping with the logic of this anamorphic-acousmatic middle—which simultaneously destroys and preserves—Karlheinz Stockhausen astutely observed that the destruction of the World Trade Center Towers was a "perfect esthetic event."[39] True to the idea of the Lacanian Real, synonymous with the obsessive "return to/of the Real," the moment of destruction was obsessively replayed. Repetition, as a means of establishing the anamorphic R_2 fold of space that had brought the airliners into the center of the two towers, was enacted on a massive public scale, with full awareness of its status as a trauma. The Trade Towers in their manner and moment of destruction resembled nothing more than the classic pre-Breughel image of the Tower of Babel—a lower structure intact, upper stories consumed in a cloud. Where Brueghel emphasized incompletion over destruction, earlier emblems had provided the bridge between the Hebrew myth and the more universal *mons delectus* derived from the Babylonian ziggurat, whose top was not unfinished, but rather invisible, because of its direct contact with the divine. Concealed within a fold of space, only those whose blindness could overlook this invisibility could see the pinnacle as purely performative.

Violence in this case is akin to the literary device of *anagnorisis*, the discovery scene, where the truth becomes evident, but remains beyond commentary or any direct symbolic recognition. In Sophocles' *Œdipus Rex*, the audience has delayed their recognition of the fearful symmetry (i.e. anamorphosis) lying behind Œdipus's anxieties and initial successes. As the philosopher Henry Johnstone noted, *anagnorisis* is not a resolution, but the discovery of an indissoluable kernel of difference that won't go away, a gap that's built in.[40] This gap is what we're after in any theoretical exploration of architecture, but in the case of violence, it's conveniently both the condition and the object of study.

The significance of *Carthago delenda est* lies in its logic. Freud's story of the borrowed kettle demonstrates the uncanny sequence of dreams, where destruction follows an inversion protocol: (1) I never borrowed a kettle from you; (2) I returned it to you unbroken; (3) the kettle was already broken when I got it from you. Žižek notes that "such an enumeration of inconsistent arguments confirms *per negationem* what it endeavors to deny—that I returned you a broken kettle."[41] Cato the Elder's habitual conclusion to every speech in the Roman Senate ended with *Carthago delenda est!* (Carthage must be destroyed). Carthage was in fact the mercantile engine behind Roman prosperity in Tunisia, but Romans were the farmers, Carthaginians were the astute businessmen. Cato, by disconnecting his admonition from any logical sequence, gained access to the collective Roman dream of social inversion.

In the same essay, Žižek recalls the story of the contest between the famous painters of the ancient Greece, Zeuxis and Parrhasius, which I mentioned earlier in the footnote related to the Turing Test. Parrhasius, like Turing's computer, wins by employing a curtain. The curtain related directly to the dream structure of the judges' demand for an object they knew to be false, but were judging in its relation to the true. The curtain was "truer than true" because it related directly—at a 1:1 scale, so to speak—to this demand. Our desire for violence is thus the curtain that is architecture, the veil that conceals the pretense we know as such, as that which we wish to expose. But, *there is only the veil*—the copied jewel is the authentic one, as Scotty discovers in Hitchcock's enigma of doubles, *Vertigo* (1958). This is the cost of truth.

The story of Babel is really quite funny from an etymological perspective. The word for the sacred towers, designed to penetrate into the *æther* of heaven and communicate directly with the gods, was Bab'El, the "gate of God"—a case of R_1 if there ever was one! The Hebrew word for speaking nonsensically was the closest counterpart, so the story of the sacred tower became a tower of foolishness that corrupted Adamic speech, whose relation to being is immediate, into prismatic fragments of imperfect languages— nonsense, which we generalize as R_2. Babel, like the adjective *heimlich*, is not a name for something else: its name contains its story! More than the architectural device to put man in touch with the divine, it immediately restores unmediated meaning through a renunciation of mediation: a destruction, literal and figurative, of the towers that are, if anything, literal places of mediation/exchange, hinges between the texts, keys to the cipher of privation and prohibition. The architecture of the inside frame, the anamorphic cipher, is nothing for the nobodies who have, from Babel to the WTC Towers, used architecture in its radical form: a fold, a password, an escape.

Endnotes

1— Aldo Rossi, *The Architecture of the City*, trans. Diane Ghirardo and Joan Ockman (Cambridge, MA: MIT Press, 1982), 22.

2— The classic trick of showing a rounded vignette when a film character looks through binoculars or a camera is an instance of an "internal fourth wall" that is implied in all fictional presentations. The shadowed edge creates a space between the viewer and viewed that, in normal conditions, is invisible. This technique was used with great effect in Alfred Hitchcock's *Rear Window* (1954), and is significantly accompanied by a circumstantial forcing of a fourth-wall effect. Suffering a heat wave, residents who share a Manhattan urban courtyard are forced to throw open their curtains, shades, blinds, and windows to the view of their neighbors. Everyone is put into the position of a potential if unwitting voyeur—or rather audience member—of a multi-screen cinema presentation.

3— Donald Kunze, "From Babel to Hitchcock: Suture, Interpolation, and Absence in the Formation of Architectural Meaning," *Intersight* 7, ed. Keith Johnson (2004): 187–200.

4— This was the idea, too, of Jeremy Bentham's "Panopticon," which worked on the idea that discipline was most efficient when prisoners could not determine when they were being observed.

5— Slavoj Žižek, *For They Know Not What They Do: Enjoyment as a Political Factor*, 2nd edition (New York and London: Verso, 1991), 58, n 28.

6— To get on the right track, the reader might recall the 2002 film, *Panic Room*, where Meg Altman (Jodi Foster), a claustrophobic resident of a mansion in New York, is trapped with her daughter in a security room, which becomes a tomb-like trap.

7— George Spencer-Brown, *The Laws of Form* (London: Allen & Unwin, 1969). Spencer-Brown's single symbol notation, defined alternatively as a cross or a call, allowed mathematicians to skip over many problems experienced in Boolean logic. The calculus was essentially a way of modeling the spaces created by framing or distinguishing and, as such, highlighted the implicit self-referential quality of *encadrement* (the frame-within-the-frame).

8— This is evident as the serpent takes up other roles in cultural imagery, namely as the Uro-boros, a world-encircling serpent familiar to many cultures. In keeping with the theme of the recursion, the Uroboros is typically shown as devouring its own tail, putting the Hegelian paradox of self-identity into a puzzle of inside-outside, or what Lacan called "the extimate" (*l'extimité*).

9— Nan Ellin, *Architecture of Fear* (New York: Princeton Architectural Press, 1997). One essay specifically addresses the case where fear is inscribed immediately within the object designed to exclude it, Anne Troutman's "Inside Fear, Secret Places and Hidden Spaces in Dwellings" (143–157). Still, Troutman avoids mentioning the references that seem to support her views most definitively: Edgar Allan Poe's fictions, such as "Masque of the Red Death" and "Fall of the House of Usher," or Anthony Vidler's *The Architectural Uncanny: Essays in the Modern Unhomely* (Cambridge, MA: MIT Press, 1992).

10— G. W. F. Hegel, *Hegel's Science of Logic*, trans. A. V. Miller (London: Allen & Unwin, 1969), 415. Hegel's involvement in the rewiring of exterior (essence) into interior (attribute) must be credited to Žižek, *ibid.*, footnote 3.

11— This is the thesis of Donald Phillip Verene's "Hegel's Recollection, A Study of Images" in *The Phenomenology of Spirit* (Albany, NY: State University of New York Press, 1985).

12— Blindness and invisibility are summarized elegantly in the film's last scene. The flower girl now owns her own shop and fantasizes about the return of her millionaire benefactor, who, she imagines, is handsome and single. When she sees Chaplin, ragged and tormented by a pack of street urchins, she takes pity and steps out to the street to give him a coin. He recognizes her, but she—of course—doesn't recognize him until she touches his hand to give him the coin. This moment of recognition, a true Aristotelian moment of *anagnorisis*, needs go no further than the symbolic repayment and the infinite distance between cost and benefit, beauty and beast.

13— Lacan's interest in usufruct goes back to Seminar XIV, April 16, 1967, where he emphasized that *jouissance* is completely negative, something that "serves no purpose." See Bruce Fink, *The Lacanian Subject: Between*

Language and Jouissance (Princeton: Princeton University, 1995), 191. On this point, we are invited to consider Eden as a case of geographical *jouissance*: "useless" (obviating any practical need) and a margin (an edge that is also a center, i.e. an inside frame).

14– Donald Kunze, "The Missing Guest: The Twisted Topology of Hospitality," in *Eating Architecture*, ed. Jamie Horwitz and Paulette Singley (Cambridge, MA: MIT Press, 2004), 169–190. To continue the reference of the note above, the purposelessness of *jouissance* relates as well to the nature and choice of sacrifice offered to the household gods at the hearth-side. The margin of cooked meat, the fat, is key to the value of sacrificial offerings for divination. In the same sense, the margin of cultivation, such as the corners of fields cited in *Leviticus* refers to a common place that cannot be used but, rather, allowed to nourish another margin, the socially marginal: the poor.

15– The acousmatic (impossible to locate) voice is, originally, a cinematic idea. See Michel Chion, *La voix au cinema* (Paris: Cahiers du cinema, 1982). For expanded use of this interesting idea, see Mladen Dolar, *A Voice and Nothing More* (Cambridge, MA: MIT Press, 2006). The acousmatic voice lies outside of linguistic analysis and typically involves the idea of authority, as in the utterances of prophets and sibyls. In ordinary speech, it is that "minimal element of ventriloquism" that creates an uncanny otherness, a warning, or a password.

16– Rex Butler, *Slavoj Žižek: Live Theory* (New York: Continuum, 2005), 44–47.

17– The most succinct description of Jaws' shark as a master signifier is Fredric Jameson's: "[T]he vocation of the symbol—the killer shark—lies less in any single message or meaning than in its very capacity to absorb and organize all of these quite distinct anxieties together. As a symbolic vehicle, then, the shark must be understood in terms of its essentially polysemous function rather than any particular content attributable to it by this or that spectator. Yet, it is precisely this polysemousness which is profoundly ideological, insofar as it allows essentially social and historical anxieties to be folded back into apparently "natural" ones, both to express and to be recontained in what looks like a conflict with other forms of biological

existence." Fredric Jameson, *Signatures of the Visible* (New York: Routledge, 1990), 26–27.

18– The meaning of *unheimlich*, for Freud, derives from the ambiguity already present in *heimlich*: "…[T]his word *heimlich* is not unambiguous, but belongs to two sets of ideas, which are not mutually contradictory, but very different from each other—the one relating to what is familiar and comfortable, the other to what is concealed and kept hidden. *Unheimlich* is the antonym of *heimlich* only in the latter's first sense, not in its second. … [T]he term "uncanny" applies to everything that was intended to remain secret, hidden away, and has come into the open." Sigmund Freud, *The Uncanny*, trans. David McLintock (London: Penguin Books, 2003), 132. The original essay was published in *Imago* 5/6 (1919).

19– The Turing Test involves a curtain that connects it to two other famous examples: *The Wizard of Oz*'s control room, where the Wizard fiddles with levers to manipulate the image of his horrible Otherness, and Parrhasius's painted curtain which, in the contest between the ancient Greek artists, won out over Zeuxis's *trompe-l'œil* bowl of fruit. The curtain conceals/reveals an "acousmatic" authority that, like the off-stage voice in cinema, gains its truth value by being impossible to locate.

20– *Dead of Night* was produced at Ealing Studios in 1945 with the collaboration of Michael Crichton, Basil Deardon, and Robert Hamer, under the general direction of the Brazilian-born Arturo Cavalcanti, famous for his film renditions of Dickens novels. The film starred many well-known British actors, including Googie Withers, Mervyn Johns, and Michael Redgrave.

21– Telling spooky tales while in a cozy home was a common practice, as Henry James indicated in his own famous spooky tale, "The Turn of the Screw" (1898).

22– For a thoroughgoing account of the centrality of the uncanny to Lacan's psychoanalysis, see Mladen Dolar, "'I Shall Be with You on Your Wedding-Night': Lacan and the Uncanny," *October* 58, Rendering the Real (Autumn 1991): 5–23.

23– Harold Bloom, *Kabbalah and Criticism* (New York: Seabury Press, 1975).

24– Jacques Lacan, *The Four Fundamental Concepts of Psychoanalysis*, The Seminar of Jacques Lacan, Book XI (New York: W. W. Norton, 1998), 59.

25– The account of "The Purloined Letter" is featured in Jacques Lacan, *Ecrits: The First Complete Edition in English*, trans. Bruce Fink in collaboration with Eloïse Fink and Russell Grigg (New York: W. W. Norton, 2006), 6–50. I have taken liberties to adjust Lacan's account of this story to an analysis by Richard Kopley (see note below), which, though initially alien and unsympathetic to Lacan's, is inadvertently illuminating.

26– See Richard Kopley, *Edgar Allan Poe and the Dupin Mysteries* (New York: Palgrave Macmillan, 2008).

27– I borrow the R_1/R_2 terminology from Ed Pluth, *Signifiers and Acts: Freedom in Lacan's Theory of the Subject* (Albany, NY: State University of New York, 2007), 17. To be fair to Pluth, my R_1 is embellished with the pre-Copernican imagery that forever sees any enclosure as a restriction of reality; reality is always a matter of escape into a larger, "contextual" set of truths, a head poking through clouds, making it invisible from below.

28– Richard Kopley, "Some details from Edgar Allan Poe's 'The Purloined Letter'" (lecture presented at Congregation Brit Shalom, State College, Pennsylvania, Spring 2010).

29– Warren H. Cudworth, "Cryptography—Mr. Poe as a Cryptographer," *Lowell Weekly Journal*, April 19 1850, 2: "The most profound and skilful cryptographer who ever lived was undoubtedly Edgar A. Poe, Esq. It was a favorite theory of his, that human ingenuity could not concoct a cipher, which human ingenuity could not resolve. The facility with which he would unravel the most dark and perplexing ciphers, was really supernatural. Out of a most confused medley of letters, figures and cabalistic characters, in any of the seven different languages, the English, German, French, Spanish, Italian, Latin, and Greek, his superhuman power of analysis would almost at once evolve sense, order and beauty; and of the hundreds of cryp[t]ographs which he received while editor of one of our popular periodicals, he never failed to solve one unless it was illegitimate, that is, unless its author put it together not intending to have it make sense."

30– Atreus served up Thyestes' sons, roasted, in revenge for Thyestes' adultery with Atreus's wife, Aerope. A version of the Thyestean feast was incorporated into Robert Harling's 1989 adoption of his own play into a film, *Steel Magnolias*. Police look for a missing man and suspect the wife, a victim of domestic violence. They are entertained at a restaurant opened by the wife and her best friend, who have dismembered and barbecued the husband and served him up to the hungry, grateful detectives, who have in this sense "found their man."

31– This is not a casual characterization. In the frontispiece to his final version of *The New Science*, Giambattista Vico showed Homer, the blind poet, gazing at the invisible helmet of Hermes, the only icon in the frontispiece that Vico did *not* describe in detail, as he had done for all the others. The blind man, Lacan somewhere notes, is not aware of the invisibility that conceals the partial object from those with "normal(ized)" sight and thus accesses divinatory powers of a Tiresius. The game of Blind Man's Bluff captures the essence of this power. The blindfolded "it" is free to roam, while all others are fixed in space, as were the victims of Medusa, whose face was "impossible to look at." Victory comes with touch, tangency, *tuché, touché*, the button that quilts layers of meaning together.

32– Kopley rejects the notion of any Lacanian connections to his work but, clearly, he has set up the opportunity to connect two seminal aspects of Lacan's work: his interest in grounding visibility in the unconscious (the study of "The Purloined Letter") and the primal origins of the gaze in the imaginary at the point of the Mirror Stage, arguably his theoretical foundation stone. The expansion of the role of anamorphosis has proven to be extremely productive, especially in its ability to link works of popular culture to the logic of the psychoanalytic clinic, as is evident in Slavoj Žižek's projects around the idea of parallax. See not only his major work on this subject, *The Parallax View* (Cambridge, MA: MIT Press, 2006), but also his earlier book, *Looking Awry, An Introduction to Jacques Lacan through Popular Culture* (Cambridge, MA: MIT Press, 1991).

33– The return of the word *psyche* as a Freudian technical term to its ancient meaning as "soul" is the famous subject of Bruno Bettelheim's critique of translations of Freud that needlessly distance psychoanalysis from the classics that Freud so revered. Bruno Bettelheim, *The Uses of Enchantment: The Meaning and Importance of Fairy Tales* (New York: Vintage Books, 1989).

34– The relation between *psyche* as soul and visibility has a rich source in antiquity, the story of Cupid and Psyche, told famously in Apuleius's third-century novel, *The Transformations of Lucius*. For a modern edition, see *The Transformations of Lucius; Otherwise Known as The Golden Ass*, trans. Robert Graves (New York: Farrar, Straus & Young, 1951), 122–143.

35– Giambattista Vico was interested in the Stoic distinction between *animus* and *anima* through the etymology of *cælum*, which could mean either "heaven" or "wedge." He reconciled the two senses by arguing that the blue ether of the sky, which was required by Roman law to be directly visible whenever oaths were made, was the substance of the gods, free of contamination by contingency. (In this sense, Vico is the proper forerunner of the science of artificial intelligence.) *Cælum* was, thanks to its sharpness, connected to *ingenium*, wit and impregnation. See *The Autobiography of Giambattista Vico*, trans. Max H. Fisch and Thomas G. Bergin (Ithaca, NY: Cornell University, 1975), 148–149.

36– The best example from contemporary culture is Douglas Gordon's remake, "24 Psycho" (1993), a conversion of the original 109-minute Hitchcock film into a series of still frames lasting 24 hours. By removing the Ø-function connectivity that constructs the illusion of motion, Gordon allowed the "alien" content of the viewer to roam among the images, in a sense creating new user-generated films.

37– Predictably, another of Douglas Gordan's experiments, "Between Darkness and Light" (1997) was the projection of two different films, *The Song of Bernadette* (Henry King, 1943) and *The Exorcist* (William Friedkin, 1973), simultaneously on either side of a single screen.

38– Don DeLillo, *White Noise* (New York: Viking, 1985). Jean Baudrillard, *Simulacra and Simulation*, trans. Sheila Faria Glaser (Ann Arbor: University of Michigan Press, 1994).

39– Karlheinz Stockhausen, "...Huuuh! Das Pressegespräch am 16 September 2001 im Senatszimmer des Hotel Atlantic in Hamburg," *Musik Texte* 91 (2002): 69–77.

40– Henry W. Johnstone, Jr., "Truth, Anagnorisis, and Argument," *Philosophy and Rhetoric* 16, 1 (1983): 1–15.

41– Slavoj Žižek, "The Antinomies of Tolerant Reason, A Glance into the Archives of Islam, http://www.lacan.com/zizantinomies.htm.

MUST ARCHITECTURE BE DEFENDED...

THE CRITIQUE OF VIOLENCE AND *AUTOIMMUNITY*

NADIR LAHIJI

What confronts us today is a life that as such is exposed to a violence
without precedent precisely in the most profane and banal ways.
Giorgio Agamben, Homo Sacer: Sovereign Power and the Bare Life[1]

Preamble

It is a vexed question: Is there a direct relationship between architecture
and violence? Are they inextricably linked? Is architecture immune to
the violence "without precedent" which, according to Giorgio Agamben,
permeates life today? How is architecture as a form of life affected by
this violence without precedent? If it is exposed to it, does it have its own
means of self-protection? Can it remain unscathed? Is architecture in
collusion with this violence or functions as its instrument?

All these questions boil down to an academic one: How should the
link between architecture and violence be framed for an analysis? In the
attempt to frame this link, it is still imperative to pose the following: What,
today, constitutes this *violence* that permeates life? Is violence *originary*, an
anthropological constant, manifest or invisible, even ineradicable? If it is
originary, does it reside *inside* architecture per se, an inherent condition
at its birth—similar to the a priori violence which is always already inside
language as such—or does it come from the *outside*, from the political
contingencies of postmodern violence in contemporary culture?

Slavoj Žižek, in his Violence: Six Sideways Reflections, makes an important
and fundamental distinction between what he names as "subjective" and
"objective" violence. He argues that subjective violence, as the most visible
acts of violence, includes two objective kinds of violence. The first he calls
"symbolic" violence that is embodied in language and its form, and has to
do with "[their] imposition of a certain universe of meaning"; the second
kind he calls "systemic" violence, "or the often catastrophic consequences
of the smooth functioning of our economic and political system."[2] Žižek
claims that subjective and objective violence cannot be viewed from the
same standpoint: "subjective violence is experienced as such against the
background of a non-violent zero level. It is seen as the perturbation of
the 'normal' state of things."[3] The objective violence, however, is invisible.
"Systemic" violence, he remarks, is "like the notorious 'dark matter' of
physics, the counterpart to an all-too-visible subjective violence. It may
be invisible, but it has to be taken into account if one makes sense of what
otherwise seems to be 'irrational' explosion of subjective violence."[4]

Relying on Žižek's instructive categorization, I contend that both
kinds of objective and subjective violence are present in architecture and

its discourse. Yet, initially, a more fundamental question must be asked: what are the constitutive elements structuring the so-called "critique of violence" within the architectural discourse? It must be made clear from the outset that architecture, as a form of culture, does not have an exclusive means over violence by itself at the subjective level; it is rather the authority of law and the sovereign exercise of power and State that are the very foundation of violence. We have learned this from Walter Benjamin, who was the first thinker to posit that it was the State that had the monopoly over violence in modern time when he wrote his landmark essay "Critique of Violence" in 1921. Hence, the question of violence is inherently a *political* question and therefore requires a *political theory* to address it. This point sets the stage for establishing the necessary relationship between architecture and violence in this essay.

I

Is the critique of architecture in the philosophy of two influential twentieth-century thinkers, Georges Bataille and Michel Foucault, a critique of the violence of architecture, whether in its modern origins as prison in a disciplinary society for Foucault,[5] or as "society's authorized superego" for Bataille?[6] Do both critiques merely address the metaphor of architecture in the discourse of philosophy?[7] How do we cut through the metaphor of architecture to the political philosophy of violence? If in this philosophy we are, with Bataille, "against architecture," then the question to be asked is this: *must architecture be defended?* In the two-page essay "Architecture," originally published in *Documents* in 1929, Bataille criticized the *expansion* of architecture and condemned the "hidden architectural skeleton" that he detected in classical painting.[8] In his essay on *informe*, or formless, he interrogated architecture's function to provide a "formal coat, a mathematical frock coat" to "*whatever exists*."[9] To say that this mathematical frock coat is omnipresent in whatever exists, is to claim that we are imprisoned in the suffocating grip of an architecture from which we cannot escape. In this view, architecture would be the *arche* of violence, the ground for all forms of violence. This simply renders architecture indefensible. Bataille argues that it is only in modern painting—namely, Manet's *Olympia*—that we see the beginning of the dissolution of this architectural skeleton.

Despite the rhetoric of the *informe* in contemporary art, analyzed by Rosalind Krauss and Yve-Alain Bois, no amount of discussion of formlessness in contemporary architecture can do away with the skeleton and its "mathematical frock coat," which saw its "second death" only in modern painting in Manet.[10] No matter how much the exponents of the discourse of *informe* hide behind sophisticated philosophies to shore up their theories and prescriptive practices, their so-called "other" geometry, in spite of themselves, is still ruled by a "mathematical frock coat." It is just a different kind of non-Euclidian mathematical "frock coat." Architecture is still the unspoken Commendatore, subtlety expressive of "society's superego." In this respect, the proponents of the discourse of *informe* not only lack a critical project, but worse, their discourse has blunted the sharp edges of Bataille's radical philosophy.[11]

Still, the dissolution of the architectural skeleton was by no means tantamount to the end of violence and the architectural metaphor. The reality through which the architectural skeleton imposes violence on the cultural-political body is that it always opens a hole in its midst, that is, the Real of violence as its traumatic kernel, which escapes the symbolic order it creates. Therefore, the idea of architecture as the superego of the society in Bataille, aptly interpreted by Hollier, is only half of the story. It has yet to go through the psychoanalytical explanation of the symbolic law. The *law* of violence, or violence *and* the law, always comes with its obscene enjoyment, as we have learned from Slavoj Žižek.[12]

Before coupling violence with architecture—only to be decoupled and critiqued later—and before the analysis of architecture can be linked with the analysis of violence, we must first examine how the discourse on violence itself was posed in the discourse of modernity. And, insofar as the question of violence is eminently a *political* one—which means also *political* in the domain of discursive practice—it cannot avoid addressing the discourse of political philosophy of our time; that is, the analysis of *power* and *force*. As I will argue below, the fashionable notions of the post-political and post-ideological in contemporary theory have effectively blocked such a political analysis, including in architectural discourse.

II

Architecture in its institutional forms can be seen to be an agent of violence while, at the same time, it is itself exposed to the same violence, whether in acts of war or not. In the first case, when architecture is an agent of violence, the discourse of the political power must be addressed directly. In the second case, when architecture itself is exposed to violence, two sets of forces must be properly distinguished: those forces which do violence to architecture from the *without*, and those which are immanent from the *within*, the visible and invisible in Žižek's categorization of subjective and objective violence.

These two cases are dialectically intertwined. The latter case will be addressed under the term of "theoretical violence," or—in Žižek's terminology—"symbolic," and what Walter Benjamin addressed under the notion of the "violence of critique." I will argue that the violence of critique is the logical consequence of another form of violence in contemporary culture, which I name the violence of image. This kind of violence is most dominant in contemporary architectural practice, and I will critique it under the concept of "autoimmunity." This latter concept was introduced by Jacques Derrida in his early work and was later discussed in relation to the "event" of September 11 (Derrida's notion is corollary to Žižek's "systemic" violence). Within this framework, the main question to be asked is: according to what parameters and in what manner can architecture be defended, if it must be defended, against external and internal violent forces; that is, at subjective and objective levels? I contend that when architecture acts as the agent of political biopower in collusion with a contemporary neoliberal order, which reduces people—to borrow Giorgio Agamben's term—to *homo sacer*, architecture is defenseless. It must plead guilty. But when the same biopower violates the right of architecture to exist from *without*, architecture must be forcefully defended. Accordingly, architecture must also be defended against the violence *internal* to its discursive practice. I term this "theoretical violence," in conjunction with the idea of violence of critique, to which this essay is mainly devoted.

If we follow Giorgio Agamben's statement quoted in the epigraph, the same power that exposes life to violence also wields its forces of destruction and death against architecture. I adopted the affirmative statement "architecture must be defended" after reading Michel Foucault's annual lecture at Collège de France delivered on power/war in 1975/76, published under the title "*Il faut défendre la société*," and later translated and published in English as "Society Must Be Defended."[13] It was in the session of 17 March 1976 that Foucault introduced the idea of "biopolitics," which he later took up again in his first volume of *The History of Sexuality*.[14] In that lecture Foucault stated: "Biopolitics deals with the population, with the population as political problem, as a problem that is at once scientific and political, as biological problem and as power's problem. And I think the biopolitics emerges at this time."[15] It was in this lecture that Foucault distanced himself from his earlier idea of "disciplinary society" and arrived at the idea of the "regularized" society. He remarked: "To say that power took possession of life in the nineteenth century, or to say that power at least takes life under its care in the nineteenth century, is to say that it has, thanks to the play of technologies of discipline on the one hand and technologies of regulation on the other, succeeded in covering the whole surface that lies between the organic and the biological, between body and population."[16] It is by following Foucault that I advance the thesis "Architecture Must Be Defended," both from the *without* in the destruction of life by biopolitics and from the *within* in the "violence of image." I will return to the latter point below. But first I must point out that the forces from outside are always-already inside. Both the "outside" and the "inside" are political, which goes to the heart of contemporary discourse on violence.

III

In *Homo Sacer: Sovereign Power and Bare Life* Giorgio Agamben takes up Foucault's idea of biopolitics and expands it into one of the most profound political philosophies of our time. Noting that the Greeks lacked a single term to describe life, Agamben makes the distinction between zoē, or natural life, naked life, bare life, common to all living beings; and *bios*, a form of life proper to the individual and the community of the *polis*, the political life. Following Walter Benjamin and Carl Schmitt on the idea of the state of exception and sovereignty, Agamben describes the structure of sovereignty as the point of exception inscribed in the law itself, the point that can suspend the validity of laws and proclaim the state of emergency.[17] At the opposite side of the sovereign we have its inverse figure, *homo sacer*—a bare life that can be killed with impunity, without entering the realm of sacrifice. Agamben writes:

> It is therefore possible to give a first answer to the question we put to ourselves when we delineated the formal structure of the exception. What is captured in the sovereign ban is a human victim who may be killed but not sacrificed: homo sacer. If we give the name bare life or sacred life to the life that constitutes the first content of sovereign power, then we may also arrive at an answer to the Benjaminian query concerning "the origin of the dogma of the sacredness of life." The life caught in the sovereign ban is the life that is originally sacred—that is, that may be killed but not sacrificed—and, in this case, the production of bare life, which is invoked today as an absolutely fundamental right in opposition to sovereign power, in fact originally expresses precisely both life's subjection to a power over death and life's irreparable exposure in the relation of abandonment.[18]

According to Agamben, the *homo sacer* is also the figure who is evicted from the life of the *polis*, from the city, from the political life proper. In architectural terms, this is the situation of war, when the building has been emptied of the life of the *polis*. War inscribes violence directly into space itself, reducing architecture to ruins.

Towards the end of his book Agamben draws a powerful and provocative conclusion: "Today it is not the city but rather the camp that is the fundamental biopolitical paradigm of the West." He then advances two theses that relate directly to my argument. The first states, "Western politics is biopolitics from the very beginning, and that every attempt to found political liberties in the rights of the citizens is, therefore, in vain."[19] The second can be related to architecture. It advances the idea that the model on which urban studies conceive the public space of the cities is without any clear awareness that at their very center lies the same bare life.[20]

We are reminded that the vast slum areas in the world megalopolises from Mexico City to Lagos are in fact camps inside contemporary cities, in which the inhabitants are reduced to bare life—the direct result of violence of the sovereign states' biopolitics and architecture as an instrument of their power. Žižek has connected Agamben's thesis to Mike Davis's writings on the subject of slums. He writes: "The defining feature of the slum-dwellers is sociopolitical; it concerns their (non-) integration into the legal space of citizenship with (most of) its incumbent rights—to put it in somewhat simplified terms: a slum-dweller, much more than refugee, is *Homo Sacer*, the systematically generated 'living dead' of global capitalism."[21] Are not these slums the symptoms of the violence of modernization, development and the world market, manifestations of the biopolitical order, and the "innermost logic of global capitalism," infecting the city and architecture, he rhetorically asks? So we can further inquire: does not architecture—through its institutional forms, implicated in the effects of the social order and often as the instrument of the global biopolitical power, with or without an aesthetic logic—act as the *agent* of that violence by reducing political life to the bare life of the slums of the contemporary metropolis?

We must now turn to the question of how the discourse of the biopolitical affects the internal discourse of architecture. I take up this question in the following sections through the analysis of the "violence of critique" from *within* the discipline, with the caveat that there is no clean distinction between inside and outside forces as I have already argued. I contend that the spectacular failure of what I call the "project of critique" in architecture is a symptom of the discourse of so-called post-ideology, and that this failure is at the center of the "violence of critique" in our time.

IV

Any discussion on violence and critique in modernity should begin with Walter Benjamin's 1921 landmark essay "Critique of Violence," on which Agamben's political philosophy is also based.[22] Benjamin witnessed the crisis of critique in his own time and his writing was a response to it. Jacques Derrida in his seminal essay, "Force of Law: The Mystical Foundation of Authority," brought Benjamin's article to the fore for political theory concerned with violence and the practice of critique.[23] There are many parallels between our time and Benjamin's. Benjamin's essay, influenced by but divergent to Carl Schmitt, articulated an anti-liberal critique of the parliamentary liberal democracy in Weimar Republic and its dissimulated institutional violence.[24] Albeit in a theological fashion (in Derrida's interpretation, "messianic without messianism," of à-venir, future to come), Benjamin sympathized with the insurrectionary counter-violence, in which he saw something recalling the sublime "violence" of divine nature.[25] It can be said that a similar gesture of counter-violence inevitably follows the institutional violence of the contemporary global neoliberal system, except that in our time technologies of the biopolitical have replaced the technologies of power that were in place at the time Benjamin wrote his text.

As Beatrice Hanssen points out, it is thanks to Benjamin's coupling of the "critique of violence" with the "violence of critique" that the discourse of power/violence (implicit in the original German word *Gewalt*) has taken the center stage in contemporary debates.[26] The other dimension of Benjamin's thought that Hanssen brings forward is the notion of *critique* and its practice. "Benjamin meant to establish a typology of different manifestations of violence that discriminated the secular from the theological, the legal from the illegal, law-preserving from law-positing force."[27] Benjamin took the term critique from the original Greek *krinein*, "to cut, rift, separate, discriminate, but also to decide."[28] However, the important lesson in Benjamin for the purpose of my argument is the notion of a crisis of critique (curiously, the two words are etymologically related). Hanssen charts the genealogy of the project of critique: starting with the genuine original notion of critique in Kant's monumental critical project, to Marxist critique of ideology, to the Frankfurt School of Critical Theory and the "immanent critique," through Hannah Arendt and Foucault's works on violence, force, and war. This genealogy culminates in the renewal of a psychoanalytically oriented "ideology critique" as analyzed and advanced by Slavoj Žižek. This is not the place to rehearse the various meanings of critique from Kant's critical philosophy through the work of political philosophers.[29] Suffice it to say that today we experience a crisis of critique, or a "violence of critique," similar to the one Benjamin faced in his time. We are concerned here with the connection between power, force, and violence in disciplinary discursive practices and how this *critique of violence* gets entangled in contemporary critical discourse. It is here that Benjamin's difficult reflections on violence can provide the conceptual tools necessary to address the nexus between violence and architecture.

After the 1921 essay, Benjamin foregrounded architecture in his work, especially in the "Work of Art in the Age of its Technical Reproducibility" essay and in the *Arcades Project*.[30] In fact, a genealogy can be drawn between the essay on violence and the "Artwork" essay.[31] If for Benjamin film had been a *pure* technological medium with its inherent potential to transform sensorial perception in the experience of modernity (which subsequently manipulated and violated by the Fascist system, lost its independence as the *pure* technological means), it could analogically be argued that architecture is *the* means of organizing technological experience in human sensorium. However, as a *pure* medium able to genuinely shape our experience, it has lost its independence in our time.[32] For Benjamin, as Howard Caygill has insightfully commented, "Architecture provides the main site for the interaction of technology and the human, a negotiation conducted in terms of touch and use. It is both a condition and the object of experience, the speculative site for the emergence of the 'technological *physis*.'"[33] As the locus of modern experience, Caygill further writes, "architecture both establishes the parameters of perception in space and time while being itself subject to constant transformation."[34] This is why Benjamin ends his "Artwork" essay by identifying architecture as "concrete a priori" or "canonical" art form.[35] Today, this role has been disrupted not by the violence of a Fascist system, but rather by another kind of violence that Žižek names "The Violence of Liberal Democracy," which in the neoliberal order of capitalism is coupled with the pervasive violence of—as Derrida called it—the "mediatized-tele-technological" culture.[36] In the light of such loss of independence, the "project of critique" has failed within the architecture discourse. This failure is the symptom of the predominant post-political discourse fashionable nowadays, which has also affected architecture's discursive practices. According to the post-political, after the loss of legitimacy by liberal institutions in recent decades, the neoliberal global order is the sole world order. As Chantal Mouffe has remarked, among the symptoms of the post-political discourse are the politics of "reflexive modernization," "risk society," or the official "third way" politics.[37] Moreover, "the lack of political channels for challenging the hegemony of the neo-liberal model of globalization is, I contend, at the origin of the proliferation of discourses and practices of radical negation of the established order."[38] As I will explore in the next section, the "violence of critique" *within* architecture discourses and practices failing the "project of critique" are the case in point, presenting an aspect of the predominant neoliberal, post-political discourse.

V

A particular example inside the discipline of architecture is the case where those who claim to represent a radical position take up the sophisticated philosophy of Gilles Deleuze and, recently, the influential works of Michael Hardt and Antonio Negri, *Empire* and *Multitude*.[39] Although these sources would seem to bestow on all followers a guaranteed revolutionary stance, in my view, they lack a critical political dimension. As Žižek, Mouffe, and others have shown, these best-selling works, while refreshing the discourse of globalization on the left, now appear to be profoundly flawed.[40] Mouffe writes: "If, as I have been arguing, what is needed today is an adequate understanding of the nature of the political which will permit grasping the conditions for an effective hegemonic challenge of the neo-liberal order, we certainly do not find in this book [*Empire*] the theoretical tools for such an enterprise. What we find is another version of the post-political perspective which defines the common sense in our post-democracies. To be sure, in this case it is a 'radical' version, formulated in a sophisticated philosophical vocabulary: hence its appeals to those who pretend that the time has come to relinquish 'old-fashioned' categories and 'rethink' the political."[41] She summarizes, "Power can be overcome, the constitutive character of antagonism is denied, and the central question of sovereignty is dismissed."[42] Žižek's criticism is even more acute:

> However, although HN [Hardt and Negri] see today's capitalism as the main site of proliferating multitudes, they continue to rely on the rhetoric of the One, the sovereign Power, against the multitude; the way they bring these two aspects together is clear: while capitalism generates multitude, it contains them in the capitalist form, thereby unleashing a demon it is unable to control. The question to be asked here is, nonetheless, whether HN are making a mistake very similar to that of Marx: is not their notion of the pure multitude ruling itself the ultimate capitalist fantasy, the fantasy of capitalism's self-revolutionizing perpetual motion exploding freely when its inherent

obstacle is removed? In other words, is not the capitalist form (the form of the appropriation of surplus-value) the necessary form, formal frame/condition, of the self-propelling productive movement?43

Elsewhere, Žižek expands his criticism of Hardt and Negri in taking them into task on their professed claims in Deleuzian philosophy and branding their work as ultimate exercise in Deleuzian politics with fatal consequences. He writes, "Back to Marx: What if his mistake was also to assume that the object of desire (unconstrained expanding productivity) would remain even when deprived of the cause that propels it (surplus value)? The same holds even more for Deleuze since he develops his theory of desire in direct opposition to the Lacanian one. Deleuze asserts the priority of desire over its objects: desire is a positive productive force that exceeds its objects, a living flow proliferating through the multitude of objects, penetrating them and passing through them, with no need for any fundamental lack or castration that would serve as its foundation."44

In recent architectural discourse we witness a proliferation of design concepts—too numerous to cite—emanating from the philosophical works discussed above. Here, the "radical" employs a sophisticated philosophical vocabulary, which amounts to "theoretical violence" in that it omits all reference to critical social theory. For example, consider the recent debate—between exponents of the above philosophy forming one camp, that of the "radicals" themselves only semi-versed in the philosophical works cited above, fashionably abandoning "ideology critique" and the critical project of the Left altogether, only in turn to be rebuffed by an opposite camp accusing them of being "discontent" with "criticality"— and you will get the picture of the post-political discourse.45 This takes us to the heart of the violence of critique *within* the discursive practice of the architecture, to Žižek's symbolic violence, and its isomorphism with the notion of "autoimmunity," which I now take up again.

VI

Must Architecture Be Defended?

In *Afflicted Powers: Capital and Spectacle in the Age of War,* our time in the aftermath of 9/11 has been defined as "the struggle for mastery in the realm of the image."46 The authors (Boal, Clark, Matthews, and Watts)—extending the argument of Guy Debord in *The Society of Spectacle*—write:

The logic of the pilots was part fantasy, we would argue, part (proven) lucidity. We would reply to it by saying that the new terrorists succumbed to the temptation of the spectacle, rather than devising a way to outflank or contest it. They were exponents of the idea (brilliant exponents, but this only reveals the idea's heartlessness) that control over the image is now the key to social power; and that image-power, like all other forms of ownership and ascendancy under capitalism, has been subjected to an ineluctable process of concentration, so that now it is manifest in certain identifiable (targetable) places, monuments, pseudo-bodies, icons, logos, manufactured non-events; signs that in their very emptiness and worthlessness (the Twin Towers as architecture were perfect examples) rule the imaginary earth; and whose concentrated, materialized nullity gives the new terror a chance—to frighten, demoralize, turn the world upside down.[47]

Extrapolating the argument quoted above, it can be said that what suffered a *spectacular* defeat on September 11 was "image-architecture." "This world of images," the authors go on saying, "had long been a structural necessity of capitalism oriented toward the overproduction of commodities, and therefore the constant manufacture of desire for them; but by the late twentieth century it had given rise to a specific polity."[48]

This is a sign of a more universal malaise. We are living in the "Society of Enjoyment," as Todd McGowan has written, building his argument on the Lacanian psychoanalytical theory of *jouissance.*[49] This society is an image-dominated society, in which the image forms the perverse factor in this enjoyment. "In this sense, an emphasis on the image is symptomatic of the society of enjoyment because it provides the illusion of total enjoyment and freedom without the kind of enjoyment that might disturb the functioning of the social structure itself."[50] In this society, the imaginary reigns in the absence of symbolic authority. Grounding the analysis of image in psychoanalytical theory, McGowan writes: "The image liberates the subject from the symbolic world of prohibition, offering a route to enjoyment that bypasses the threat of castration. ... The imaginary provides a way for the subject to respond positively to command to enjoy, offering the immediate enjoyment that the symbol denies."[51]

Image-power and its discourse in "the society of spectacle" are precisely the power which affects the discursive practice of architecture, not only from *within*, but also from *without*. Not only the critique of this image-power after 9/11 is disarmed in Ground Zero, but worse, competing with the terrorists' "image-victory," it exemplifies the "violence of critique" on the occasion of the projects proposed for Ground Zero.[52] In competing with the "image-victory," the architect/master planner of Ground Zero, Daniel Libeskind, wrote: "in some circles it is fashionable to interpret the attack as the inevitable result of U.S. imperialism, or the nation's oil policy, or its global arrogance. I do not buy that. The strike on the World Trade Center was an attack on democracy—on global democracy and global freedom. New York was a target because it is the center of the free world."[53] With equally blunt language, we must not buy this apology of power and facile pseudo-analysis. We see that the image and its violence in culture are also affecting architectural discourse and practice. The architect/master planner of Ground Zero, entrenched in a kind of pathological narcissism that Žižek describes as a typical subjectivity of our permissive society, enjoys his created image of "freedom."[54] But, ironically, as McGowan writes, in the society of enjoyment "narcissism precludes the possibility of actual enjoyment because it obscures the subject's relation to the *objet petit a*, the lost object, that is the sources for the subject's enjoyment. Even though the subject can never attain this object, it nonetheless opens the sole avenue through which the subject can access enjoyment in the Real."[55] Moreover, "narcissism closes off this openness in the Other and thus also closes off the possibility of enjoyment."[56] We can link the image in the society of enjoyment with the notion of spectacle in the society of spectacle. Spectacle, Debord wrote, is "capital accumulated to the point where it becomes an image." Hal Foster, discussing the role of image in contemporary architecture, added that today the reverse is equally true: "spectacle is an image accumulated to the point where it becomes capital."[57] Elsewhere, Foster insightfully traces the genealogy of the pervasive image in architecture from 1960s to recent contemporary practices under the notion of "Image Building."[58]

I contend that the violence of image in practices of architecture is the symptom of the indefensible "violence of critique" in discursive practice of the discipline. Here the answer to the interrogative mode in my title is flatly affirmative: *Yes, Architecture Must Be Defended*. That is, architecture must be protected against this indefensible practice of "violence of critique." Here, we must return to the question I posed in the preamble: where does such violence originate from today? Following the late Jacques Derrida, I want to argue that this violence of image is the agent of the "autoimmunity" in the internal discourse of the discipline. That is, the violence of image functions in what I name the "*architectural autoimmunity*" in contemporary society. In an extraordinary reflection in "Faith and Knowledge: The Two Sources of 'Religion' and the Limits of Reason Alone," Derrida opens his notion of "autoimmunity" for the analysis of the "return of religion" and offers a remarkable analysis of the nature of violence in contemporary society.[59] Derrida writes, "The same movement that renders indissociable religion and 'tele-technoscientific' reason in its most critical aspect reacts inevitably *to itself*. It secretes its own antidote but also its own power of auto-immunity. We are here in a space where all self-protection of the unscathed, of the safe and sound, of the sacred (*heilig*, holy) must protect itself against its own protection, its own police, its own power of rejection, in short against its own, which is to say, against its own immunity. It is this terrifying but fatal logic of the *auto-immunity of the unscathed* that will always associate Science and Religion."[60]

Derrida acknowledges that the notion of immunity comes from the domain of biology: "As for the process of auto-immunization, which interests us particularly here, it consists for a living organism, as is well known and in short, of protecting itself against its self-protection by destroying its own immune system."[61] Hence, we are authorized, Derrida adds, to speak of a general logic of auto-immunization. Derrida repeatedly makes clear where this general logic of autoimmunity originates. It is lodged in the *digital and cyberspatialized culture*, in "tele-technological-scientific-capitalist-mediatic" power in its globalized dimensions controlled by panoptical visualization and telecommunication. In this respect religion allies itself with the tele-technological. And in the so-called "wars of religion," Derrida clearly traces "two ages" of violence. He writes, "The one, already discussed above, appears 'contemporary', in sync or in step with the hypersophistication of military tele-technology — of 'digital' and cyberspaced culture. The other is a 'new archaic violence', if one can put it that way. It counters the first and everything it represents."[62] Verbatim, we can trace the sources of the violence of image in the same "mediatized-capitalist-digital-tele-technological" culture, infecting and contaminating discursive practice of architecture, causing its autoimmunity, and disarming its "project of critique," which—I repeat—constitutes the "violence of critique" in the discipline. Once architecture *allies* itself with the reason of mediatized digital culture, infatuated with the image and its *enjoyment*, it loses its self-protection and its *publicness*. The more architecture builds images, the more it violates the principles of the critique, the more it becomes autoimmune against the same forces from which it is supposed to protect itself.

Derrida took up the notion of autoimmunity in analysis of the "event" of September 11 in a dialogue with Giovanna Borradori.[63] The assault of

September 11 was violence against the image of architecture, or architecture as image, translated as an image of power, this time not coming from the violence of biopower but from the side of fundamentalists who ally themselves with tele-technological-scientific Reason in a mediatized spectacle. Any restoration of this image of power through architecture is an exercise in absurdity. Yet the architect/master planner engages in futility to restore this spectacularly failed image-architecture after the terrorists' violence. In his analysis of September 11, Derrida writes: "What will never let itself be forgotten is thus the perverse effect of autoimmunity itself. For we now know that repression in both its psychoanalytical sense and its political sense—whether it be through the police, the military, or the economy—ends up producing, reproducing, and regenerating the very things it seeks to disarm."[64]

Borradori extends Derrida's argument and remarks that 9/11 "is the symptom of an autoimmune crisis occurring within the system that should have prevented it. ... Autoimmune conditions consist in the spontaneous suicide of the very defensive mechanism supposed to protect the organism from external aggression."[65] Derrida refers to an article by Terry Smith, "Target Architecture: Destination and Spectacle before and after 9/11," which speaks of an "architecture of trauma."(See the published version of Smith's article "The Political Economy of Iconotype and the Architecture of Destination.").[66] Citing the commentary of Joseph B. Juhas on Minoru Yamasaki (the architect of the Twin Towers) written in 1994, Derrida claims, "The WTC had been our Ivory gates to the White City. ... Though, at least when viewed from distance, the TWC still shimmers—it is at the moment thoroughly besmirched by its unfortunate role as a target for Middle East terrorism."[67] And further, "Of course, any 'stability' based on the suppression of open systems becomes an element in a drama which in its own terms must terminate in cataclysm. In an allegorical sense, the vast, twinned doubled ghostly presence of WTC presents a sepulcher from which ghosts will not rise on the day of cataclysm as the resurrected dead: rather as a tombstone it prophecies the raising of Golems and Zombies."[68] Derrida continues to offer his own comments, "Without considering the architectural problems (urban, technical, political, aesthetic) posed by the World Trade Center, we must at least recognize this: the affect, indeed the affection, the love that it inspires (a love whose double specter has invaded my own memory, for example, for more than ten years) cannot exclude the at least unconscious feeling of a terrible vulnerability, the fascinating exposure of these two enormous vertical bodies to heinous or loving aggression."[69] Echoing Terry Smith's analysis, Derrida further notes: "How can one not 'see' these two towers without 'seeing' them in advance, without foreseeing them, slashed open? Without imagining, in an ambiguous terror, their collapse? That is to say, their sublime sublation in the filmed archive, a film more unforgettable than ever for giving, idealizing memory of the worldwide-ization (*mondialisation*) of the world."[70] Our philosopher in this architectural-political commentary demonstrates an insight otherwise lacking in our architect/master planner.

Epilogue

Yes, architecture must be defended!

We must now return to Walter Benjamin. How do we extricate architecture, the mediality of its medium—analogous to the modality of the film medium for Benjamin—and its discursive practice from their manipulative exploitation of the Image and its perverse enjoyment, from the force of neoliberal sociopolitical order and its discourse of post-political? How do we save it from the mediatized culture of "tele-technological-capitalist-digital" reason? How must architecture be defended against the violence in its own internal discourse, against the symbolic violence permeating its language of criticism and its universe of meaning? How should its critical project be restored?

Here, against the discourse of post-political, the political left must demarcate its own discourse. That is, the radical discourse of critique must be reconstructed against its neoliberal opponents. This is what Benjamin attempted in his "Critique of Violence" and in his famous afterward to the theses in the "Artwork" essay. Is there a *legitimate* mode of violence as Benjamin envisioned through his "politics of the pure means"? In his final analysis in the "Critique of Violence," he speculated that "pure violence" beyond the exchange of means and ends attains the level of revolutionary or "divine violence."[71] Benjamin wanted to separate the unalloyed technological means—that is, the medium of film in his time—from its illegitimate exploitation by Fascist propaganda. Can the same argument, today, be valid in its analogical extension to architecture, notwithstanding the fundamental difference that exist in respect to the reception between film and architecture? Can we call for the politicization of the pure medium of architecture, *architecture as distinctively a media in its* particular Benjaminian sense—architecture as a priori *technological* means for the organization of experience (ironically, after the "destruction of experience" in modernity[72])—towards an injunction to *pure* revolutionary violence?[73] Is such a project viable? It was Fredric Jameson who, a long time ago, argued that while Nazism corresponded to an earlier primitive stage of the emergence of the media (which Benjamin attacked with his strategic idea of technologically advanced art), in today's increasingly media-totalizing societies it is no longer possible to maintain such an optimistic view. But Jameson further adds that "without it, however, the project of specifically political modernism becomes indistinguishable from all the other kinds—modernism, among other things, being characterized by its consciousness of an absent public."[74] Nevertheless, perhaps architecture must maintain its *pure mediality* against the mass audience of the "total system" of media society and the current forms of exploitation by the mediatized culture. Moreover, it must protect itself against the violence of the uncritical and misguided "image-victory," expropriated in competition with the same exploitative mediatic discourse.

The discourse of the aesthetic in architecture should be grounded in the political discourse and should be protected from falling into the "theoretical violence." What would enable the discursive practice of architecture to internally counter the "violence of critique" in this thesis? The project of critique requires that we reconstitute the discursive practice when architecture as social practice stands between the discourses of the *political* on the one hand, and discourse of *technological-aesthetics*, on the other. Yet, under what condition can architecture maintain its *pure* technological mediality to protect itself against the violence of the *biopower*? Can Benjamin's utopian-messianic project of critique of violence for an injunction of the *pure* revolutionary violence in the "politics of pure means," save the "project of critique" for discursive practice of architecture?

Endnotes

I would like to thank Donald Kunze for his valuable editorial intervention in this essay.

1— Giorgio Agamben, *Homo Sacer: Sovereign Power and the Bare Life* (Stanford: Stanford University Press, 1998), 114.

2— Slavoj Žižek, *Violence: Six Sideways Reflections* (New York: Picador 2008), 2.

3— Ibid.

4— Ibid.

5— Michel Foucault, *Discipline and Punish: The Birth of The Prison* (New York: Vintage, 1977).

6— Denis Hollier, *Against Architecture: The Writings of Georges Bataille*, trans. Betsy Wing (Cambridge, MA: MIT Press, 1989).

7— For an exposition of the metaphor of architecture see Kojin Karatani, *Architecture as Metaphor: Language, Number, Money* (Cambridge, MA: MIT Press, 1995).

8— Georges Bataille, "Architecture," in *October* 60 (Spring 1992). See also Hollier's analysis of this article in *Against Architecture*.

9— George Bataille, "Formless," in *Visions of Excess: Selected Writings, 1927–1939*, ed. Allan Stoekle (Minneapolis: University of Minnesota, 1985). Emphasis is mine.

10— Yve-Alain Bois and Rosalind Kraus, eds., *Formless: A User's Guide* (New York: Zone Books, 1997).

11— To this effect see also Anthony Vidler, "Diagrams of Diagrams: Architectural Abstraction and Modern Representation," *Representation* 27 (Fall 2000).

12— For more on this, see Slavoj Žižek, *The Parallax View* (Cambridge, MA: MIT Press, 2006), especially Chapter 1.

13— Michel Foucault, *Society Must be Defended: Lectures at the College de France, 1975–1976*, trans. David Macy, ed. Arnold I. Davidson (New York: Picador, 2003).

14— Michel Foucault, *The History of Sexuality, Volume One: An Introduction* (New York: Vintage Books, 1980).

15— Foucault, *Society Must be Defended*, 245.

16— Ibid., 253.

17— Also see Giorgio Agamben, *State of Exception*, trans. Kevin Attell (Chicago: The University of Chicago Press, 2005).

18— Agamben, *Homo Sacer*, 83.

19— Agamben, *Homo Sacer*, 181.

20— Ibid., 181–182.

21— Slavoj Žižek, *The Parallax View*, 269. Also see Mike Davis, "Planet of Slums: Urban Revolution and the Informal Proletariat," in *New Left Review* 26 (March/April 2004) and more recently his *Planet of Slums* (London and New York: Verso, 2006).

22— Walter Benjamin, "Critique of Violence," in *Walter Benjamin, Selected Writings: Volume 1. 1913–1926*, ed. Marcus Bullock and Michael W. Jennings (Cambridge, MA: The Belknap Press of Harvard University Press, 1996).

23— See Jacques Derrida, "Force of Law: The 'Mystical Foundation of Authority,'" in *Deconstruction and the Possibility of Justice*, ed. Drucilla Cornell et Al. (New York & London: Routledge, 1992).

24— For this and what follows I rely on excellent work of Beartice Hanssen, *Critique of Violence: Between Poststructuralism and Critical Theory* (New York and London: Routledge, 2000).

25— For further elaboration of this point see Žižek, *Violence*.

26— Hanssen, *Critique of Violence*.

27— Ibid., 4.

28— Ibid.

29— See Hanssen for more, ibid.

30— Walter Benjamin, "The Work of Art in the Age of Its Technological Reproducibility: Second Version," in *Walter Benjamin, Selected Writings: Volume 3. 1935–1938*, ed. Michael W. Jennings (Cambridge, MA: The Belknap Press of the Harvard University Press, 2002).

31— Hanssen draws this connection, see *Critique of Violence*.

32— For a sustained analysis of architecture in the Benjamin's "Artwork" essay, see Howard Caygill, *Walter Benjamin: The Colour of Experience* (London and New York: Routledge, 1998).

33— Caygill, *Walter Benjamin: The Colour of Experience*, 116.

34— Caygill, ibid.

35— See Howard Caygill, *Benjamin: The Colour of Experience*.

36— Slavoy Žižek, "The Violence of Liberal Democracy," in *Assemblage* 20, ed. Mark Wigley (April

1993). See also Giovanna Borradori, *Philosophy in a Time of Terror, Dialogue with Jürgen Habermas and Jacques Derrida* (Chicago: The University of Chicago Press, 2003).

37– For more on the notion of post-political see Chantal Mouffe, *On The Political* (London and New York: Routledge, 2005).

38– Mouffe, *On The Political*, 82.

39– See Michael Hardt and Antonio Negri, *Empire* (Cambridge, MA: Harvard University Press, 2000) and *Multitude: War and Democracy in the Age of Empire* (New York: Penguin Books, 2005).

40– See Mouffe in ibid. and Žižek, *The Parallax View*. Also see the collection of essay in *Empire's New Clothes*, eds. Paul A. Passavant and Jodi Dean (New York: Routledge, 2004).

41– Ibid., 109.

42– Mouffe, *On The Political*,107.

43– Žižek, *The Parallax View*, 263. Also see Žižek "Objet a in Social Links," in *Jacques Lacan and the Other Side of Psychoanalysis: Reflections on Seminar XVII*, ed. Justin Clements and Russell Grigg (Durham: Duke University Press, 2006).

44– Žižek, "Objet a in Social Links," in *Jacques Lacan and the Other Side of Psychoanalysis: Reflections on Seminar XVII*, 126–27.

45– See for example George Baird in his "'Criticality' and Its Discontent," in *Harvard Design Magazine* (Fall/Winter 2004).

46– Iain Boal et al./Retort, *Afflicted Powers: Capital and Spectacle in A New Age of War* (London and New York: Verso, 2005), 19.

47– Iain Boal et al., *Afflicted Powers*, 28–29.

48– *Afflicted Powers*, ibid.

49– See Todd McGowan, *The End of Dissatisfaction? Jacques Lacan and the Emerging Society of Enjoyment* (Albany, NY: State University of New York Press, 2004).

50– McGowan, *The End of Dissatisfaction?*, 59.

51– Ibid., 66.

52– The story of the failure, or better, the fiasco of the Ground Zero at the level of architectural, institutional, political, and cultural is too large to be tackled here.

53– Daniel Libeskind, *Breaking Ground* (New York: Riverhead Books, 2004), 274.

54– See Slavoj Žižek, *Looking Awry, An Introduction to Jacques Lacan through Popular Culture*

(Cambridge, MA: MIT Press, 1992). See also McGowan, *The End of Dissatisfaction?*

55– McGowan, *The End of Dissatisfaction?*, 67.

56– Ibid.

57– Hal Foster, "Master Builder," in *Design and Crime And Other Diatribes* (London and New York: Verso, 2002), 41.

58– Hal Foster, "Image Building," *Artforum International* 43: 2 (Oct. 2004): 270–3, 310–11.

59– Jacques Derrida, "Faith and Knowledge: The Two Sources of 'Religion' at the Limits of Reason Alone," in *Religion*, eds. Jacques Derrida and Gianni Vattimo (Stanford: Stanford University Press, 1998), 1–78.

60– Derrida, "Faith and Knowledge: The Two Sources of 'Religion' at the Limits of Reason Alone," 44.

61– Ibid, 73, n. 27.

62– Ibid.

63– See Giovanna Borradori, *Philosophy in a Time of Terror, Dialogue with Jürgen Habermas and Jacques Derrida* (Chicago: The University of Chicago Press, 2003).

64– Borradori, *Philosophy in a Time of Terror*, 99.

65– Ibid., 150.

66– Terry Smith, "The Political Economy of Iconotypes and the Architecture of Destination," *Architecture Theory Review* 7: 2 (2002): 1–44. This article contains many insights by Smith in his comprehensive analysis of the "image-architectural trauma" of 9/11 in relation to the convergence between "spectacle architecture and a spectacularizing media." Smith comments concerning the Twin Towers as architecture that invited its own obliteration also confirms the point I have discussed around the notion of "autoimmunity."

67– Borradori, *Philosophy in a Time of Terror*, 187.

68– Borradori, *Philosophy in a Time of Terror*, 186–87.

69– Ibid., 187.

70– Ibid.

71– See Hanssen, *Critique of Violence*.

72– See Giorgio Agamben, *Infancy and History: On the Destruction of Experience* (London and New York: Verso 2007).

73– See Caygill, *Walter Benjamin: The Colour of Experience*.

74– See Fredric Jameson in *Aesthetics and Politics* (London and New York: Verso, 1980), 208.

HEARTLESS IN HAVENWORLD™; OR, THE BULLET-RIDDLED ARMOR OF THE SUBURBS

WILLIAM B. MILLARD

> *I am convinced that the future is lost somewhere in the dumps of the*
> *non-historical past; it is in yesterday's newspapers, in the jejune*
> *advertisements of science-fiction movies, in the false mirror of our*
> *rejected dreams. Time turns metaphors into things, and stacks them up*
> *in cold rooms, or places them in the celestial playgrounds of the suburbs.*
> *Has Passaic replaced Rome as the Eternal City?*
> Robert Smithson, "The Monuments of Passaic"[1]

How much degradation can an environment sustain and remain hospitable to civilization? Human beings can adapt to an enormous range of climates, densities, structural patterns, and levels of resource availability, but it would be biologically and sociologically naive to claim that the behavioral effects of all these adaptations are matters of indifference. The more radically *Homo sapiens* reshapes its environment, the more drastically the species reshapes itself. The stranger, harsher, and more antisocial its built environments become, the harder it becomes to do justice to them in the decorous languages of scholarship and journalism, and the likelier it may be that some artists will outperform more prosaic types of analysts in providing compelling critiques of those environments.

The contemporary United States, for better or worse, is a largely suburban nation. Any serious understanding of the individual and collective behavior of Americans requires a deep, nuanced understanding of suburban mindsets. Demographic and developmental shifts toward suburbs, away from both dense urban settings and smaller agrarian towns, have been the norm in the U.S. since the first few decades of the twentieth century, and suburban ways of life have distinct consequences for practically every important aspect of a civilization: energy use, economic variables, sociopolitical attitudes, cultural formations. The hyperconsumption, social stratification, anomie, and automobile dependence that suburban land-use patterns encourage have come under such heavy criticism from environmental and communitarian perspectives that some commentators view the clash between proponents of restoring urban density (e.g., Andres Duany, Dolores Hayden, Kenneth Jackson, Jane Jacobs, James Howard Kunstler, David Owen, and others) and defenders of sprawl (Robert Bruegmann, Joel Kotkin) as the defining battle of twenty-first-century sociocultural politics.[2]

Scholars of suburbia such as Hayden, Jackson, Herbert Gans, Richard Harris, and Robert Lewis have anatomized the history, typologies, and pathologies of these environments to a degree that social novelists might envy.[3] However, suburban archetypes in both canonical and popular cul-

HEARTLESS IN HAVENWORLD™

ture—the upper-middle-class cocktail hours of John Cheever and John Updike, the "little boxes" of Malvina Reynolds and Pete Seeger, the reassuring blandness of nuclear-family settings in television programs like *Father Knows Best* (1954–1960) and *Leave It to Beaver* (1957–1963), or the menacing blandness of later cinematic representations such as Bryan Forbes's *The Stepford Wives* (1975) and Todd Solondz's *Happiness* (1998)—only begin to sketch the meanings of these environments. Whether whitewashed or dark, the suburbs in most such works are generalized caricatures of the specific places represented, if they represent specific locations at all. For all the attention the mass media pay to generic Suburbia, their representations of how suburban environments shape behavioral repertoires are rarely site-specific.

The Home Box Office series *The Sopranos* has attracted attention for its close attention to physical and cultural signifiers, its combinations of horror and comedy, and its faithfulness to its primary setting, the cities and suburbs of northeastern New Jersey.[4] I am primarily concerned with its rendering of the physical environments of North Jersey and New York City, and of the ways it presents the relations between built environments and multiple forms of violence. The series presents disturbing images and events; it also gives a sophisticated and realistic portrait of a regional suburban environment. How can these qualities coincide, since violent crime is something suburbs were supposedly built to exclude? *The Sopranos*, I am convinced, has attained much of its appeal by taking an underappreciated setting, the North Jersey suburbs, and rendering a fictive version of this place in ways that reveal its complexities and internal contradictions. North Jersey has long existed in the cultural shadow of New York City, where America's organized-crime mythos lives. *The Sopranos* has extended that mythos to a place that is more typical of the middle-American environment, yet bears the marks of an informative and troubling history.

The Domesticated Beast in Me

Many qualities of *The Sopranos* have evoked hyperbole, but evaluative criticism is not the point of this analysis. By rendering the built and natural environments of northern New Jersey and New York City concretely, *The Sopranos* raises questions of spatial history and environmental change in the suburban settings where most Americans now live—critical contested zones in national debates over development policy, transportation, energy use, and cultural politics.

At the nexus of the series's plot is Tony Soprano's decision, after a series of fainting spells with no somatic cause, to explore their etiology in conversations with psychiatrist Jennifer Melfi, M.D.—a breach of the mob's *omertà* (code of silence) and thus an exposure to the risk of murder by either rivals or DiMeo Family colleagues. The name Soprano draws multiple levels of meaning into juxtaposition. The obvious meaning, the high female vocal range, connotes "singing" in the sense of betraying Mafia secrets, with the implication that any mobster caught singing risks castration as well as murder. Less obvious, however, is the translation of *soprano* as "high," derived from *sopra* (above) and the Latin *super*, not confined to the musical idiom but used geographically, in opposition to *sottano*. The Sicilian town of Corleone, from which the crime family in Francis Ford Coppola's *Godfather* films (1972, 1974, 1990) hailed and took its New World name, was once surrounded by defensive walls connecting two fortifications known as the Castello Soprano (now in ruins) and Castello Sottano; the *Godfather* saga, naturally, is one of the most frequently cited cultural touchstones in the intertextual reference field of *The Sopranos*, the subject of recurrent homages, quotations, and even interpretations by the characters. Much of Tony's life among the upper middle class calls to mind Michael Corleone's remark in the least appreciated of the films, *Godfather III*: "The higher I go, the crookeder it becomes."

The Soprano home in North Caldwell, N.J., appropriately, is located atop a hill, emphasizing privacy, exclusion, and elevation. Tony and his family have risen through the various strata of the American class system, and through the associated residential environments, to reach the upper bourgeoisie. The location of their house in a suburban zone bordering a wooded area brings wild animals into the yard and the pool; the migration flight of a family of ducks that Tony had become fond of, an event that triggers the first of his psychosomatic blackouts, initiates a recurrent motif of animals, feral or domesticated, as signs of the mobster's half-civilized nature. Tony is psychically troubled by his culture's estrangement from nature; his daughter's name, Meadow, implies that at least some of the 1960s generation's green sensibility rubbed off on Tony and Carmela.[5] Toward fellow humans, however, Tony is a violent predator and a relentless parasite. Befittingly, the soundtrack under the pilot episode's closing credits is Nick Lowe's "The Beast in Me."

The Sopranos is thus both a crime saga and a soap opera, superimposing two genres with gender specific audiences and conventions. Much of the show's black comedy derives from how readily the Mafiosi have adapted to the American suburbs—both individual Mafiosi like Tony and the organization they call simply "this thing of ours," *cosa nostra*, still fearsome, but in an acknowledged state of decline:

> The Sopranos, of course, is self-consciously farcical. The series is constructed out of characters who know they are witnessing a "Family breakdown" and who know how bourgeois lifestyle precludes the appropriate gravitas.... The Sopranos represents a world in which the logic of the market is everywhere triumphant, and where loyalty (whether corporate or familial or, as in the case of the Mafia, both of these at once) is increasingly treated as a commodity to be bought or sold.[6]

Professional criminals in their fictional and cinematic representations, as Fred Gardaphé points out, have a long history as icons of ethical and cultural otherness: trickster figures whom the vast majority of non-mobbed-up citizens of any socioeconomic class can perceive from a safe distance.[7] The unabashed, unregulated self-interest of the mobster can also provide useful contrast for the citizen within an economic order that is premised on the assumption of universal greed yet conceals that motivation beneath at least some veneer of civility. The fascination of mobsters, who operate according to behavioral codes that are foreign to "legit" civilization yet also reflect the acquisitiveness and ruthlessness of modern capitalism, may increase in direct proportion to their proximity to observers—provided some impermeable barrier still exists between Us and Them. Many people thrill to the sight of large predatory animals in zoos, but few actively seek their company in the wild.

To an important degree, in both mythology and reality, the Us/Them, citizen/outlaw barrier has been spatial. As a phenomenon of immigrant cultures in the United States, traditional criminal groups like New York's Five Families, Chicago's Outfit, Cleveland's Porrello and Lonardo families and their successors, the Carollas of New Orleans, the DeCavalcantes of Elizabeth, N.J. (widely assumed to be the real-life model for the DiMeo/Soprano group), and their equivalents in other cities have been associated with specific neighborhoods, most memorably New York's Italian East Harlem at the beginning of the twentieth century and, later, the Little Italy/Five Points areas of the Lower East Side. (Despite the concentrated media attention to Sicilian and Italian organizations, no single ethnic group or neighborhood ever monopolized this type of activity, as evidenced by the Irish Westies on New York's West Side, comparable Irish groups in South Boston, and, more recently, Russian/Ukrainian, Japanese, Colombian, Mexican, and other ethnically defined "mafias" in various cities.)

Localism was one of the distinctive characteristics of the informal neighborhood *padrone* traditions that evolved into the recognized and much-mythologized Mafia of the Kefauver Commission and the *Valachi Papers*. George De Stefano, drawing on historian Robert Orsi's studies of Italian East Harlem, emphasizes one particular tradition drawn from the southern Italian communities from which most immigrants to America had come after Italy's unification in 1861: a belief that moral authority and loyalty reside with the "domus," the local community bound by blood ties, and not with any affiliative groups at the level of nation or religion.[8] Filiations grounded in southern Italian villages were maintained at the neighborhood level in the New World in both legitimate and criminal affairs. This territorial tendency, combined with pervasive nativist prejudice against immigrants, augmented the Jeffersonian distrust of city life that Jackson has called "the anti-urban tradition in American thought,"[9] contributing to the popular association between urban spaces and crime. If the city was the place of excitement and opportunity, in contradistinction to the assumed safety of more homogeneous small towns and suburbs, it was also the territory of risk, a space harboring thugs whom the official legal mechanisms rarely came close to governing.

In the light of these realities and perceptions about urban space, another meaning of *The Sopranos* arises from the converse of its central observation. If the show scores comedic points by placing Mafiosi, the horrific Others, right alongside suburban homes, its tragedy and menace also derive from how readily the suburbs have accepted the Mafiosi. Surprise and titillation at viewing killings, beatings, arson, and all the other patented forms of mob intimidation so close to the supposedly sacred hearth-and-home realm of the suburbs, I would argue, become less counterintuitive when one gives close attention to the way the series represents, historicizes, and demythologizes its environments. In its vision of how North Jersey organizes its built spaces, *The Sopranos* makes some of the dominant myths about suburbia as unsustainable as the particular technologies that transformed and dominated those spaces in the first place.

Fight and Flight, Decline and Fall

As Sam Jacob of the British architecture firm FAT has written, "Suburbia has a reputation as a place of duality: of surface happiness with something darker lurking below the radar. This sensation isn't just a convenient artistic device, or a left wing metropolitan smear. It is hardwired into the very foundations of suburbia."[10] Describing the development of suburbs as a psychological dialectic between "technology and nostalgia, [...] desire and fear," as expressed by early proponents such as John Ruskin and Ebenezer Howard, Jacob echoes the analyses of Hayden and others in identifying two complementary motivators: the positive attractions of nature, familial space, and whatever sense of community suburbs could offer, coupled with moral panic over urban slum behavior and industrial squalor.

Propagandists in praise of the intermediate spaces between country and city, from Andrew Jackson Downing, Catharine Beecher, and Samuel Gross in the nineteenth century to Sears, Roebuck and Company, the Levitts, and contemporary packaged-luxury developers like Toll Brothers, are all in the business of selling class aspiration as well as building plans and materials, using positive attractions of bucolic residences and upward mobility—often intermingled with the overwrought imagery of religious salvation, as Hayden drily recounts.[11] The corollary of such positive aspiration is status anxiety, and the long effort to persuade members of the working class to consider the *embourgeoisement* of a move to newly developed suburbs has also depended on a series of powerful negative images: squalor, debt, dependence on landlords, residential instability, and vulnerability to both the sinful habits and the predatory violence of the urban underclass. Fear has always been the underside of the drive toward suburban privatism and domesticity.[12] Suburbs arose in part as a safe private space for families, in contrast to the hazards of public space and economic life; as middle-class economic formations increasingly separated the masculine realm of work from the feminized, idealized realm of the home, these allegedly peaceful spaces close (but not uncomfortably close) to domesticated nature became the natural site for the "cult of domesticity" critiqued by Christopher Lasch in *Haven in a Heartless World*. Versions of that title phrase recur throughout Lasch's study in ironic contexts, as he scrutinizes a succession of psychological, ideological, and institutional trends that he finds have rendered the concept of an innocent familial haven practically a self-parody, but the phrase has a certain tenacity in the realm of myth and belief.[13] Sadly, the dominant spatial manifestation of this idealized haven, particularly through the construction practices of the post-WWII period that replaced the denser, more centripetal "streetcar build-out" pattern with the automotive "sitcom suburb" (nodally distributed, centerless, and widespread in northern New Jersey) has a history that is anything but innocent.

In the United States, the dualistic carrot-and-stick appeal to foster preferences for suburbs over cities has historically included race-based fears ("white flight") as well as class-based ambition. Nowhere has that fear had more explicit consequences than in and around Newark, NJ, the childhood home of Tony Soprano and the real-life location of some of the nation's severest riots in 1967. Newark's unique combination of concentrated poverty, geographic compression (its area measures less than 24 square miles), an inability to incorporate its surrounding suburbs and their higher tax bases within the city limits, and a series of critical building decisions on a citywide level made it the poster child for urban blight from the 1950s through the 1990s—a time when the city lost 160,000 people, or over a third of its population, including a sixth of it in the 1980s alone.[14] The violent events that mark this city's history cast long and influential shadows, both in the real world and in the fictional realm of The Sopranos.

In conversations with longtime New Jersey residents, I have been struck by how large the Newark riots (and the related, arguably harsher violence[15] in nearby Plainfield during the same year) loom in their experience and consciousness. The rioting was a transformative event in the decision of many families to move, the hardening of antisocial attitudes, and the exacerbation of spatial segregation. Sopranos series creator Chase (born David DeCesare, raised in Clifton and North Caldwell) knows these patterns of behavior intimately. The real-world migration of Italian-Americans out of Newark's First Ward or Seventh Avenue district, a local Little Italy that is now only a memory, is an essential process in the formation of the show's imaginary suburbanized Mafia. The Sopranos gestures toward the Newark area's history at least once per episode through its opening "drive" sequence as well as throughout its long-range plot arcs, and that history intertwines urban-planning decisions (particularly those involving the highways that have come to define North Jersey) with reciprocal processes of both official and popular violence.

Newark and its suburbs have long been among the most socially polarized of America's metropolitan areas. Postwar Newark, as Kenneth Jackson recounts,

> built more units of public housing per capita than any other city in
> the nation. Because its neighbors were more protective of their image,
> however, Newark attracted an even larger percentage of the very poor,
> and by 1970 it was the most troubled metropolis in the United States
> by any of a half-dozen measures of urban pathology.[16]

Despite its mayor's recommendations in 1900 favoring the same process of annexation that allowed New York and other cities to diversify demographically while expanding physically, Newark actually lost territory over the twentieth century, a pattern shared only with Washington, D.C. Separate governmental status allows Newark's outlying neighborhoods to zone out lower-income residents and public housing projects, rejecting larger cities' methods of spreading and sharing responsibility for the poor. Within Newark's borders, while the African-American population tripled in less than two decades as migrants arrived from the rural South, jobs became steadily scarcer in midcentury as local brewing, tanning, manufacturing, and other industries left the city; the city's housing stock had been deteriorating for decades, often through insurance-driven arson or "landlord lightning," with an average of 3,620 structural fires per year between 1961 and 1967.[17] Prejudicial redlining practices by the Federal Housing Administration, rating essentially the entire city as a bad risk, created formidable barriers to property ownership or renovation by African-Americans, immigrants, and the working class as a whole.[18] These economic and physical conditions combined with incidents of police brutality (many real, some amplified by rumor), exclusion of the city's black residents from city government despite promises from mayor Hugh Addonizio, and an urban-renewal policy that local residents equated with "Negro removal"[19] create optimal conditions for insurrection.

The most devastating blows to Newark's neighborhoods involved plans to demolish occupied homes and traditional pedestrian-friendly blocks for new building projects, particularly highways: the New Jersey Turnpike in the early 1950s, the Turnpike's Newark Bay extension from 1954 to 1956, Interstate 78 from 1956 through 1989, and Interstate 280 from 1958 to 1980. Arguably, these roads were largely unnecessary, since the intercity commuter-rail lines that merged into New Jersey Transit in 1979 made a streetcar-build-out pattern of first-ring suburbs viable, but federal and state transportation officials had other priorities. Neighborhood representatives and city officials wrangled for decades, before and after the riot year, to prevent residential areas from suffering the kind of fate that Robert Moses had notoriously imposed on the Bronx.[20] They did not succeed. After the conversion of fifteen First Ward blocks to three Corbusier-style superblocks in the early 1950s for the high-rise Christopher Columbus Homes (cut off from the rest of the city, quickly blighted, and now demolished), a plan to place a 150-acre campus for the University of Medicine and Dentistry in Newark's Central Ward ghetto made it clear that the African-American community was slated for the same kind of official assault that had already decimated Little Italy. The systematic destruction of urban territory for conversion to automotive territory, in short, was a politically sanctioned urbicide. Under such conditions, the racially tinged police-beating incident that provoked the 1967 riots was simply the spark in an extremely dry tinderbox, transforming one sustained form of structural violence into the more obvious variety.

One may also note that the roadbuilding that made centerless suburbs possible was never in any meaningful sense a peacetime activity. Viewing the entire Interstate Highway System in its historical context requires a recognition of Cold War military imperatives. Roads had to be sufficient to move large populations and large armaments, much as Haussmann's boulevards had allowed troops to fire straight at Parisian insurrectionists. After World War II's expansion of the field of warfare into territory previously considered civilian—under the shadow of nuclear "total war"—the Interstate system essentially militarized the American landscape. President Dwight D. Eisenhower had been impressed by the German autobahns and the efficient military mobility they enabled; he was also responsive to the argument, raised by a special "Defense through Decentralization" issue of the *Bulletin of the Atomic Scientists*, that dispersing the population from cities to smaller, lower-density satellite communities decreased the desirability of urban missile targets.[21] After decades of pro-highway pressure on congressional committees by the road-building, automotive, trucking, parking, real-estate, and construction industries, these defense considerations may have decisively tipped the political balance. Eisenhower's advocacy of a nationwide highway system, realized with the Federal-Aid Highway Act of 1956, explicitly included civil-defense planning, as reflected in its official name, the "National System of Interstate and Defense Highways," expanded in 1990 to the "Dwight D. Eisenhower System of Interstate and Defense Highways."[22] Countless pop-cultural paeans to the freedom and independence of the open road may have erased this history from the public consciousness, but the form of freedom that automobility confers has always been a side effect of the government's interest in transporting weapons and moving bomb-traumatized populations away from cities as rapidly as possible.

The built environment that appears throughout *The Sopranos* may evoke the mythology of the family haven—the affluent housewives of the series exert considerable effort sustaining that mythic image through design, deploying ceaseless floral pattern decorations and Martha Stewart-style amenities in their tract homes—but this environment always had a doubled identity as a form of war zone. The act of automobilizing a territory, structuring it to favor the convenience of persons driving private vehicles between suburbs over the interests of inhabitants of older urban forms of space, has been socially and aesthetically destructive in ways that James Howard Kunstler and others have shouted themselves hoarse describing and decrying.[23] The car is the structure in these spaces that forces all other structures to accommodate to it, rather than accommodating to them. Any auto-dominated building or setting sends the message that specific places matter less than movement between them. The implicit meme *You are somewhere* yields to *You are here for now, but you won't be here long.* Kunstler poses the essential question regarding this sustained campaign against the sense of community: "if Americans loved their cars, perhaps it was because the machines allowed them to escape from reality – which raises the more interesting question: Why did America build a reality of terrible places from which people longed to escape?"[24]

Taking a step closer to the military meaning of *mobilization*, and considering the policy choices and informational campaigns that were necessary to sell the automotive age to Americans, it does not unduly stretch one's metaphoric capacity to interpret automobilization as an act of class warfare, waged from above. The history of Newark's rebellions indicates that such acts of war do not occur in a vacuum. As violence nearly always begets further forms of violence, the 1967 riots answered the automotive lobby's attack on American territory in the form of neighborhood destruction, racial and class antagonism, and erosion of communal bonds.

The Sopranos anchors its plot in Newark's violent history early on. A prolonged flashback sequence in the first-year episode[25] "Down Neck" (the phrase names a Newark district along the Passaic River) establishes the milieu of Tony's youth in Newark's Little Italy in 1967. Soul-rock from the period is on the radio; riots in the Springfield Avenue ghetto are on his family's television screen; bystanders in one scene, the arrest of Tony's mobster father Johnny-Boy Soprano, shout about how the police should concentrate on arson by *mulignans* (Italian for "eggplants," a racist term for African-Americans) instead of on mob activity. The entire community is shown focusing on the riots, and even the toughest of the wise guys fear the rioters; some of the Sopranos' neighbors are already making plans to leave.

Johnny-Boy, his wife Livia, and their children live in a paneled row house closely packed among neighboring buildings—a residence that could easily have been among those depicted in the show's opening montage, early in the sequence of housing forms, well before Tony and Carmela's North Caldwell house appears onscreen. As the "Down Neck" flashback makes the harsh events that formed modern New Jersey explicit, setting the stage for the Sopranos' own white flight and migration up the ladder of stratified residences, the opening sequence makes the physical consequences of that process palpable.

A Jersey Barrier

The opening credit sequence creates a sense of place through strategic exclusion and inclusion. Its transitions between urban and suburban sites, combined with highly selected details and moments of Eisensteinian intellectual montage, superimpose a personal journey, a class migration, and a societal rejection of communitarian development patterns in favor of the fragmentation, privatism, and technological mediation associated with suburban building forms. It is a literal and metaphorical journey from New York City to North Jersey, and it marks a critical transition point in how Americans view the relations of physical and social environments. It encodes the violent transformation of the Newark region in just 98 seconds of video and music (Alabama 3's "Woke Up This Morning," inscribing Tony's destiny and frustrations in both a blues-based melodic tradition and the jarring artificial timbres of 1990s electronica).

The sequence shows one brief Manhattan skyline view (over a slab of rough concrete) and a single landmark: the Statue of Liberty as seen from the New Jersey side at a distance over Meadowlands foliage. Otherwise, it focuses on locally familiar structures, establishing the environment that Tony drives through on his way home from the city, chiefly Hudson and Essex Counties. In representing this environment through rapid jump cuts over a powerful soundtrack, Chase and colleagues have done what few besides William Carlos Williams and Bruce Springsteen have accomplished: they have iconicized New Jersey.

They have not rendered it beautiful, at least by any nonironized definition of the term. Much of this industrial landscape would qualify as brownfields or "drosscape," to use Alan Berger's term for abandoned and damaged land, or in the discourse of Rem Koolhaas, as "junkspace," a tightly yet randomly packed collection of industrial-era eyesores largely gone to seed in the postindustrial/automotive era.[26] The Meadowlands area is polluted severely enough, with both industrial waste and, legendarily, the bodies of Mafia victims, to make reclamation for most uses forbiddingly difficult, but Chase reclaims it as a cultural touchstone.

The choices of roads and the visual angles shown from Tony's Chevrolet Suburban do not add up to a realistic single drive unless Tony is making multiple irregular stops in the areas of Jersey City, Newark, Kearny, and

Elizabeth. The shots are a jumbled composite, only roughly directional between the Lincoln Tunnel origin and the North Caldwell destination, and an improbable combination of clear sunlight and overcast skies establish that the sequence is a spatial and temporal *bricolage*. Nevertheless, the sequence has become famous as an analogue of the movement of America's immigrants from urban communities—New York's Lower East Side being the most heavily mythologized—through the distinctive settlement patterns of traditional first-ring suburbs and later exurbs. Tony's drive shows him rising through social strata, steadily accumulating sufficient wealth to buy into exclusive suburbs with extensive landscaping, long private driveways, swimming pools, and other upper-middle-class comforts.

The full set of opening-sequence shots is as follows, with each episode's credits speeding left to right in automotive fashion, pausing just long enough to be read[27]:

1 Ceiling of Lincoln Tunnel (two shots of the same subject)
2 Emergence from Lincoln Tunnel into bright sunlight, curving "helix" ramp (three shots, first two separated by fade to white, including midtown Manhattan above a concrete Jersey barrier in the third)
3 New Jersey Turnpike sign
4 World Trade Center towers (first three seasons only), seen occupying whole screen at first, then with camera drawing back, establishing that the towers are reflected in Tony's side mirror: the shot places Manhattan unambiguously behind him
5 Tollbooth (two shots); Tony takes his Turnpike ticket; a sticker on the tollbooth reads "Vote 1998 The Brown Slate,"[28] and two stickers express opposition to "FUR" with a red slash
6 Signs, plane
7 New Jersey Turnpike, heading south; oncoming trucks in mirror view
8 Lighter
9 Goethals Bridge (linking Elizabeth, N.J., with Staten Island, N.Y.), window view
10 Parallel road, more trucks
11 Industrial landscape, Hydro-Pruf roof sign with one letter missing: "HYDRO-P UF DURABLE WATER REPELLENT"
12 Interior as Tony drives through Elizabeth refinery district, exhaling cigar smoke
13 Overhead lights
14 Plane taking off from Newark Airport

15 Statue of Liberty seen from New Jersey angle, rear view, over local trees and plants
16 Exit 13 sign
17 Tony's hairy hand on wheel
18 Refinery drum, DRIVE SAFELY sign
19 Road, white lines passing fast
20 Port Newark: rail yard and power-line towers, either reflected in a ridged/mirrored surface or viewed through segmented glass
21 Smokestacks (two shots)
22 Pulaski Skyway above water
23 More Elizabeth smokestacks above traffic; cigar again, reiterating the concept that Tony is also a polluter, entirely at home in this environment
24 Signage above, as viewed from Pulaski Skyway, headed toward Newark: North Truck 1 & 9; To South 440
25 Routes 1 & 9, elevated roadway again; more trucks
26 Wheel with downtown Newark reflected in hubcap
27 Tony in mirror, with smoky interior (he carries his form of pollution with him, and he is not immune to self-reflection)
28 Overhead bridge, Route 280 into Newark, clear sky
29 Passing railroad bridge
30 Church: Sacred Heart Basilica Cathedral, Newark
31 Rail yard of Newark Penn Station
32 Meadowlands panorama, gray sky, water, plants in foreground
33 Overhead bridge
34 Signage on Route 21 north, Newark: Linde Volkswagen billboard, Valley Landscape Inc., and Sunoco station (offering 97.9-cent gasoline, now a poignant memory),
35 Tony interior again with cigar, turning
36 Statue of large "Muffler Man" near Wilson's Carpet and Furniture in Jersey City, formerly holding an auto muffler and clad as a lumberjack, now holding a rolled-up green carpet
37 Sky, clear again, pole and wires, overhead bridge
38 Cemetery, Route 7, North Arlington; industrial buildings in background
39 Urban corner, Pulaski Savings branch, Harrison; pedestrian (working-class man carrying small bag, perhaps lunch)
40 Satriale's Pork Store, Kearny. pig sculpture on roof, satellite antenna on adjacent building (Satriale's is fictional, though its real-life model, Centanni's in Elizabeth, appeared in the initial episode)

HEARTLESS IN HAVENWORLD™

41 Urban sidewalk, possibly Jersey City, Union City, or Newark; parked cars, multiethnic teenage pedestrians

42 Fade to road again, white line

43 Tony, interior

44 Pizzaland,[29] North Arlington: frontal view, slower speed

45 First residential block, lower-middle-class area with closely packed houses, flag on porch

46 Second residential block, higher socioeconomic level (possibly Belleville, Maplewood, or Montclair), more diverse styles, 2½-story houses, driveways; some lawns maintained better than others

47 Third residential block, 1½-story bungalow-style houses with porches, probably West Orange; house proximity and socioeconomic level intermediate between first and second residential blocks

48 Fourth residential block, larger yards, 1½-story but larger and more widely separated houses, further west; possibly Wayne or West Caldwell

49 Fifth residential block, similar area; point of view is further from the houses (larger); power lines and traffic light; shot shows more of the road and infrastructure than the blocks

50 Tony in silhouette with cigar

51 Woods (two shots: second over the unchanging credit "Created by David Chase"), sunlight viewed through taller trees, roughly 30'–40': nature insulates the next residential block from the previous ones

52 Fade, approaching Tony's driveway

53 Tony's house, North Caldwell, coming into view as writer credits appear; long tracking shot approaching pseudo-gated driveway with California-style front-facing garage at right; Tony in rear-view mirror; close proximity of neighbors' houses in background: with its large scale but decidedly un-aristocratic settlement pattern (crowding other large houses on nearby lots), this is an "estate home," i.e., McMansion

54 Tony's face in clear sunlight as he exits the SUV with a grim expression, looking ready for a struggle as he enters his home over final repetition of the lyric "got yourself a gun"

55 Title of show; fade to black

Of the 54 brief scenes (some comprising more than one shot), 27 include explicit automotive content (I count only shots directly relevant to vehicles, parts of vehicles, roads, Tony's driveway, etc.) If the railroad and bridge imagery is added, the role of transportation modalities as an environmental determinant is inescapable. The overwhelming impression of this sequence is dominance of the local environment by motor vehicles. Tony's SUV is more than a conveyance; it mediates his vision in all directions, insulates him from the noise and danger of other vehicles and from the famously vile-smelling air of Elizabeth's refineries, provides private space within which he can enjoy his cigar, music, and private thoughts, and delivers him to a home whose design and façade emphasize the importance of automobility by foregrounding the driveway and garage. The pervasiveness of private transportation in this world is so complete that to notice vehicles *qua* vehicles risks stating the obvious, but this sequence highlights the vehicular aspect of North Jersey life in ways that heighten critical attention.

On symbolic and metaphorical levels, it is difficult to dissociate any emergence out of a tunnel into daylight from the imagery of birth. One should tread carefully in attaching a biological interpretation to scenes of an environment that is so relentlessly inorganic; on the other hand, the plot lines treat psychiatric sessions, intrafamilial (particularly maternal) conflicts, and filiative themes so centrally that it would be perverse to exclude obstetrical associations entirely. Tony's emergence from the Lincoln Tunnel leaves New York City and its familiar Mafia mythologies—the ethnic solidarity, the codes of honor, the moments of heroism despite loathsome deeds—decisively and irreversibly behind. No one ever crawls back into a womb, and no one who has left New York for North Jersey retains quite the same direct connection to the city. Manhattan remains visible only at a distance and across barricades, separated by more than a river.

Tony travels through an unwelcoming realm, ascends through first-generation neighborhoods, and arrives at a contrived place where the semi-public *domus* has yielded to the private domicile. Death surrounds him, both the deaths his profession requires and the physically encoded death of all the biological matter that the Earth has spent millennia heating and compressing into petrochemicals. Tony's voyage, however, does not end in symbols of his own death—unless one views that final shot of the garage (its dormer windows positioned like eyes, its central flagpole socket a diminutive proboscis, and the garage door a closed maw on the verge of gaping) in the same way Kunstler viewed his family's Long Island suburban development: "The houses, with a few exceptions, were identical boxy split-levels, clad in asphalt shingles of various colors, with two windows above a gaping garage door, affording the façades an aspect of slack-jawed erotinism."[30] Domesticity and automobility, the inseparable governing principles of the outer-ring suburban existence, are on the brink of swallowing Tony whole.

HEARTLESS IN HAVENWORLD™

People Come Here to Die

Tony's house is a goal that many Americans would strive to attain. It is large by almost any measure, garish by traditional Anglophile-American standards of taste, dominated by its driveway and garage, separated from street grids by a cul-de-sac development pattern, difficult to approach without a vehicle (it has neither a front sidewalk nor a rear alley), well-nestled in woods but surprisingly close to its neighbors, considering its scale. It sits at the end of a curvilinear road, a street design associated with bucolic privacy since Alexander Jackson Davis's undulating design for the foundational American exurb, Llewellyn Park in West Orange, N.J., in the mid-nineteenth century.[31] It has ostentatious driveway gate piers, but no actual gate; its gestures toward the country retreats of older cultures and more snobbish classes are entirely for show. It is a McMansion, the type of *nouveau-riche* residence that has attracted energetic critiques for excessive scale, energy inefficiency, and pseudoaristocratic pretension. The Soprano house[32] is one of several McMansions depicted in the series. In the episode "The Knight in White Satin Armor," Tony's sister Janice and temporary fiancé Richie Aprile purchase an even larger home, an indicator of Aprile's recurrent desire to one-up Tony; New York mob underboss John "Johnny Sack" Sacrimoni, having moved to New Jersey, shows off his new exurban McMansion to Tony in "Employee of the Month," complete with two-story great room and backyard view of farmers on tractors. Domestic one-upmanship among the mobsters takes the same form it takes among Tony's physician and stockbroker neighbors: the house is a shrine to its owner's ego and finances, whether legitimately or illegitimately acquired, and the affluent spare no expense in displaying their status.

Tony and Carmela's house is upper-middle-class gaudy, with a living room full of pseudo-Roman fluted columns (one of which has a secret compartment containing an automatic rifle), overstuffed furniture, Murano glass knickknacks, multiple mirrors, gold-on-white decor, a stylized wall sculpture of a curving musical staff above the fireplace (though only one person in the family, Meadow, shows any musical talent, and only briefly), and unnatural-colored floral motifs in all directions. (Offered a deal on antiques in "Mr. Ruggiero's Neighborhood," Carmela respectfully declines: "Oh, I don't have antiques; my house is traditional.") Carmela's taste in home design is an updated version of the kind that compelled Frank Lloyd Wright to refer to interior decorators as "inferior desecrators," though it remains just within the bounds of middlebrow respectability, pulling up short of the broad parvenu caricatures depicted in *Goodfellas* (1990), Jonathan Demme's *Married to the Mob* (1988), and other representations of Mafia domesticity. Beyond the class signifiers of decoration, the house is a finely tuned machine for living. The large kitchen is supplied with culinary conveniences, the verdant backyard includes a swimming pool and deck, and the living spaces are thoroughly wired with home electronics; both children and parents are frequently shown using computers, video-game stations, DVD players, and other entertainment media. However much violence, hypocrisy, and agonizing intrafamilial drama haunt this building, it is a self-contained consumer utopia for the affluent twenty-first-century nuclear family. It is a mediated parody of the spatial prize an economic striver was supposed to have earned in moving out to the edge space between city and country, a theme-parkish simulacrum of a family haven.

Attention to domiciles throughout the show's environment is obsessive, particularly in early episodes establishing the settings. Invasion of the sanctity of domestic space (in the form of a home phone call from Tony's ex-mistress in "Whitecaps") is the one thing that can drive Carmela, a committed Roman Catholic, to take steps toward divorce and throw Tony out, although she has previously tolerated countless crimes, infidelities, and lies. Earlier in the timeline ("Nobody Knows Anything"), Tony draws the distinction between the home and the outer world as sharply as a fissure in time: admonishing his children not to talk frankly about sex in the home, he tells them, "Out there it's the 1990s. In this house, it's 1954." In episodes organized around questions of social class like "A Hit Is A Hit," houses are charged with fetishlike energy: even the rational and sophisticated Dr. Melfi, during a dinner party at the Sopranos' next-door neighbors' house, surreptitiously cranes out a bathroom window to gawk at the Sopranos' property. In the same episode a rap-music mogul, having invited Tony's nephew Christopher Moltisanti to his manse in Englewood Cliffs for business reasons, makes sure to answer Moltisanti's compliment over the property by mentioning casually that his other house in the Hamptons is larger. Conversely, separation of a character from a house becomes an intrafamilial capital offense when Tony's aged mother, the borderline-psychotic Livia, manipulates her brother-in-law Corrado "Uncle Junior" Soprano into putting out a contract on her own son as retribution for his decision to move her from her Verona bungalow to an assisted-living facility ("Isabella" and other first-year episodes). If home ownership in this world, as in the nineteenth-century advertisements identified by Hayden, is tantamount to personal salvation, a house can signify hell as well. A wounded and comatose Tony in "Mayham" [sic], hallucinating that he is trapped in an alternate existence riddled with Catholic and Buddhist death symbols, is nearly ushered into a large, ominous house by a politely insidious man (resembling his cousin Tony Blundetto, a troublemaking loose cannon whom Tony himself killed). A figure resembling Livia is visible in the doorway, but the voice of a child causes him to recoil, and he emerges from his coma. Most interpreters of the series, and of this dream, view this house as Tony's narrowly avoided death and damnation. Nonviewers of The Sopranos may reasonably find their eyes glazing over at the dense knots of plotting, dreams, and symbols; the gist is that houses in Sopranos New Jersey are always much more than houses.

Any member of a criminal organization must play constant cat-and-mouse games with law enforcement personnel. Tony's friendly nemesis, FBI Agent Harris, conducts his investigations of the Soprano home not with the obsessiveness of an Eliot Ness, but with alternating deference and intensity. The contrast between the gravity his duties require and the tame domestic setting where they take place is sometimes played for laughs, sometimes for poignancy. A federal "sneak and peek" operation to install a hidden microphone in the house ("Mr. Ruggiero's Neighborhood") requires spying on family members to ensure that no one is home when agents enter; Harris's crew consequently don utility-company disguises, coordinate movements by radio using code names, and tail such unmenacing figures as schoolchildren and an errand-running housewife (over a soundtrack that beat-matches the detective-film jazz of the "Peter Gunn Theme" to the Police's stalker anthem "Every Breath You Take"). Executing a search warrant in Tony's home ("The Legend of Tennessee Moltisanti"), Harris comes discreetly to the back door and explains to the elder Tony that he'll give him a few minutes to send his son upstairs under some appropriate pretext: "We don't think it necessary to traumatize kids by kicking in doors." The difficulty of imagining real-world investigators from harder-nosed eras (Harry Anslinger? Robert Kennedy? Rudolph Giuliani?) backing off out of sensitivity to the emotions of children is only part of the point here. Underlying both the humor and the humanizing of the suburban mobsters is the tacit assumption that the privacy of domestic space trumps all other values, sometimes even the law.

The metaphoric power of construction and demolition extend beyond the residential realm. Tony's immigrant grandfather and great-uncle were stonemasons, and in the pilot episode he shares a moment of pride with Meadow in a Newark church where the elder Sopranos worked on the construction crew. Italian stone and marble workers, he tells his daughter, "didn't design [the church], but they knew how to build it." After a pause, with Meadow marveling at the sculptured interior and beginning to understand the depth of her father's connection to the place, he continues: "Go out now and try to find me two guys who can put decent grout around your bathtub." This scene is followed by a cut to his *consigliere* Silvio Dante setting a restaurant on fire, but the abrupt transition from construction to arson is practically unnecessary to drive home the theme: greatness, in the form of either public works or superb craft in any field, belongs to the past. The present and its typical structures, from McMansions to commercial facilities, are debased and antiheroic—a cheap and transitory architecture appropriate to both the auto age and the era of *il declino del padrino*, the "decline of the Godfather."[33] Kunstler, with the history of the Interstate system in his own rear-view mirror, provides salient commentary:

> *The public realm suffered in another way with the rise of the automobile. Because the highways were gold-plated with our national wealth, all other forms of public building were impoverished. ... Public buildings such as the Philadelphia water works or Jefferson's Virginia state capitol at Richmond were expected to endure for generations, perhaps centuries, as the Greek temples had endured since antiquity. These earlier American building types were set in a different landscape, characterized by respect for the human scale and a desire to embellish nature, not eradicate it. Try to imagine a building of any dignity surrounded by six acres of parked cars. The problems are obvious. Obvious solution: Build buildings without dignity.[34]*

Aside from private homes, little of enduring substance is built in the *Sopranos* world. Public space is ignored or plundered; in "Another Toothpick," when Tony discusses a Newark redevelopment project with Johnny Sack and bought-and-paid-for local politician Ronald Zellman, Zellman jokes that the architect's scale model should include "little hookers giving little blowjobs," as the idea of a safe noncriminal pedestrian realm on the streets of Newark strikes him as inherently absurd.[35] To these men, urban redevelopment has value only as a ripe source of graft. Any public or semi-public facility in this world is vaguely sinister and dishonest, no matter how ostensibly pleasant: the retirement community Green Grove, for example, where Livia Soprano and other relatives of mobsters end up living, resembles a three-star hotel or a collegiate social center in its outer areas but conceals starkly functional medical facilities behind an internal door. (Livia, taken for an introductory visit in the pilot episode, is not fooled: "This is a nursing home! People come here to die!")

Another of the show's most frequently shown structures is the Bada Bing strip club, bar, and crew headquarters, a repurposed warehouse close to a barren state highway[36] and a scene of commercial sexual sordor. Bada Bing appears in contrast to a built environment only a few miles away physically but light years away culturally, the Columbia University campus, in the episode "University," which juxtaposes an undergraduate Meadow's growing sophistication against the harsh fate of a girl roughly her own age but much further down the socioeconomic ladder. The naive Tracee (pregnant, wearing dental braces, and already supporting one child as a nude dancer) is beaten to death by sociopathic mobster Ralph Cifaretto behind Bada Bing, next to the steel guardrails and chain-link fencing. The ugliness pervading this environment, both physical and behavioral, has rarely been more apparent than in this incident; even Cifaretto's fellow Mafiosi are appalled.

Where domestic space is sacred and public space is degraded, everything depends on the technology that connects and organizes all those spaces, the automobile. The car is not only ubiquitous but, from the outset, weaponized. Out of the many murders and injuries shown in the series, the pilot episode's first act of violence—Tony's attack on Mahaffey, a middle-management executive who is behind on gambling debts—is not a beating or a shooting, but a leg-breaking vehicular assault in an industrial park. Parking garages are ominous: in the disturbing episode "Employee of the Month," Dr. Melfi is viciously raped in one. In "Pax Soprana," the sole intrusion that is allowed to interrupt one of her psychiatric sessions with Tony is a phone call about an auto-repair emergency, which she discusses in medical terms involving "diagnostics" and a "second opinion." Automotive needs outweigh those of humans here, even with the meter running on the psychiatric hour, and neither party gives this implicit priority ranking a second thought. Cars may be indispensable, but they are the all-purpose source of trouble, the convenient excuse for absences and unexplainable injuries (including Melfi's after her assault, when she invents an auto-accident story to keep the incident private), and of course a source of violence in their own right, accepted as an unfortunate but unalterable fact of life. In "Another Toothpick," driving appears even more dangerous than wet work: a retired mobster battling lung cancer, Bobby Baccalieri, Sr., performs one last double murder (winning a struggle against a much younger, healthier man), but loses control of his getaway car during a coughing fit, hits a roadside sign, and dies behind the wheel. Cancer and gunfire could not kill this man, but North Jersey's crowded roads could.

In what Chase called "the ultimate *Sopranos* episode,"[37] "College," Tony by chance encounters Fabian Petrulio (a turncoat ex-colleague displaced from New Jersey by the federal Witness Protection Program) while taking Meadow, the Soprano family's high-flying academic achiever, on college visits in Maine. Travel motifs proliferate so insistently that "College" might as easily have been labeled "Mobility and Its Discontents." Ample time passes in a rental car, where Meadow asks Tony the key question naming the term that mobsters' offspring traditionally never use ("Daddy, are you in the Mafia?") and receives a not-entirely-dishonest answer. Petrulio is now working as a small-town travel agent and a traveling lecturer with a "confessions of an ex-mobster" program; his office is a mobile home, the humblest and least stable of American building forms. A parallel plot has Carmela Soprano and her parish priest, Father Phil Intintola, spending a rainy night in each other's company at the Soprano house, a technically chaste but sexually charged overnight visit in which she confesses sins of omission (complicity in Tony's life of crime for the sake of material comfort) and receives two Catholic sacraments, confession and communion, that are normally performed in churches (Father Phil is carrying a portable "sacrament kit" including communion wafers and wine). The priest makes a confession of his own after awakening on Carmela's couch, admitting that he has just struggled with sexual temptation. The episode superimposes multiple revelations of information (Tony's to Meadow about his mob membership, Meadow's confession of amphetamine use to her father, Carmela's informal and formal confessions to Father Phil, his reciprocal admission of desire, Tony's discovery of Petrulio's secret whereabouts, and Carmela's discovery that Tony's psychiatrist is female, a fact he had previously concealed) upon multiple scenarios where characters have roamed far from their customary roles. The aspect of "College" that customarily receives commentary is its juxtapository humor: at the moment Meadow is interviewing at Bowdoin, Tony is busy committing a murder. More remarkable may be the deployment of settings and indicators of rootlessness, travel, and migration, all of which destabilize the quotidian conventions that allow concealment. Mobility here does not equal escape, but is instead an efficient channel for instability and disruption. At the moment Tony has finished garroting Petrulio, he hears the familiar sound of quacking (recalling the backyard waterfowl whose departure triggered his first panic attack) and looks skyward to find an orderly V-formation of migratory ducks. He, too, is far from home, taking his daughter to Bates, Colby, and Bowdoin, but his murderous nature, values, and bad conscience have followed him.

HEARTLESS IN HAVENWORLD™

An episode suggesting how smoothly Mafia values can mesh with middle-class institutions, "Bust Out," dramatizes one of the organization's bread-and-butter economic processes, particularly in the current era of the "white-collar Mafia": the acquisition and steady financial exhaustion of legitimate businesses when their owners assume unsustainable debts. David Scatino, a former schoolmate of Tony's with a severe gambling addiction, finds himself in that position after pressing Tony to invite him into a high-stakes poker game where he is financially out of his league. Scatino owns a prosperous sporting-goods store,[38] and Tony's crew assumes partial ownership in order to use its credit lines, purchase large quantities of goods for quick resale, and bleed the firm dry, along with Scatino's personal assets and college fund for his son. Late in the episode a desperate Scatino, on the verge of exile from his family and reduced to spending nights in a camping tent in the store rather than at home, asks Tony how he could treat an old friend this way, and Tony tells him the ancient fable of the frog and the scorpion crossing a river ("This is what I am. This is what I do"). Scatino exchanges residences like the contemporary equivalent of the Depression-era "Okie" migrants, moving from the stability of the North Jersey upper middle class to the transience of a tent, and ultimately the road: he is last seen in a parking lot, strapping personal belongings to the roof of his car.

After the initial invitation into an illegal poker game (and presumably some high-interest loans), Tony breaks no laws in assuming his parasitic ownership position in Ramsey Outdoor. The distinction between his crew's economic conduct toward Scatino and that of non-Mafia lenders toward financially troubled borrowers may be only a matter of degree. Indeed, some commentators (e.g., Diego Gambetta, working close to the anarcho-libertarian school of economists Ludwig von Mises and Murray Rothbard) have argued that all the Mafia really does, analyzed as a business enterprise, is supply services privately that public institutions are unable or unwilling to supply, such as "protection," socially proscribed pleasures (gambling, prostitution, recreational drugs), or loans at usurious rates.[39] Unsupportable debt, of course, was historically one of the urban ills that suburban homeownership, at least in developers' "Why Pay Rent?" advertisements pitched at urban workers was supposed to remedy.[40] The reality of America's suburban migration for many, of course, was that a bank could be at least as heavy a burden as a landlord (if one could obtain financing at all, and Federal Housing Administration driven redlining practices ensured that many, particularly members of minorities, could not). The organization of all residential space as a subdivided and privatized commodity has proved all too compatible with the reproduction of parasitic conditions in the very spaces where personal freedom was supposed to flourish. Indeed, ineradicable consumer debt is not an anomaly in the hyperconsumption economy of places like North Jersey, but the very engine of that economy, and the United States has the low savings rates, high personal-bankruptcy rates, and burgeoning levels of both public and private debt that one would expect under such conditions. Scatino's fate is perhaps an extreme case, but by no means one confined to the entertainment realm.

One New Jersey journalist, Steven Hart,[41] connects the Scatino parable to the revival of *laissez-faire* economic policies under Republican administrations, calling a bust-out on a national scale "the natural outcome of a quarter-century of rhetoric about how government is the problem, not the solution; how government doesn't work; how deregulation is the only way to build the economy."[42] Hart identifies the Sopranos' business methods explicitly with trickle-up, "take the money and run" policies. Partisanship aside, the more public services, public spaces, and public-sector social supports are deliberately eroded, the more Scatinos are scattered throughout the nation, and the harder it becomes to distinguish one variety of private service provider from another.

The Triumph of the Ugly and Ordinary

Many aspects of this deeply cynical fictional world have struck a nerve with audiences in New Jersey and beyond. The opening sequence's mimetic potential extends into the amateur sphere: fans of the series have prepared at least fifteen parodic YouTube versions set in different locations.[43] Any one of these homemade parodies makes for fairly tiresome viewing for anyone not personally acquainted with the locations, videographers, and drivers; a sampling of all fifteen induces a strange combination of numbness and grim fascination. Aside from the desire to inhabit the Tony Soprano role vicariously for a few minutes, why would anyone take the trouble to film themselves driving through environments where nothing is of visual interest?

The banality of the amateur videos' settings, like that of the North Jersey settings in the official version, is essential to the aesthetic effect of this sequence. Yet Lance Strate, one of academia's first-generation Sopranologists, cites "the simple pleasure of seeing your local environment depicted on TV"[44] and notes how the sites have gained the kind of aura that Walter Benjamin wrote about, in this case an aura gained through electronic reproduction. The act of driving on the New Jersey highways is no longer simply a matter of transportation. It has become a ritual reenactment of the program's opening. Put The Sopranos: Music from the HBO Original Series CD on the car stereo, turn the volume up as A3 comes on with "Woke Up This Morning (Chosen One)," and the experience is complete.[45]

The well-known Benjaminian observation about the relation between an aesthetic aura and the act of mechanical reproduction is precisely inverted here. North Jersey had no particular aura, one might even claim,[46] until The Sopranos conferred one.

The homemade parodies extend this pleasure to other locales, but the interest is parochial in a pure sense of the term: being televised elevates the scenes, seizing our interest because they are in some sense privately ours, not because they hold any broader inherent interest. Were any of the shots to show a striking or monumental structure rather than Pizzaland, Satriale's Pork Store, or the Pulaski Skyway, such a shot would disrupt the mood and the qualities imputed to Tony: grittiness, unpretentiousness, comfort in the presence of ugliness both visual and ethical. The mundanity and local familiarity of each site his car passes support another critical point: the sequence does not focus on places per se, but on the act of moving through places. Among the memes that The Sopranos has placed into circulation is thus a heightened attention to the ordinary act of moving in a vehicle through public spaces that are chiefly and merely of private interest. The transposition of these environments from the real world into the iconic realm also offers an opportunity to study them in detail, to note how they echo the violence and ugliness of the processes that formed them, and to reflect on how many forms ugliness can assume. If post-urban environments can be viewed, according to Lars Lerup's formulation, as a combination of "stim" and "dross," in this rendering of North Jersey the points of stimulation and the background drosscape are one and the same.[47]

One universally recognizable structure, the twin towers of the World Trade Center, did appear in the sequence during the first three seasons (Chase removed this shot after the September 11 attack). Significantly, the WTC did not appear in direct view, but in Tony's rear-view mirror. As noted above, Tony is leaving New York City behind and striking out for a territory known for being undifferentiated. For all the resonance the scenery of New Jersey may have for those who have lived there,[48] it has no compelling visual symbols, no Golden Gate Bridge or Sears Tower or Gateway Arch. The state's natural beauties are substantial—the shore, the Watchung mountains, the Pine Barrens—but they are known mainly to residents; they are not publicly iconic. In many minds, perhaps most, the primary built forms of New Jersey are highways, malls (both enclosed and strip), and factories, not towers or bridges or public sculpture. The single national icon to which New Jersey might lay claim, the Statue of Liberty, is officially considered part of New York State, despite its closer measurable proximity to Jersey City, whose mayor and congressional representative lost a 1987 U.S. Supreme Court lawsuit to claim jurisdiction over Liberty and Ellis Islands.[49] New Jerseyans' generalized sense of disrespect has some basis in documented fact as well as in behavioral observation.

A New Jersey identity appears premised on anti-iconicity, an absence of publicly recognized grandeur and distinction. To the extent that built environments can be classified according to Robert Venturi, Denise Scott Brown, and Steven Izenour's famous polar terms "Heroic and Original" (H&O) and "Ugly and Ordinary" (U&O), New Jersey may in some sense be the national capital of U&O.[50] Derision toward New Jersey has a long history in American popular culture, tracing at least as far back as Benjamin Franklin's reputed comment that the state resembled a "barrel tapped at both ends" because its resources and its most talented citizens tend to flow toward Philadelphia and New York.[51] The state's residents have long contended with New Jersey jokes, Manhattanites' cultural condescension, incessant headlines trumpeting political scandals and environmental disasters, out-of-staters' inference that the entire state resembles the degraded portions seen from the Turnpike, and the assumption that driving is the defining experience of New Jersey life. In the media realm, New Jersey takes most of its information from the metropolitan areas at either end; it has no major television stations of its own, relying on those from New York and Philadelphia, and its newspapers occupy a similar second stratum, ceding much national and world coverage to the *New York Times* and the *Philadelphia Inquirer*. To outsiders, the state has earned the title of "the Great Wrong Place" that W.H. Auden once bestowed on the other capital of automobility, Los Angeles, and voices raised in its defense often attract replies along the lines of "thou dost protest too much, methinks." Political columnist Chris Suellentrop, writing of New Jersey's then-junior senator Frank Lautenberg, captured the customary tone succinctly, even Hobbesianly: "Because of this perpetual junior status [overshadowed by Senatorial colleague William Bradley and others]—or perhaps simply by disposition—Lautenberg, despite his grandfatherly reputation, is scrappy,

HEARTLESS IN HAVENWORLD™

sometimes mean, unpopular, occasionally nasty, and insecure. In short, he's New Jersey."[52]

If disproportionate numbers of New Jerseyans habitually speak in pugnacious tones—as the characters on The Sopranos undoubtedly do, sometimes with jaw-droppingly uninhibited personal attacks on each other's vulnerabilities—is it because they resent outsiders' disdain, or because on some level they agree with it? A combination of self-critique and perverse pride seems hardwired into the state's DNA; a popular t-shirt sold there reads "New Jersey: Only the Strong Survive." This sentiment implicitly endorses the Spencerian version of Darwinian evolution—survival not of the species best suited to their niches, as in Darwin's original formulation, but merely of the toughest, the most combative—and even though this is obviously a tongue-in-cheek attitude, it fits remarkably well with the amoral, asocial modus operandi of a Tony Soprano. The caricatured New Jersey personality not only accepts, but vehemently defends the U&O environment, prizing the ordinariness as unpretentiousness and ridiculing any effort to rise above the general degradation individually or collectively. In the world of The Sopranos, cultural elites and traditional centers of authority reek of hypocrisy, and anyone not frankly on the make is a fool and a mark. There is no room for heroism, sincerity, or originality here, or for any deviance from the fundamental command of the marketplace: maximize your private gain by any means necessary. Violence against other citizens is as legitimate as violence against the natural environment or the visual violence of the roadside eyesore: indeed, here, one may identify aesthetic violence as the logical culmination of historical, ecological, and economic as well as physical forms of violence. No one exhibits qualities that could be confused with nobility here, and nothing built here is ennobling. Ethics and aesthetics are optional. More to the point: they are commodities, which a few can afford and most cannot.

The U&O-ness that defines Sopranos North Jersey differs in certain important respects from the Venturi/Scott Brown/Izenour sense of U&O, which reacted to the perceived impracticality and arrogance of H&O high modernism, aiming to revalue the relatively honest functions of mundane suburban design. In the U&O Sopranos world, there are no revolutionary forms from which to recoil, with the sole exception of Dr. Melfi's stark, round modernist office interior (the site not of aspiration or rationalism, but of endlessly circular attempts at private purgation through self-combat). Venturian U&O, grounded in a tolerant and pretension-puncturing populism, resists the move from "decorat[ing] construction" to "construct[ing] decoration."[53] The McMansion is a construction decorated within an inch of its life, but it is a constructed decoration as well: it brings the hollowness of the theme park into wooded areas cleared physically by bulldozers and conceptually by haven-myth propaganda. Such a house is an ethical whitewashing job translated into painted brick and mirrored glass, a message Carmela Soprano must continually send herself to gain assurance that the economic processes that placed her here are peaceful, natural, and clean (and since she knows that Tony is monstrous and this message is false, she can never stop sending it, and she can allow no detail in the building to speak in dissent: domestic perfection as small-scale semiotic totalitarianism). The house hermetically seals its occupants against unpredictable exchanges with others, against the unruliness of a democratic polis; it is a strictly private monument, commemorating nothing but its owner's accumulation of financial and cultural capital. Public monumental structures implicitly inspire either civic pride or social prudence and exert a silent threat of official violence, but what the anti-monumental U&O architecture of the *Sopranos* suburbs inspires is a volatile blend of restlessness, defensiveness, anomie, and amorality, a condition that is both disorderly and overly orderly, and perhaps one that calls for disruption. Yet in its centerlessness, its paucity of publicly visible nodal spaces, it offers no Bastilles to storm. More often, it simply evokes a desire to flee: to escape mentally through whatever forms of entertainment are available, to drive to malls and shop oneself into submission, or to leave.

This cultural milieu—obviously not limited to North Jersey, merely inscribed memorably by the *Sopranos* version of the place—makes no room for the kind of long-range localized commitments that characterized Tony Soprano's stonemason ancestors. Its constructed embodiment is not only conducive to pathological selfishness and social atomization,[54] but physically and legally resistant to any effort to reverse the existing patterns and build more humane spaces. As New Urbanists point out, the human-scale urban environments prized since Jane Jacobs's day would be unbuildable under most contemporary zoning and construction codes.[55] A redesign and reconstruction of the highway-based settlement pattern of North Jersey and comparable spaces—even if either petroleum-market economic variables or a long-overdue grasp of global environmental imperatives should lead transportation policymakers to rethink the long-range sustainability of an automobile-based infrastructure—would be formidably costly. Compounding the unlikelihood of such a decision, the U.S. public sector faces budgetary shortfalls after decades of reduction in federal and state revenue (not to mention the financial hemorrhage of exorbitant military expenses). Decisions made decades ago have ensured that this environment will remain largely U&O, at least for the foreseeable future.

Celebrating the hardnosed U&O-ness of this region is simultaneously irresistible and problematic. North Jersey as represented in *The Sopranos*—and longtime residents who have written about the show insist its representation is realistic[56]—is an environment predicated on multiple forms and levels of violence: the violence that automobilization and poorly regulated industries have done to the natural world, the violence against community and civility that a hyperprivatized society has wrought, the aesthetic violence of structures like McMansions, malls, and Bada Bing. In these conditions, the conjecture that the different forms are correlated—that behavior takes U&O directions when, and where, people are thoroughly accustomed to the U&O—may be more plausible than the converse conjecture, which defenders of a U&O suburban environment must implicitly make: that no correlation between environmental and behavioral ugliness exists at all.

Addressing these senses of the relation between violence and the built environment as more than metaphorical, one might invoke an interdisciplinary analysis from a field directly concerned with societal responses to violence. James Q. Wilson and George Kelling's "Broken Windows" theory of urban environmental change, based in part on observations in Newark during its most precipitous decline, has influenced strategies of social control since the early 1980s. I would view the Wilson/Kelling argument as a form of applied semiotics, interpreting the message that a broken window or graffiti-tagged wall sends to inhabitants and translating it into urban policing strategy. Allow one broken window to persist unrepaired, Wilson and Kelling assert, and the message goes out to the community that further decline will go unopposed. The Wilson/Kelling meme can logically be applied not only to the urban underclass, as it has traditionally and prejudicially been applied (most visibly, by the New York Police Department under Commissioner William Bratton during the Giuliani mayoralty), but also to the middle and upper classes wherever they may reside. Redirecting a comparable analysis socioeconomically upward might yield powerful policy implications regarding any built environment, urban or suburban. The broader unexamined premise of the broken-windows theory is that people's conduct (violent or nonviolent, creative or destructive, interesting or boring, socially complacent or critical or constructive) is, at least in part, a response to the signals they pick up from their surroundings. This observation may appear so obvious as to need little further elaboration, but its practical extension need not occur in only a top-down direction.

If, as Wilson and Kelling state, "one unrepaired broken window is a signal that no one cares," what kind of signal is one ugly building?[57] An entire neighborhood, town, or region full of them? What signal do people infer—consciously, unconsciously, or semi-consciously, but constantly—when they see the physical consequences of automobile dependence, the indistinguishability and garishness of suburban sprawl, the visual assaults of the parking lot, the antisociality of the cul-de-sac? The message is probably quite similar: that no one cares, that little or nothing here commands respect. Banality breeds more than more banality. Banality breeds indifference to standards, and such indifference has ways of metastasizing from one realm to another.

One passage from Wilson and Kelling outlines the connection between patterns of development (urban, mass-transit-based suburban, or automotive suburban) and breakdowns of community self-regulation:

> The process we call urban decay has occurred for centuries in every city. But what is happening today is different in at least two important respects. First, in the period before, say, World War II, city dwellers—because of money costs, transportation difficulties, familial and church connections—could rarely move away from neighborhood problems. When movement did occur, it tended to be along public-transit routes. Now mobility has become exceptionally easy for all but the poorest or those who are blocked by racial prejudice. Earlier crime waves had a kind of built-in self-correcting mechanism: the determination of a neighborhood or community to reassert control over its turf. Areas in Chicago, New York, and Boston would experience crime and gang wars, and then normalcy would return, as the families for whom no alternative residences were possible reclaimed their authority over the streets.[58]

The social channeling that auto-dependent development encourages, in this view, redirects the historic and potential participants in the maintenance of urban civility toward suburban life instead, leaving a troublesome underclass to rule the city streets unchecked. Rising urban crime rates in the era of suburbanization appear consistent with this analysis, but perhaps the analysis is incomplete and one-sided. What if the ground premise on which the Wilson/Kelling formula rests—the propensity of certain people for violent behavior—did not take such an orderly class-based form? There is violence and there is violence; each class has its preferred forms. Urban and suburban history suggests that the house-worshiping, auto-driving classes and the decision-makers who have favored their interests have perpetrated forms of violence against other classes, against the national sense of public space, and against the Earth. These assaults may be subtler and harder to detect than the street crimes Kelling considered while accompanying foot-patrol officers in Newark, but they have ultimately done more severe damage. If there is a logical analogue to the alliance of peaceful citizens and police that Wilson and Kelling hail as preservers or restorers of livable space, it would be a partnership of architects, urban planners, social critics, community activists, and public officials who view a built environment's U&O-ness with as comprehensive and penetrating an eye as David Chase and his colleagues have brought to their not-entirely-fictional version of North Jersey.

The charisma, drama, black humor, and sheer strangeness that pervade the atmosphere of *The Sopranos* reflect human capacities for enduring (and, rarely, rising above) any setting, no matter how banal and beaten-down. There is an energy in these characters and stories that illuminates even such a drosscape as this exaggerated version of North Jersey. It would be a misplaced act of gross sentimentality to describe any qualities of Tony Soprano as redemptive, but one quality to be counted among his strengths is his capacity for remembering the place he comes from. Understanding, in turn, the place that has been built for the likes of him, and that harbors him without judgment, calls for a critical recognition of just how that place manages to accommodate the destructiveness that he brings to a space, not just as a fictional Mafioso, but as a representative suburbanite. The place was built on false and bloody foundations, and it takes a shape in which a peaceful community cannot rise.

Endnotes

1— Robert Smithson, "The Monuments of Passaic: Has Passaic Replaced Rome as the Eternal City?" *Artforum* 6: 4 (Dec. 1967): 51. During his 1972 interview with Paul Cummings for the Archives of American Art/Smithsonian Institution (http://www.robertsmithson.com/essays/interviews.htm), Smithson's recollection of this quote contains a telling error: "I know there is a sentence in 'The Monuments of Passaic' where I said, 'Hasn't Passaic replaced Rome as the Eternal City?'" One is tempted to ask what (aside from a minor lapse of memory) happened between 1967 and 1972, in Passaic or elsewhere, to convert Smithson's original open-ended question to a rhetorical question, phrased to expect affirmation.

2— See, among others, Andres Duany, Elizabeth Plater-Zyberk and Jeff Speck, *Suburban Nation: The Rise of Sprawl and the Decline of the American Dream* (New York: North Point Press, 2000); David Owen, "Green Manhattan," *New Yorker* (Oct. 18, 2004): 111–123; David Owen, *Green Metropolis: How Living Smaller, Living Closer, and Driving Less Are the Keys to Sustainability* (New York: Riverhead, 2009); Robert Bruegmann, *Sprawl: A Compact History* (Chicago: University of Chicago, 2005); Joel Kotkin, *The City: A Global History* (New York: Modern Library, 2005).

3— See Herbert Gans, *The Levittowners: Life and Politics in a New Suburban Community* (New York: Pantheon, 1967); Richard Harris, "The Making of American Suburbs, 1900s–1950s: A Reconstruction," in *Changing Suburbs: Foundation, Form and Function*, eds. Richard Harris and Peter J. Larkham (New York: Routledge/Taylor & Francis e-Library, 2004), 91–110; Dolores Hayden, *Building Suburbia: Green Fields and Urban Growth, 1820–2000* (New York: Pantheon, 2003); Kenneth T. Jackson, *Crabgrass Frontier: The Suburbanization of the United States* (New York: Oxford University Press, 1985); Robert Lewis, "Running Rings around the City: North American Industrial Suburbs, 1850–1950," in *Changing Suburbs: Foundation, Form and Function*, eds. Richard Harris and Peter J. Larkham (New York: Routledge/Taylor & Francis e-Library, 2004), 146–167.

4— *New York Times* critic Stephen Holden goes as far as to claim that the show is "so perfectly attuned to geographic details and cultural and social nuances that it just may be the greatest work of American popular culture of the last quarter century." See Stephen Holden, "Sympathetic Brutes in a Pop Masterpiece," *New York Times*, June 6, 1999, sec. 2, 23. For the reverberations of Holden's quote see: George De Stefano, *An Offer We Can't Refuse: The Mafia in the Mind of America* (New York: Faber and Faber/Farrar Straus & Giroux, 2006), 5.

5— For an ecopsychological perspective on Tony's malaise see Jeremiah Creedon, "The Greening of Tony Soprano," in *Utne Reader* (May / June 2003): http://www.utne.com/2003-05-01/the-greening-of-tony-soprano.aspx.

6— Steven Hayward and Andrew Biro, "The Eighteenth Brumaire of Tony Soprano," in *This Thing of Ours: Investigating The Sopranos*, ed. David Lavery (New York: Columbia University Press, 2002), 205–206.

7— See Fred Gardaphé, "Fresh Garbage: The Gangster as Suburban Trickster," in *A Sitdown with The Sopranos: Watching Italian American Culture on T.V.'s Most Talked-About Series*, ed. Regina Barreca (New York: Palgrave Macmillan, 2002), 89–111.

8— Robert A. Orsi, *The Madonna of 115th Street* (New Haven: Yale University Press, 1985) referenced in George De Stefano, *An Offer We Can't Refuse: The Mafia in the Mind of America* (New York: Faber and Faber/Farrar Straus & Giroux, 2006), 19–36.

9— See Kenneth T. Jackson, *Crabgrass Frontier: The Suburbanization of the United States*, 68–70. Thomas Jefferson's view of cities as "pestilential to the morals, the health, and the liberties of man" (letter to Benjamin Rush, Sept. 23, 1800) is well known, but Jackson (70) cites an even more pungent quote from nineteenth-century Congregationalist clergyman (and strident Anglo-Saxon supremacist) Josiah Strong, who, along with finding Catholicism a graver threat to the nation than even socialism or alcohol, explicitly associated urbanity with the mark of Cain: "The first city was built by the first murderer, and crime and vice and wretchedness have festered in it ever since." See Josiah Strong, *Our Country: Its Possible Future and Its Present Crisis* (New York: Baker and Taylor, 1875). See also Harvie M. Conn, *The American City and the Evangelical*

Church: A Historical Overview (Grand Rapids, MI: Baker, 1994), 55–56.

10– Sam Jacob, "The Psychotic Utopia of the Suburbs and the Suburbanisation of War," Strange Harvest, March 30, 2006, http://www.strangeharvest.com/mt/archive/the_harvest/the_psychotic_u.php.

11– See Dolores Hayden, Building Suburbia, 26–44, 79–88, 103–110; Kenneth T. Jackson, Crabgrass Frontier, 234–243; Jon Gertner, "Chasing Ground," New York Times Magazine, October 16, 2005, E46 ff. In an ironic inversion of Frankfurt School Marxian base/superstructure theory, the actual construction in these sites would not take place without the ideological component. "We're really a marketing company that happens to build houses," one New Jersey Toll Brothers official told Gertner, admitting that his firm subcontracts out all its actual construction work to electricians, framers, roofers, painters, masons, and plumbers.

12– Political fears animated some of the developers, too: William Levitt, whose vertically integrated firm mass-produced the houses in the famously homogeneous, all-white Levittown, N.Y. and its sister communities in New Jersey and Pennsylvania, is quoted in a Harper's article to the effect that "No man who has a house and lot can be a Communist. He has too much to do." Eric Larrabee, "The Six Thousand Houses that Levitt Built," Harper's 197 (1948): 84; quoted in Hayden, Building Suburbia, 135.

13– See Christopher Lasch, Haven in a Heartless World: The Family Besieged (New York: Basic Books, 1977).

14– Brookings Institution Center on Urban and Metropolitan Policy, Newark in Focus: A Profile from Census 2000. Living Cities: The National Community Development Initiative series. (Washington, DC: Brookings Institution, November 2003).

15– The Plainfield riots were extraordinarily violent, in part because a break-in at the Plainfield Machine Company, a small manufacturer of military-style M1 carbines, resulted in the informal distribution of weapons on the street. In one incident, a fire station sustained gunfire for five hours before New Jersey National Guardsmen in armored personnel carriers broke the siege.

16– Kenneth T. Jackson, Crabgrass Frontier, 225.

17– Winters, Stanley, ed., From Riot to Recovery: Newark After Ten Years (Washington, DC: University Press of America, 1979), 5.

18– Kenneth T. Jackson, Crabgrass Frontier, 201–203.

19– See Max Herman, "The Newark and Detroit 'Riots' of 1967" (multimedia web resource); Newark section: http://www.67riots.rutgers.edu/n_index.htm.

20– Robert Caro, The Power Broker: Robert Moses and the Fall of New York (New York: Knopf, 1974), 837–849.

21– Kenneth T. Jackson, Crabgrass Frontier, 249.

22– Richard F. Weingroff, "Federal-Aid Highway Act of 1956: Creating the Interstate System," Public Roads 60: 1 (Summer 1996), http://www.fhwa.dot.gov/publications/publicroads/96summer/p96su10.cfm.

23– James Howard Kunstler, The Geography of Nowhere: The Rise and Decline of America's Man-made Landscape (New York: Simon and Schuster, 1993), 113–131.

24– James Howard Kunstler, The Geography of Nowhere, 106.

25– After the initial pilot episode, Sopranos episodes are known by titles, which do not appear among the rolling credits but can be found at http://www.hbo.com/sopranos/episode/index.shtml.

26– See Alan Berger, Drosscape: Wasting Land in Urban America (Princeton: Princeton Architectural Press, 2006); Rem Koolhaas, "Junkspace," in Content, ed. Rem Koolhaas et al. (Köln: Taschen, 2004), 162–171. New Jersey's population density is by far the highest in the U.S., averaging 1,134.4 persons per square mile of land area on a statewide basis according to the U.S. Census for the year 2000 (U.S. Census Bureau, Census 2000 Summary File 1). The counties chiefly depicted in The Sopranos are denser still: Hudson (Jersey City and environs), 13,043.6; Essex (Newark and environs, including the Soprano home in North Caldwell), 6,285.4; Union, 5,059.0; Bergen, 3,775.5. New York City density data are naturally higher—New York County (Manhattan), 66,940.1; Kings (Brooklyn), 34,916.6; Bronx, 31,709.3; Queens, 20,409.0; Richmond (Staten Island), 7,587.9—but New York State overall has only 401.9. For purposes of comparison, as Gertner mentions in a profile of the Toll Brothers residential construction company, India has 914 persons per square mile and Japan 835.

27– I am greatly indebted to Norman Basch for assistance in identifying the New Jersey locations in the opening sequence. Two other partial lists of these locations, one at HBO's site (http://www.hbo.com/sopranos/credits/index.shtml) and one compiled by "Soprano Sue" Sadik (http://www.sopranosuessightings.com/openingcredits.htm) filled in some sites with which Norm and I were unfamiliar. Any errors or omissions are my own.

28– "The Brown Slate" in this social milieu would refer to a local union election. Stickers and graffiti about union elections, often pitting reform slates against established leadership, have long been common sights in northern New Jersey, and the placement of this one gives the tollbooth shot a touch of remarkable (if serendipitous) significance. The Brown Slate sticker is a reference to International Brotherhood of Teamsters Local 560 anticorruption candidate W. Pete Brown, elected president in 1998 (rather than the 1996 United Auto Workers election at Ford Motor Company's Cuautitlan, Mexico, plant in which the similarly named "Brown Slate" was the Ford Workers Democratic Movement, another reformist ticket ultimately thrown off the ballot). The shot that includes the Brown Slate sticker also emphasizes Tony's cigar, perhaps an unsubtle allusion to the smoke-filled room as a common symbol of either corporate management or corrupted leadership; Local 560 of Union City, N.J., has a long history of mob influence, specifically involving the Provenzano faction of the Genovese *cosa nostra* family of New York. See Michael H. Belzer and Richard Hurd, "Government Oversight, Union Democracy, and Labor Racketeering: Lessons from the Teamsters Experience," *Journal of Labor Research* 20. 3 (Summer 1999): 343–365.

In 1999, around the time *The Sopranos* first appeared, Local 560's 13-year court trusteeship under the Racketeer Influenced and Corrupt Organizations Act (RICO) was released by the federal courts, with Brown's reform presidency cited as evidence that Local 560 was finally freeing itself of mob violence and graft. All three stickers on the tollbooth, small but significant clues to local opinion and events, indicate that Tony Soprano—unlike Anthony Provenzano and other Mafia predecessors—now inhabits a political milieu where union corruption and luxurious animal-skin clothing are no longer taken for granted by the public.

29– This simple structure should logically be close to Robert Venturi and Denise Scott Brown's hearts, with a sign wildly disproportionate to the diminutive size of its simple shed volume.

30– James Howard Kunstler, *The Geography of Nowhere*, 11.

31– Kenneth T. Jackson, *Crabgrass Frontier*, 76–78.

32– Exterior shots of the Soprano house are taken at an actual residence, a five-bedroom, 6,000-square-foot, more-or-less-Mediterranean single-family house in North Caldwell, built in the 1990s by its occupant at an estimated cost of $3.5 million; see Michael Frank "Creating a Mobster's Scene: On the Set of HBO's Dramatic Series *The Sopranos*," *Architectural Digest* 59.9 (Sept. 2002): 98 ff. Interior shots use a reconstruction on a stage set at Silvercup Studios in Queens.

33– George De Stefano, *An Offer We Can't Refuse*, 4.

34– James Howard Kunstler, *The Geography of Nowhere*, 121.

35– The same politician announces the same redevelopment effort in "Employee of the Month" and mentions that it will include a Museum of Science and Trucking—not, as in other cities, a Center of Science and Industry or a Science Education Center or an Exploratorium. *Sopranos* Newark erases the real Newark's manufacturing history; it is not a place that produces things, merely a place for hauling them.

36– Actually the real-life Satin Dolls club on Route 17 in Lodi, where location shots set in Bada Bing are filmed.

37– De Stefano, *An Offer We Can't Refuse,* 155.

38– Ramsey Outdoor, a real-life business on Route 17 for which the *Sopranos* writers did not bother to invent a pseudonym. Ramsey is roughly 15 miles north of Lodi and several notches higher socioeconomically.

39– Diego Gambetta, *The Sicilian Mafia: The Business of Private Protection* (Cambridge, MA: Harvard University Press, 1996).

40– Dolores Hayden, *Building Suburbia*, 88–92.

41– In the interests of full disclosure, the author is a former colleague of Steven Hart at the Forbes Newspapers chain based in Plainfield.

From 1987 to 1994 Hart edited the arts section that included my music-review column.

42– Steven Hart, "United Scatinos of America," blog entry, The Opinion Mill (Aug. 2, 2005): http://theopinionmill.wordpress.com/2006/12/26/united-scatinos-of-america-8205/.

43– Nashville; Cleveland; Baltimore; the San Francisco Bay Area; San Diego/La Jolla, Calif.; Lansing, Michigan; Raleigh, N.C.; Ermesinde, Portugal; Sheffield, England; Luton, England and environs (broadcast on British digital channel E4); "the Niagara Region"; an unspecified location, identifiable as part of a Spanish-speaking nation only from glimpses of signage; Oakwood, Ont. (a Toronto suburb, with a teenager's bicycle and lollipop substituted for Tony Soprano's car and cigar); Middletown and Red Bank, N.J.; and, naturally, North Jersey. Sampled from http://YouTube.com on September 1, 2006, using the search terms "sopranos opening" and "sopranos credits." The sequence has also become a familiar enough cultural meme to attract numerous parodies, not limited to a 2002 episode of the Simpsons cartoon (a form of pop-culture apotheosis that places the series alongside Stephen Hawking, Tony Blair, Thomas Pynchon, and countless classic films).

44– Lance Strate, "No(rth Jersey) Sense of Place: The Cultural Geography (and Media Ecology) of The Sopranos," in This Thing of Ours: Investigating The Sopranos, ed. David Lavery (New York: Columbia University Press, 2002), 179.

45– Lance Strate, "No(rth Jersey) Sense of Place," 182.

46– Sources quoted by Boston Globe cultural reporter Renee Graham have made exactly that claim. One described how he had "long harbored a sense of shame about his home state, which has always seemed 'neither here nor there, infinitely paved-over, a gunk corridor between points north and south.'" The Sopranos phenomenon, he said, erased that sensation. See Renee Graham, "Now it's cool to come from 'Joisey,'" Boston Globe, March 28, 2001, C3.

47– See Lars Lerup, "Stim and Dross: Rethinking the Metropolis," Assemblage 25 (Cambridge, MA: MIT Press, 1991), 82–101.

48– The author resided in New Jersey for 13 years.

49– Guarini vs. State of New York. 484 U.S. 817 (1987).

50– See Robert Venturi, Denise Scott Brown, and Steven Izenour, Learning from Las Vegas: The Forgotten Symbolism of Architectural Form (Cambridge, MA: MIT Press, 1977. Rev. ed.; original ed. 1972).

51– For further discussion of the Franklin "barrel" quotation, see Jean R. Soderlund, "'A Barrel Tapped at Both Ends': New Jersey and Economic Development," Reviews in American History 24: 4 (Dec. 1996): 574–578.

52– Chris Suellentrop, "Frank Lautenberg: Scrappy, Mean, and Insecure: He Truly Represents New Jersey," Slate, Oct. 11, 2002, http://www.slate.com/?id=2072237.

53– Venturi et al., Learning from Las Vegas, 163.

54– Compare, for example, the "bowling alone" argument of Robert Putnam: Robert D. Putnam, "Bowling Alone: America's Declining Social Capital," Journal of Democracy 6. 1 (Jan. 1995): 65–78.

55– See Jane Jacobs, The Death and Life of Great American Cities (New York: Random House, 1961).

56– See De Stefano, An Offer We Can't Refuse; Gardaphé, "Fresh Garbage: The Gangster as Suburban Trickster"; Strate, "No(rth Jersey) Sense of Place"; also Jay Parini, "The Cultural Work of The Sopranos," in A Sitdown with The Sopranos: Watching Italian American Culture on T.V.'s Most Talked-About Series, ed. Regina Barreca (New York: Palgrave Macmillan, 2002), 75–87.

57– See James Q. Wilson and George L. Kelling, "Broken Windows: The Police and Neighborhood Safety," Atlantic Monthly 249: 3 (March 1982): 29–38, http://www.theatlantic.com/doc/198203/broken-windows. [The printed article lists Wilson's name first; Kelling's appears first in the electronic version.]

58– Wilson and Kelling, "Broken Windows," 33.

EARTH AND DEATH: THE ARCHITECTURE OF GATE PA

SARAH TREADWELL

This is a story about a collection of drawings made by a soldier in colonial New Zealand; the drawings record the aftermath of a battle named Gate Pa. The events of the fierce encounter are recounted through a scrutiny of the images, understood not so much as pieces of history but rather as imbricated conditions of architecture and earth: overlapping, both conditions are implicated in the nearness of death that the images portray. Violence, which is inherent in colonial occupation, is discovered in the drawings through a twinned sense of both clarity and reluctant visibility.

The battle of Gate Pa was primarily about the land that indigenous Maori held and colonial settlers wanted. For the indigenous people, the tribes of Tauranga Moana, land might be described as continuity, identity, and *whenua* (placenta) while for the colonial soldiers and settlers in the Tauranga district, on the east coast of the North Island of New Zealand, land was a commodity, a future, and the possibility of prosperity. In the battle of Gate Pa the earth itself was marshalled as an architectural resistance to occupation; the *pa*—generally described as a fortified village— was modified and activated.

Figure 1. Horatio Gordon Robley, Breach at Gate Pa – looking east. Early 30 April, 1864. Pen and wash drawing, 180 x 255 mm, Alexander Turnbull Library, Wellington, NZ.

Earth and Death 1

In what must be the most reproduced of Horatio Gordon Robley's (1840–1930) drawings,[1] *Breach at Gate Pa – looking east. Early 30th April 1864*, a rising sun casts bleak light on soldiers guarding the abandoned earthworks of Gate Pa the morning after the battle.[2] The subject of Robley's drawing, that which rose above his eyeline and on which the soldiers perched, is the recently galvanic earth. Robley sketched it (and in its immediacy and dependence on linearity it seems to be a sketch) mounded up like a beached whale with its flanks carved away. With his drawing Robley rendered the earth incipiently active as it was previously dangerous.

Lodged in the cut of the ground, human figures can just be discerned—dead and alive. At first glance they seem to be complications of the earth, a collection of shadows. There is both a necessity and a resistance to looking into the earth (into the drawing of the earth), where not only corpses but also the wounded are discovered; immobilized, trapped but sentient, staring back at Robley. Despite the fact that this is a drawing made in the open, a landscape image of hills and distant prospects, there is a categorical disturbance in the reception of the image. Robley's view of cut-open earth is constituted perspectivally as landscape and yet, with its breached boundaries, articulated interiority, and controlled subdivisions, it is also emphatically an image of architecture. Robley drew the convoluted surface of the earth at Gate Pa repeatedly, worrying away at the opening crevices.

Drawing as a medium for landscape depiction will always be found wanting, according to landscape theorist James Corner, who suggested that the full plenitude of landscape cannot be drawn without simplification or reduction.[3] The genre of landscape painting might allude to immensity, invoking the sublime, but its radically abbreviated relationship to the viewer will be at odds with the constructed experience of the physical place. The image of Gate Pa the morning after battle should suggest a more amenable landscape scale—it is a drawing of a small corner of immensity in relationship to the hills and the bay beyond. But rather than being apprehensible, it is the very material interiority, the small and deep network of trenches, that is unsettling in the image; the figures lodged in the dark folds of land suggest a limited, yet infinite extension into death. Interiority is a rendering of architecture as occupiable, but occupancy here has a grim finality: the holes, in which the dead and dying are caught and which the soldiers guard, open up—in popular imagination—to the underworld; for the soldiers the marked passage is also a vanishing point.

The sense of estrangement implicit in the viewer's position within the devastated earth unsettles the familiar spectator/landscape relationship that is said to tame and domesticate. The bringing to form is, in this case, inherent in the earth that is also *pa*. The drawing that Robley made may assert control through an unspoken narrative and active placement, but the pictured hybrid—landscape/architecture—also seems to refuse to settle into a recognizable material condition. Addressing the landscape that is also architecture, the pictorial image remains organized for a different, elusive state. The scale of the earth construction suggests its operation as a collective space, tending to a civic scale with its unseen but evident depth and its half-seen extension. The inhabited image could be interpreted as revealing the foundations of a past important construction; the drawing is however a contemporary image of a new architectural form—the modern fighting *pa*.

The maker of the image, Horatio Robley, was a soldier in the 68th Regiment of the Imperial troops, which had been positioned at the rear of the *pa* on the day of the battle and he drew what he encountered when, on the early morning of 30 April 1864, the day after the battle, his regiment was set to guard the site. Robley's drawings, often taken as accurate records but nevertheless caught by conventions, were forwarded at speed to the office of *The Illustrated London News* to be published with commentaries on colonial affairs.[4] Robley, as a sort of embedded war correspondent, ran from the battlefield to the Tauranga waterfront and gave the images, with notes, to the captain of a ship bound for London.

The engraved version of the image of *Breach at Gate Pa – looking east* was published on the front page of *The Illustrated London News* under the inaccurate title "The War in New Zealand: Interior of Puke Wharangi Pah After the Conflict of April 29." Separated from the text that described the battle, the image was positioned above an editorial questioning of the nature of the war: "Whatever may be adduced by way of special argument to show that the existing hostilities in New Zealand may have been excited immediately by acts of Maoris, which, as being the deeds of dark-skinned men whom we are pleased to designate as savages, are assumed to be at once treacherous and gratuitous, it is impossible to talk away the fact that the real or occult cause of the war is to be found in the coveting of their neighbours land by the English settlers."[5] The critical editorial commentary on the war was given gravity by the engraved Robley image, from which corpses and the injured had been eliminated. The soldiers are pictured standing withdrawn, heads cast down, on the edge of an emptiness, at the rim of alienated and abandoned earth.

Preparations for War

The battle at Gate Pa was part of a larger conflict that has been known variously as the Maori Wars, the Land Wars, and the New Zealand Wars. At the time of the battle of Gate Pa, the 1860s, war was already being waged in Waikato (in northern New Zealand) and some inhabitants of Tauranga (Ngati Ranginui of Takitimu descent and closely linked Ngaiterangi of Mataatua descent) were involved in fighting for Waikato. Despite some doubt about which iwi (tribes) in the Bay of Plenty were "loyal" or "disaffected," Governor George Grey and his ministers eventually decided to send a punitive expedition to Tauranga with the troops landing there in January 1864. The arrival of troops in the area caused local inhabitants to attempt to precipitate battle on their own terms and with architectural bait.

Twentieth-century historian James Belich has argued that the arrival of the British expeditionary force in the district provoked a strategic response from local iwi of Tauranga Moana. Because the terrain at Tauranga did not favor the pattern of warfare previously employed in the Waikato and because local Maori were outnumbered and unable to maintain their warrior force indefinitely, Ngaiterangi and others strategically encouraged the British to attack a specially prepared position.[6] An existing pa at Waoku was fortified and a message sent to the British inviting battle. The message pointed out that a road had been built so the English soldiers might more easily move to the pa. This taunting invitation was not acted upon. Ngaiterangi moved nearer the troops and fortified a pa at Poteriwhi, and another challenge was sent to the British. The delay suited the colonial forces that were awaiting the arrival of more troops. Ngaiterangi and Ngati Ranginui then moved much closer to the English fortifications adjacent to Te Papa, the mission station; they started to build at Pukehinahina, two miles from the Tauranga landing. On April 3 Ngaiterangi were observed entrenching on the Pukehinahina ridge, where a ditch had been inscribed into the ground dividing missionary land from Maori land.[7]

The Construction of Gate Pa

In descriptions of Gate Pa it is generally agreed that the pa was so named because it was located at the point of a "gate," a slip rail in a fence, that was designed to keep apart Mission and Maori land. The Church Missionary Society block of land, of approximately 250 hectares, had been purchased by Archdeacon Brown in 1838 and 1839 for tobacco, scissors, razors, adzes, spades, hoes, trousers, and iron pots, among other things. According to local historian R. D. McCully, writing on the centenary of the battle, "the land ... extended from Sulphur Point out to Gate Pa, the boundary being defined by a deep ditch and a bank, with a gate."[8] The ground that was formed into Gate Pa was already a fortification.

James Cowan, in his history of the event, pointed out that the fence on the Pukehinahina ridge "had originally been built by the Maoris to block the way against *pakeha* (a term for New Zealanders of European descent; non-Maori New Zealanders) trespassers."[9] Cowan describes the fortification of the line as an enlargement of an existing condition; the ditch and bank structure became amplified into the form of a modern fighting *pa*. Already defensive, the line accurately acknowledged anxiety about future trespass, future alienation of land; it was a sore point in the earth at which general issues of acquisition and loss became intensified. The small slip gate in the line that allowed passage and trade was closed, and the gate, that would lend its name to the battle, became an opening into war.[10]

On the line at Pukehinahina two *pa* were built—a more substantial structure towards the centre of the ridge and a smaller one to the west. The ditch and bank and its elaboration formed a connecting link between the two positions.[11] The building of the *pa* has been described by Hori Ngatai, a Ngaiterangi chief, and a survivor of the battle. In 1903 Ngatai recounted his story to Captain Gilbert Mair (1843–1923), who translated it and then incorporated it into his book about the battle. (Mair uses the term redoubt to stand for the *pa* and for the British fortifications, and he also uses the Maori word *pa* in his translation: the forms that would come to literally overlay each other are seen subsequently by Mair as corresponding.) Ngati wrote of the construction of Gate Pa: "In the evening we set out for ... [Pukehinahina], every person carrying bundles of flax, small manuku, and tupakihi poles and sticks for building our redoubt – you know how scarce timber is at Tauranga. ... We reached the position about midnight and started at once to build two pa's."[12]

Ngatai describes the acquisition of timber from nearby the British soldier's camp: "With the material so obtained we built a light low fence enclosing the two redoubts. Beside the fences there were parapets, ditches and rifle pits, and within the redoubts shelters were built for the protection of the garrison. Men went to Pukereia to collect timber to roof over our rifle pits and covered ways."[13] The architecture emerges in the words of Ngatai through the process of construction and naming of the elements of the new form of *pa*; the translated words—"redoubt," "parapet," "rifle pits"—making the architecture of Ngaiterangi equivalent to the fortifications of the British. Belich, writing in the late twentieth century, also refers to the pa as a redoubt. He described Gate Pa at the point of the battle as "the major work, ninety by thirty yards in size, ... manned by about 200 Ngai-te-Rangi warriors at the time of the British attack. The lesser redoubt – about twenty-five yards square – was garrisoned by thirty-five warriors, mainly Ngati Koheriki."[14] The architecture in Belich's description is presented as a container of warriors. Soldier Horatio Robley turned to the discipline of architecture to represent Gate Pa, describing it conventionally on a much-copied drawing.[15]

Architectural Drawings

On a landscape-format sheet of paper Robley drew together, using architectural conventions, site plan, plan, elevation, section, and two details of the pa. Drawings that survey an existing landscape or architecture are said by Corner to be projections *from* the ground whereas an architect's drawing that precedes the making of the architecture/construction—the constructive drawing—is projected *into* the ground.[16] Robley drew an existing condition and so his pictorial images might be seen as survey drawings, yet, with his use of projective drawing techniques, he revealed both the pa as architecture and the ground as material structure, exceeding its usual location as site. He made a plan that demonstrated the spatial disposition of the pa, a section which negotiated between interiority and exteriority, and which shaped matter. With his architectural drawings he opened the pa to interpretation and analysis even as he revealed its embedded condition.

Confirming the drawings as projective, Robley named the engineer/architect of the pa. Unusually, in terms of both architectural documentation and the attitudes of the time, he drew a portrait of the designer, Pene Taka".[17] Pene Taka Tuaia (?–1889) has been described as a "Ngai Te Rangi warrior, military engineer, land protester,"[18] and Belich pointed out that "Pene Taka deserves to rank as an innovative master of field-fortification in the tradition of Kawiti."[19] Pene Taka was not a singular genius designer but rather an expert in a line of experts; Kawiti had defeated the British at Ohaeawai with a modern pa that, as Belich points out, included anti-artillery bunkers as protection against severe bombardment. It has been suggested the Pene Taka learnt his architecture from Kawiti.

Robley's portrait shows Pene Taka as a man partaking in two cultures, with his moko (tattoo), and cap and necktie. The act of portraiture records both his innovation and his status—this is a respectful portrait, even if it could also be seen as a form of beheading and re-inscription. (Robley

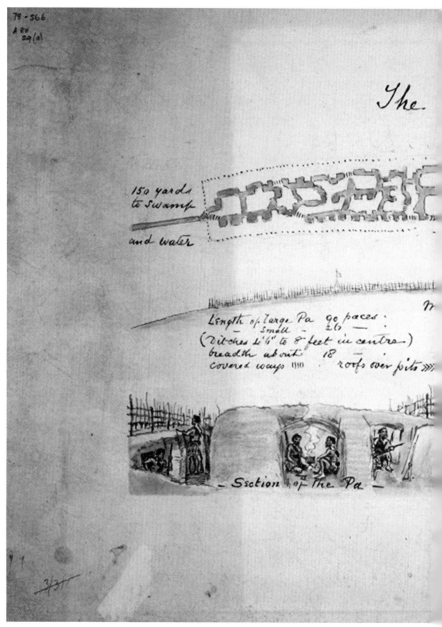

The.

150 yards
to swamp

and water

Length of Large Pa 90 paces.
— small — 26 —
(Ditches 4'6" to 8 feet in centre)
breadth about 18
covered ways 𝄃𝄃𝄃 roofs over pits ⟫⟫

— Section of The Pa —

Figure 2. Horatio Robley, The Gate Pa [1864]. *Ink and wash*, 292 x 465 mm, *Ref. No. B-077-027, Alexander Turnbull Library, Wellington, NZ.*

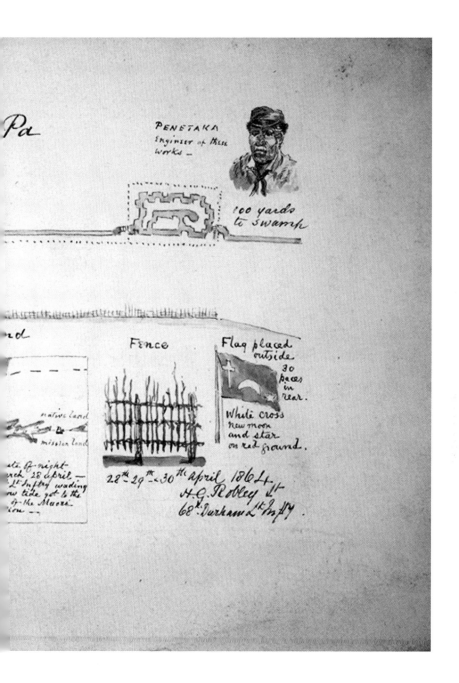

Pa

PENETAKA
Engineer of these
works —

100 yards
to swamp

Fence

Flag placed
outside
30
paces
in
rear.

White cross
new moon
and star
on red ground.

native land

mission land

nd

28ᵗʰ 29ᵗʰ & 30ᵗʰ April 1864
H.G. Robley Lt
68ᵗʰ Durham Lt Infᵗʸ

became a skilful recorder of *moko* and he also collected *momokai*, "tattooed heads.") Pene Taka is named and his occupation is given even though his tribal affiliation is not written down. His portrait, located in a supervisory position above the drawings, signs the design even as he—decapitated—is disconnected from ground and context.

The drawings on the sheet record and collect the innovative design of Pene Taka. In the elevation a *pekerangi* (light fence) can be seen concealing the two *pa* and the gap between. In its frailty, it signals weak resistance and minimal obstruction thereby inviting attack: in its extent, it suggests a formidable construction, stretching across the ridge unifying the two separated *pa*. On the same sheet Robley included a detail of the fence. About three to four feet high, the bottom of the fence was approximately 12–18 inches above the ground, so that shots could be fired from underneath. The fence was designed to deaden effects of cannon and shot, and to delay storming parties. Robley drew the lashing, the spacing of the vertical timbers, and the consequent, slightly elastic net-like nature of the fence, making it apparent how the fence might absorb the force of the ammunition, even as it looked inconsequential.

Below the elevation is positioned a drawing of an inhabited section—the architecture that the British troops could not see. It shows a trench, about four feet deep, from where shots could be directed at an advancing force. Returns that maintain the strength of the wall and provide shelter for reloading are clearly depicted. Behind the trench a parapet of mounded earth, about six feet high, conceals an underground chamber, where two relaxed-looking men can be seen cooking on an open fire. In copies of Robley's drawing the chambers, corridors, and passages become elaborated; in a subsequent print the structures appear as arched masonry and the scale approaches the monumental.[20] The underground chambers that served as shelter from muskets and cannon balls were covered with low pitched roofs made from timber covered with layers of fern and earth about two feet thick. Robley's section cuts through the earth showing the substantial volume of material that had been moved and shaped. The section—that is, an instance—attends to materiality and to life as a momentary construction: Robley imagined lively inhabitation in the sectional cut (a productive furrow in which life thrives) and he witnessed death in his pictorial perspectives. The depicted ground, already active and volcanic,[21] in which the warriors were lodged, exhaled smoke from their fire.

Running along the top of the drawing is Robley's plan of Gate Pa. Unlike conventional architectural plans (which the drawing resembles at first glance) in which enclosing walls are marked with black or hatched lines, in Robley's drawing it is excavated space that is made solid with darkness. In the plan of Gate Pa the enclosing wall is also the earth, which is also the paper on which Robley drew: the edges of the excavation extend under the ink marks that indicate the *pekerangi* (light fence) and become the ground for the breach that Robley pictures in the elevation. The enclosing substance is limitless, not linear, and the enclosed space is—like a *moko* (tattoo)—a calligraphic, linear opening. Carved into a ground/surface was an interiority that, like a scar, became defensively overlaid. Occupiable space, usually depicted with whiteness and light, is at Gate Pa imagined as a dark condition.

The plan shows connecting tunnels and covered ways within the trench system facilitating the defenders' movement within and between the two *pa* sheltered by earthworks. The covered ways are noted with a series of straight lines while the roofed-over pits are indicated with chevron patterns. With his use of notation Robley's drawing indicates the systematic nature of the *pa*—its division into "figures"; groups of trenches separated from each other, each with their own pattern. The interior of the trenches was said to be like a maze, designed to confuse an attacking force. The plan, with its capacity to see everything at once and its clarifying notation, denies the confusion that the invading troops experienced and on which subsequent commentators tend to dwell.

The architectural drawing set was presumably made by Robley after the fighting, after he had guarded the *pa* and looked into its damaged forms; into the mud, blood, maimed bodies, and corpses. The architectural drawing structured by measurement, rationality, and exactitude carries no trace of the mayhem of battle: it winds back time to the hours before the British attack.

Sequence of the Battle

According to Belich, the colonial force consisted of 1,700 elite infantry and naval brigades, and "the most powerful artillery train ever used in New Zealand."[22] By April 21 General Cameron and his staff had arrived in the area of Gate Pa bringing with them one 110-pounder Armstrong gun and two 40-pounder Armstrong guns, which "with fourteen other guns, landed previously, were taken out by 800 troops to within easy distance of the Gate Pa."[23] The guns were emplaced and blinded with green ferns. Within the *pa* were between 200 and 230 warriors from different iwi.[24]

28 April 1864 was occupied by a sham attack on the thin, fragile-looking Gate Pa and further repositioning of British troops to the rear. At day-

break on April 29 firing commenced on the Ngaiterangi position. The bombardment was fierce and continuous, and involved 24-lb howitzers, 8-inch mortars, along with the massive Armstrong guns. Ngatai described the effect of the bombardment on those inhabiting the pa. "An awful fire was concentrated on our redoubt. Eighteen big guns (so we learned afterwards) were hurling their projectiles at us and shells were bursting all around. Our fences and parapets crumbled away under the heavy artillery fire, and splinters and earth were continually flying through the air."[25] The pounding from the artillery was relentless and the air grew thick with smoke and drizzle.

While British soldiers were initially drawn to direct fire at the flagpole, which, as Robley noted on his architectural drawings, was strategically "placed outside [the pa] 30 paces in rear," this ruse did not prevail and—with what is generally agreed to have been accurate bombardment—eventually a breach was made in the surrounding fence. At three o'clock that afternoon the 110-pounder ceased firing, as it had by then released a hundred rounds, and at 4:00 p.m. two covering columns of 150 and 170 men set off to left and right, and concealed themselves in the fern. At a signal the storming party—four abreast, two soldiers and two sailors with officers to the flanks—charged at the double towards the breach in the palisade caused by the bombardment. Two other companies (one of them Robley's) opened up heavy fire front and rear. Mair described the storming party as being lead by officers rushing into the pa and initially driving back Ngaiterangi who "sought shelter in their covered ways, traverses and underground shelters, from whence they opened a severe fire on our troops."[26]

Ngatai remembered the attack of storming party and the Ngaiterangi defence: "Then we loosed our fire on them when they got well within range – still they charged on, with bayonets fixed and swords waving, cheering as they came. Through and over the breach walls they rushed; they entered the ruins of the larger pa; most of it was in their possession. But all at once the tide of war changed. Up leaped our men from the rifle pits as if vomited from the bowels of the earth."[27] From their positions concealed within the active earth, within the maze, Ngaiterangi warriors fired upon the soldiers in the pa above them.

Mair described the British reaction to the sudden encounter with subterranean fire: "It was now almost dark, and most of the officers had fallen, the assaulting column supports and reserves were all crowded into a small space, and appear to have lost control, and a panic ensued, caused, it is said, by a subaltern calling out: – 'My God, here they come in thousands.' Others again say the order 'Retire! Retire!' was given, when the disordered mass, instead of holding on to the earthworks already won, retreated..."[28] Flight followed, with the colonial troops pouring out of the *pa* in panic. General Cameron finally rallied his men outside the *pa* and threw up earthworks, within a hundred yards of the Ngaiterangi position, where the British waited uneasily until daybreak.

Meanwhile Ngatai recollected: "In the night we collected arms, accoutrements and ammunition from the British dead. Then recognising that our defences no longer existed we abandoned the ruined pa under cover of darkness, retiring in good order and spirits."[29] At 5:00 a.m. the following morning a British sailor entered the works and "found the place had been abandoned by the defenders, who had crept through the spaces between the lines ... during the darkness."[30] On taking possession, the British found only the dead and the dying. In the days following the encounter, a toll was taken: the battle had led to the death of thirty-five British soldiers and the wounding of eighty-three men. Approximately twenty-five Maori warriors had been killed. The numerically and seemingly technically superior force had suffered what was to be considered a humiliating defeat and it was in full knowledge of this that Robley made his drawings of the architecture of Gate Pa.

Earth and Death 2

Guarding the *pa* as a belated trophy of a lost battle, Robley drew *Scene in the Pa*.[31] He depicted two wounded Ngaiterangi warriors in the trenches with their dogs. At the front of the image is a dead man—his face caught in a horrific grimace and the flesh of his legs shredded. Above and beyond Robley, seated within the trenches, men are pictured carrying off bodies on stretchers.[32]

The sketch has something of the quality suggested by Vietnam War correspondent Michael Herr: "You know how it is, you want to look and you don't want to look. I can remember the strange feelings I had when I was a kid looking at war photographs in *Life*, the ones that showed dead people or a lot of dead people lying close together in a field or in a street, often touching, seeming to hold each other. Even when the picture was sharp and cleanly defined, something wasn't clear at all, something repressed that monitored the images and withheld their essential information."[33]

A similar entwining of denial and attraction percolates in Robley's drawing *Scene in the Pa*. While the title of the image suggests a picturesque construction, in which the *pa* is depicted as an exotic assemblage of costume and artifact, in this drawing the event is disturbing and uncanny. Robley is sitting on the ground and observed by the wounded man at the centre of the image who turns his head towards the soldier and artist. Caught in the fold of the paper (blue paper like a blueprint—a construction or foundational drawing), the man is grotesque as his arm and a dog's head protrude at odd angles from the cloak that covers him; blood drips down his arm onto the ground. Robley drew a conjunction of dog and cloak, and recalled the *kahu kuri*, the dog-skin cloak associated with battle as a fighting garment. The cloaks of the wounded men, marked with blood, are, in the drawing, a form of housing—a protective lining between the body and the cut earth in which they are fixed.

Robley wrote on the back of the drawing: "Sketch in the pah / Wounded Maories & their dogs / Several wounded Maories that have not been carried off by their friends lay in the burrows of the pah and the two I have ... sketched had their dogs remaining beside them, though of course very frightened. They allowed themselves very reluctantly to be led away by the pakehas (Europeans). The white dog in the picture ran away from his captor and for some days kept sight of the works waiting for his master and causing some alarm amongst the [outlying?] sentries in the fern at night. The dead man close to the cooking place in front was killed by a shell passing through his right knee and carrying away a great part of the left

Figure 3. Horatio Robley, Scene in the Pa [1864]. Pencil drawing on blue paper, previously folded, 210 x 344 mm, Ref. No A-033-022, Alexander Turnbull Library, Wellington, NZ.

EARTH & DEATH

leg – the wounded are being carried away in stretchers out of the pah. The different hiding places you can see in the passages where they remained safe from shot & in the assault raked our stormers."[34] Robley's interest seems curiously detached. He commented on the dogs as much as on the wounded men who had remained in the pa overnight and only reluctantly removed. The wounds of the dead man are mentioned alongside the discussion of the (deadly) architecture. Robley wrote as if to a distant viewer, across space and time, with detachment and in an informative vein.

The wounded man is located at the centre of the image at the bottom of a v-shaped cut into the ground. Above his head repeating, rounded voids are slices of the system of tunnels or covered ways for navigation from the bunkers to the firing stations. The architecture of the pa is demonstrated by a drawing that opens into the underground, revealing the foundations as convoluted and occupiable, rather than a stable bearing condition on which to build. The construction that historian James Cowan had described as having a "really weak character," had withstood the heaviest bombardment used in the war of 1863–64.[35]

The dead man who has no cloak lies on the ground beneath the hearth, his eyes staring. The fine detail of his active hands and curling beard is at odds with the legs from which the skin spreads out horizontally, like cloth; blood of the man darkens the earth. The weight of the earth to which he returns is in contrast with the frailty of the palisade, past which silhouetted figures with laden stretches carry bodies—alive and dead—out of the pa. Like a frieze they mediate between the earth in which Robley drew and the sky—the only way out of the trap.

Defeat

Given the overwhelming numerical superiority of British men and guns, the loss of the battle at Gate Pa was seen as a devastating defeat by the colonial and British public. The battle had ended in retreat and the reasons that were suggested for the loss of what had been anticipated as an easy British victory were numerous, including the cowardice of the troops. Accounts of the defeat indicate that the timing of the attack might have been at fault—the storming was left too late and darkness was a problem; rain and smoke destroyed whatever visibility there was. It was also espoused that heavy ammunitions were ineffective on light earth and that the mixed forces land and sea—lacked unity and cohesion. Mair suggested that prior to actual hostilities the soldiers had too closely fraternized with Ngaiterangi and a strong mutual regard had sprung up;

hence, consequently, the battle had not been regarded enthusiastically. Little attention was given to the architecture of the pa where the defeat had taken place.

Mair, writing in the early twentieth century, recognized that military skill was involved, claiming that "probably there was never an instance in modern warfare where more deliberate and carefully conceived plans had been devised for securing a crushing defeat of the enemy."[36] James Belich, in his 1986 revisionist history,[37] extended the argument pointing out that "the British consistently sought to avoid the conclusion that the Maori possessed the higher military talents, despite the fact that a major manifestation of these talents, the modern pa, was constantly before them. Instead they searched widely and desperately for alternative explanations for their defeats and difficulties."[38]

Belich points out that the defeat at Gate Pa occurred because of a piece of architecture—the modern pa. Constructed especially for the battle, it operated by stealth and was an ensnaring ruse, a disposable killing field. Surrounded with a relatively fragile palisade "the interior of the pa was in fact a trap – a maze-like confusion of trenches dominated by hidden firing positions. The British were allowed in and shot down. In terms of protecting the garrison, modern pa were trench and bunker systems; in terms of repelling assault, they were carefully prepared killing grounds."[39]

Robley's drawings agree with Belich's commentary on the efficacy of the modern pa; they pay attention to the intelligence of the architecture of war. The details and operation of the design are demonstrated in his drawings, both in his eyewitness sketch of the morning-after and in his sheet of architectural plan and section. Further, Robley's war reportage does more than offer a dry recitation of a sequence of events. His drawings catch the still dankness of the trenches and the superficial indifference to death that war momentarily brings. The technically innovative architecture of Gate Pa that Robley appreciatively presented in his architectural drawings was also the confining space of an abattoir leading inexorably to death.

Earth and Death 3

In the drawing *Sketch in Trenches, Gate Pa. 30th April 1864,*Robley moves further into the earth.[40] Beneath the image he described the scene: "wounded Maori (Reweti in centre was second in command at Gate or Pukehinahina Pa) He had been shot by Dr Manley V.C. 29th April 1864 outside when the stormers had retired. Sketch taken early 30th – artist divided his flask with these and others, but young warrior looked curiously on at taking portraits in a hurry (see watching portrait) signed HGR." The notes beneath the drawing seem to suggest that Rewiti had been shot outside the *pa* and that he was placed in the trenches by the British—in a holding cell—and he may be the man that Ngatai listed as one of the twenty-five men killed, "Petarika – Te-Rewiti Manatini taken the next day to Te Papa, where he died."[41]

The two men in the drawing are in or of the ground—the underground has been accessed and the doors of war are still ajar. A spade as a measure of the prodigious amount of physical work involved in the construction of the *pa* is leaning against the face of the cut ground—it seems to be more than an inconsequential detail. The technology of the *pakeha* has been put to work against them. The spade is also the tool of the gravedigger—the ground that has opened for war could also be closed.

The young man looks at Robley with sadness and weariness, and Rewiti watches him with compassion and wariness. The two men seem to be fixed in the trenches, held in the trap of their making. In the space

Figure 4. Horatio Robley, Sketch in trenches, Gate Pa. 30 April 1864. Watercolour, 192 x 242 mm, Ref. No. A-033-036, Drawings & Prints Collection, Alexander Turnbull Library, Wellington, NZ.

beyond is a third figure—someone lying on the ground looks through a small aperture to Robley. Apertures, openings from the underground, had provided the undoing of the colonial forces. The drawing of the wounded men in the trenches does not seem to be a trophy. Robley observes named and known men who look back at him; there is equivalence in the scene. The drawing is of the moment when and where the life of Rewiti was still present—his humanity is caught by the image. The depicted furrow in the earth in which he lies, acts as premonition of his death even as the ground is an incubator of life. Caught in excavation, in a trench that carves passage to the underworld, the drawing of Rewiti acknowledges both the persistence and the transitory nature of life.[42]

Robley's drawings make the consequences of war explicit and are even more disturbing because of his indifference to the effects of war: there is neither glorification nor sentimentality. *Robley* drew British soldiers lying dead in the mud outside the *pa* and he depicted hand-to-hand combat within the fortification. He worked with sketches, a genre of immediacy and presence, and yet the subsequent re-drawings and paintings point to a deliberation in his making of images. Robley scored the surface of the paper in vivid, linear marks that are considered to be lively, but which—in the crosshatching—seem to cancel out the life lines of the furrow in which the wounded lay.

Te Ranga

The loss of the battle at Gate Pa and the humiliation that followed probably account for the invariable coupling of the defeat at Gate Pa with a subsequent British victory at Te Ranga—a victory achieved at a nearby site of an unfinished *pa*. Caught by surprise, in the act of constructing a modern *pa*, local Maori lost important chiefs as well as many men. It was following this defeat that a formal surrender of the people of Tauranga Moana to the British occurred and land confiscation followed. The confiscations were severe and, although presented as an act of restraint on the part of Sir George Grey, a substantial amount of land was lost: "The 'confiscated land retained by the Crown', ... comprised some 50.000 acres, 20,235 hectares, ... but insufficient land was available for farms promised to military settlers and the additional area was retained west of the Wairoa."[43] The confiscations and subsequent compulsory land purchases by the Colonial Government continue to cause grief to the people of Tauranga Moana.[44]

Despite the victory at Te Ranga, the defeat at Gate Pa remained in the imaginary of British soldiers and six years after the battle naval officer

Herbert Meade, in an act of military tourism, visited Pukehinahina ridge. In a publication that recorded his travels there is a chromolithograph titled *Gate Pa Redoubt, Tauranga*.45 Red-brown land under a cadmium yellow sky camouflages a fortification that, in turn, covers over a *pa*. The depicted ground had not only been contested through military engagement and technology but also with architectural form and representation. Architecturally the British redoubt in the chromolithograph was constructed over the remnants of the earthworks of Gate Pa and the ground is tested in the title of the image where Maori "Pah" (*pa*) is succeeded by Pakeha "Redoubt," with both words meaning fortification. The title registers the complex relationship between the two cultural forms of warfare. The redoubt observed by Meade, that was built over the *pa*, was itself built over—years later—by a church.

The line of division between Mission and Maori elaborated into a modern *pa* was subsequently filled to provide foundations for the English redoubt that anticipated a Christian church—the cut of the earth gathered form like a wound. The ground at Gate Pa wrapped and folded around Ngaiterangi, Te Ranginui, and British warriors—both protectively enveloping them and transmitting them to an underworld. In the battle that would ultimately lead to both loss and acquisition, the contested earth was shaped into patterns of ownership, resistance, and death. The earth that vomited forth men, that was internally alive, that had received blood, that was coded as maternal, became shaped into the architecture that slowed, but could not stop, its own alienation.

Neither an open field for warfare nor a closed city space, the architecture of the modern *pa* was inhabited collective space that operated with spatial ruses, through disconnections between the visible and the material. Robley, a detached and yet active participant in the battle, made drawings detailed in both the empirical and the human nature of the event. He depicted Gate Pa from differing standpoints, detachedly appraising and approximating death even as he evoked the painful loss of war. The architecture of Gate Pa, as drawn, played out the tensions inherent in his attempts to pin down the imbricated conditions of landscape, architecture, and our transient interiority.

Endnotes

1— Horatio Gordon Robley (1840–1930), Breach at Gate Pa – looking east. Early 30th April 1864. Pen and wash drawing, 180 x 255 mm, Alexander Turnbull Library, Wellington, New Zealand.

2— See discussion in Leonard Bell, Colonial Constructs: European Images of Maori 1840–1914 (Auckland: Auckland University Press, 1992), 119.

3— James Corner, "Representation and Land-scape," in Theory in Landscape Architecture: A Reader, ed. Simon Swaffield (Philadelphia: University of Pennsylvania Press, 2002), 147.

4— See the extended discussion on Robley's work in Leonard Bell, Colonial Constructs: European Images of Maori 1840–1914 (Auckland: Auckland University Press, 1992), 118.

5— The Illustrated London News, 23 July 1864, 1.

6— James Belich, The New Zealand Wars and the Victorian Interpretation of Racial Conflict (Auckland: Penguin Books, 1988), 177.

7— A number of accounts exist of the initial moves to battle. The description in this paper is informed, primarily, by James Cowan and James Belich, the two major authorities in the field.

8— R. D. McCully, The Centenary of Gate Pa (Pukehinahina) 1864–1964: the Mission House, the Roman Catholic Mission, the Battle Story: programme of events (Tauranga: Bay of Plenty Times, 1964), 4.

9— James Cowan, The New Zealand Wars: A History of Maori Campaigns and the Pioneering Period, reprint, (Wellington: P. D. Hasselberg, Government Printer, 1983), 432.

10— "The boundary was later defined by a deep ditch, where the Maori erected a fence and gate to separate the Mission property from the Pa; hence the name Gate Pa." Stanley Bull, "The Venerable A. N. Brown," in Pukehinahina: Historic Gate Pa 29th April 1864, second edition, (Tauranga: St. George's Memorial Church, 1968), 11.

11— Pukehinahina: Historic Gate Pa, 9.

12— Hori Ngatai, "A Maori Survivor's Story: How the Ngaiterangi repulsed the Pakeha at the Battle of Gate Pa," in Captain Gilbert Mair, The Story of Gate Pa, April 29th, 1864 (Tauranga: Bay of Plenty Times Office, 1926), 22.

13— Ngatai, "A Maori Survivor's Story," 22.

14— Belich, The New Zealand Wars, 178.

15— Horatio Robley, The Gate Pa, [1864]. Ink and wash drawing, 292 x 465 mm, ref. no. B-077-027, Alexander Turnbull Library, Wellington, New Zealand.

16— Corner, "Representation and Landscape," 152.

17— Text under the caption of the image copied from Robley's drawing. The caption reads: "The War in New Zealand: Interior of Puke Wharangi Pah After the conflict of April 29..." The London Illustrated News, No. 1270, vol. XLV, 23 July 1864, 81.

18— Alister Matheson, "Tuaia, Pene Taka ?–1889," in Dictionary of New Zealand Biography, accessed December 5, 2010, http://www.dnzb.govt.nz/dnzb/alt_essayBody.asp?essayID=1T107.

19— Belich, The New Zealand Wars, 188.

20— Horatio Gordon Robley, Puke Hina Hina Pah (or Gate Pah), lithograph from a sketch by Lieut. Robley 68th Regt, April 29, 1864. Lithograph at the Topographical Depot of the War Office. Copy, ref. no 50792 1/2, in Alexander Turnbull Library, Wellington, New Zealand.

21— Tauranga is within the Taupo Volcanic zone.

22— Belich, The New Zealand Wars, 178.

23— Captain Gilbert Mair, Tauranga, The Story of Gate Pa, April 29th, 1864 (Tauranga: Bay of Plenty Times Office, 1926), 13.

24— Dame Evelyn Mary Stokes, DNZM (5 December 1936–15 August 2005), Te Raupatu o Tauranga Moana: The Confiscations of Tauranga Lands. A Report Prepared for the Waitangi Tribunal (Hamilton, NZ: University of Waikato, 1990), 33.

25— Ngatai, "A Maori Survivor's Story," 24.

26— Mair, The Story of Gate Pa, 15.

27— Ngatai, "A Maori Survivor's Story," 25.

28— Mair, The Story of Gate Pa, 15.

29— Ngatai, "A Maori Survivor's Story," 26.

30— Mair, The Story of Gate Pa, 16.

31— Horatio Robley, Scene in the Pa, [1864]. Pencil drawing on blue paper, previously folded, 210 x 344 mm, ref. no. A-033-022, Alexander Turnbull Library, Wellington, New Zealand.

32— Robley, Scene in the Pa.

33— Michael Herr, Dispatches (London: Pan Books Ltd., 1978), 23.

34– Robley, *Scene in the Pa*.

35– Cowan, *The New Zealand Wars*, 425.

36– Mair, *The Story of Gate Pa*, 13.

37– Belich, *The New Zealand Wars*.

38– Belich, *The New Zealand Wars*, 316–7.

39– Belich, *The New Zealand Wars*, 296–297.

40– Horatio Gordon Robley, *Sketch in Trenches, Gate Pa. 30th April 1864*. One watercolor and one photocopy of handwritten notes, 192 x 242 mm, ref. no. A-033-036, Alexander Turnbull Library, Wellington, New Zealand.

41– Ngatai, "A Maori Survivor's Story," 26.

42– "In contemporary western societies [land-scapes] involve only the surface of the land; in other parts of the world, or in pre-modern Europe, what lies above the surface, or below, may be as or more important." Barbara Bender, "Landscape–Meaning and Action" in *Landscape, Politics and Perspectives*, ed. Barbara Bender (Providence: Berg, 1993), 1.

43– Stokes, *Te Raupatu o Tauranga Moana*, 3.

44– An extensive account of the losses is contained in Dame Evelyn Stokes's research for the Waitangi Tribunal (a permanent commission of inquiry set up in 1975 and charged with making recommendations on claims brought by Maori relating to actions or omissions of the Crown that breach the promises made in the Treaty of Waitangi). See Stokes, *Te Raupatu o Tauranga Moana*.

45– Text with chromolithograph: "The Gate pah has been built up into a small sand-bag redoubt, mounting an Armstrong field-piece." Lieut. The Hon. Herbert Meade, RN, *A Ride through the Disturbed Districts of New Zealand; Together With Some Account Of The South Sea Islands* (London: John Murray, 1870), 8.

INDEX

A

Abdel Rahman, Omar,
  Sheik, 191
Addonizio, Hugh, 227
Adorno, Theodor, 22–23,
  38, 40, 45;
  Minima Moralia, 23
aerial photography, 128,
  134
*Afflicted Powers: Capital and
  Spectacle in the Age of War*
  (Boal, Clark, Matthews,
  and Watts), 209–210
Agamben, Giorgio, 200,
  203–206
Agrest, Diana, 118, 120
Alabama 3's, "Woke Up
  This Morning", 230
Alfieri, Dino, 29
Al-Maārri, 154
Al-Mutalammis, 160
Alsop Architects
  Peckham Library, 73,
  78–81
American Association
  for the Advancement of
  Science (AAAS), 133–134,
  138–139, 143
Amnesty
  International, 129, 136,
  138–139, 140, 143
anamnesis, 190
Andreu, Paul, 163
Apollodorus of
  Damascus, 162
Arcades Project
  (Benjamin), 207
Archigram, 62–63, 65–67,
  70–72, 83
Architecture and Modernity
  (Heynen), 105
Architecture of Fear
  (Ellin), 13, 179, 192
Arendt, Hannah, 206
Artaud, Antonin, 101, 104,
  108, 113 116, 118–120, 123
  Theater and its Double, 103,
  117

*Theater and the Plague,
  The*, 109
Theater of Cruelty, 98,
  100, 102–103, 109–112,
  121
*To Have Done with the
  Judgment of God*, 109
Auden, W. H., 244
Augustine, 156
autoimmunity, 203, 209,
  211–213

B

B-018 (Khoury), 88–95
Babel, Tower of, 176,
  193–194
Balbo, Italo, 35, 36
Balibar, Etienne, 16
Ballard, J. G., 71
Barkhin, Mikhail, design
  for Meyerhold (1932), 107
Baroque horseshoe
  theater, 101–102
Basset, René, 161
Bataille, Georges, 15, 83,
  87–90, 92, 94–95, 101,
  108, 201, 202
  "Abattoir", 60
  "L'Amérique
  disparue", 153
  "Musée", 60
  Tears of Eros, The, 87
Baudelaire, Charles, 23,
  25;
  "Double Room", 14
Bauhaus, 94, 107
Beecher, Catharine, 225
Beirut, 88, 95
Belich, James, 259–261,
  265, 270
Benjamin, Walter, 21, 23–
  24, 32, 35, 38, 48–49, 90,
  104, 147, 163, 203–204,
  215, 243–244
  Arcades Project, 207
  "Critique of
  Violence", 173, 201,
  206–207, 214

"Narrator, The", 22
"Storyteller, The", 116
"Work of Art in the
  Age of its Technical
  Reproducibility", 207
"Work of Art in the
  Age of Mechanical
  Reproduction", 129, 147
Berger, Alan, 230
Bernini, Gian
  Lorenzo, 158–159
Bevan, Robert, 13
biopolitics, 203–206
biopower, 131, 142, 144,
  203, 213, 215
Birth of Tragedy
  (Nietzsche), 101, 106
Boal, Iain A., 209–210
Body in Pain, The
  (Scarry), 115
Bois, Yve-Alain, 201
Borradori, Giovanna, 212–
  214
Borromini,
  Francesco, 158–159
Bosnia, 128, 132
Bouazizi, Mohamed, 160
Bouphonia, 152
Brandt, Carl
  (Commissioner,
  New York Police
  Department), 106
Bratton, William, 247
Breton, André, 117
Breughel, Pieter, 193
Britain, Festival of,
  (1951), 67–68, 70
"Broken Windows"
  theory, 247–249
Bruckwald, Otto, 106
Bruegmann, Robert, 220
Burma (Myanmar), 129,
  133, 135, 139–140

C

Campbell, David, 133
Carceri (Piranesi), 117–118,
  176

ARCHITECTURE AND VIOLENCE

Y

Z

Published by
Actar
Barcelona—New York
Part of ActarBirkhäuser
www.actar.com

Edited by
Bechir Kenzari

Copyediting
Dorota Biczel

Design and Production
ActarBirkhäuserPro

ISBN 978-84-92861-73-6
DL B–22596–2011

Printed and bound in the EU

Cover pictures (clockwise):
—Peckham Library's plaza on 27 November 2000, the day of Damilola Taylor's murder. Courtesy PhotoNews Service.
—Mario Sironi, *Mostra della rivoluzione fascista* (Exhibition of the Fascist Revolution), Salone d'Onore, Rome, 1932.
—"Crater formation within the CSZ (Civilian Safety Zone) between May 6 and May 10, 2009," Sri Lanka. Image from American Association for the Advancement of Science, Science and Human Rights Program, "High-Resolution Satellite Imagery and the Conflict in Sri Lanka" (2009). Image courtesy DigitalGlobe, Inc.
—Victoria and Albert Museum, London. Courtesy Annette Fierro.
—B-018, Beirut. Courtesy Bernard Khoury.

Distribution

ActarBirkhäuserD
Barcelona—Basel—New York
www.actarbirkhauser.com

Roca i Batlle 2-4
E-08023 Barcelona
Tel. +34 93 417 49 93
Fax +34 93 418 67 07
salesbarcelona@actarbirkhauser.com

Viaduktstrasse 42
CH-4051 Basel
Tel. +41 61 5689 800
Fax +41 61 5689 899
salesbasel@actarbirkhauser.com

151 Grand Street, 5th floor
New York, NY 10013, USA
Tel. +1 212 966 2207
Fax +1 212 966 2214
salesnewyork@actarbirkhauser.com